FOR THOSE WHO DARE

FOR THOSE WHO DARE

101 GREAT CHRISTIANS AND HOW THEY CHANGED THE WORLD

JOHN HUDSON TINER

First printing: September 2002

Copyright © 2002 by Master Books, Inc. All rights reserved. No part of this book may be used or reproduced in any manner whatsoever without written permission of the publisher, except in the case of brief quotations in articles and reviews. For information write: Master Books, Inc., P.O. Box 726, Green Forest, AR 72638.

ISBN: 0-89051-369-4
Library of Congress Number: 2001098885

Printed in the United States of America

Please visit our website for other great titles:
www.masterbooks.net

For information regarding author interviews,
please contact the publicity department at (870) 438-5288.

Dedication

To Jeanene, again

TABLE OF CONTENTS

ABOUT *FOR THOSE WHO DARE*

Recounted here are the stirring stories of 101 individuals who made an impact on their — and our — world. Individuals were selected because of their lasting heritage. The people came from a variety of occupations: barefoot pioneers, kings of countries, blind storytellers, lawyers, and scientists. These individuals recognized that God had given them a work to do. They put their trust and faith in Him into action.

The book captures the religious beliefs of these towering individuals. Often, the religious foundations of history are sacrificed to make the facts acceptable to a secular society. *For Those Who Dare* shows how the notable advances of the past arose from the basic Christian beliefs of key individuals.

The 101 biographies are arranged in chronological order. This puts a person's contribution in context with other events of the same period. Each of the powerful biographies gives essential information about the person along with an exciting account of the person's life. The name, birth and death dates, nationality, occupation, and major accomplishment quickly show who and what the biography is about. Although written to be read straight through, a specific individual can be located with the alphabetical index at the back of the book.

For Those Who Dare can be kept as an enduring reference book for every Christian home and school.

ROGER BACON

1220–1292
ENGLISH SCHOLAR
MAJOR ACCOMPLISHMENT: FIRST MODERN SCIENTIST,
PROPONENT OF SCIENTIFIC EXPERIMENTATION

ROGER BACON INSISTED that the future of science lay in the experimental method with mathematics as a scientist's most important tool.

Roger Bacon was born in England during the bleak period of European history known as the Dark Ages. Most people eked out a living on land they did not own. The struggle for survival left little time for education. Only a few people could read and write. The scholars who did gain an education found that what they learned was full of errors.

Despite the desperate conditions, Roger Bacon enjoyed a life far better than most. His family was well to do, and his father served under King Henry III. Roger received the best education then available. He attended Oxford University and traveled to Paris where he earned a master's degree. He lectured at the University of Paris on philosophy of Aristotle. He became knowledgeable in mathematics, astronomy, optics, chemistry, and music.

When he returned to Oxford in 1251, Bacon had the benefit of studying copies of books that had been translated directly from Greek into Latin. Bacon had a "built-in doubter" and insisted on testing the ancient authorities. He expended great effort and vast sums of money in this research. His studies convinced him that science was a quagmire of misinformation and superstition. He pressed for changes in the school system, but he encountered stiff opposition.

He even studied the reason new ideas are ignored. Bacon identified four hindrances to separating truth from fiction: blind belief in flawed authority, prejudice, resistance to change, and pretentious writing and vain speculation to disguise ignorance.

He developed a clear and convincing writing style. Unlike others of his day, Bacon lectured to inform his students, not impress them. His students enjoyed his teaching and gave him the title "Doctor Mirabilius," Latin for "Wonderful Teacher."

Bacon was the first European to describe how to make gunpowder. He studied optics and constructed a magnifying glass for reading small print. Scholars who read books began wearing eyeglasses. The convex lens of Bacon's magnifying glass became the lenses in telescopes and microscopes.

Bacon pointed out that the Julian calendar made the year too long by about 11 minutes. Seasons and the calendar were growing out of step with one another at the rate of three days every four hundred years. Farmers depended on the calendar as a guide to planting crops. Bacon proposed a change to the way leap days were added to the calendar. His change was eventually adopted 300 years after his death.

He estimated the size of the universe and found the stars to be far more distant than anyone had imagined. He restored the Greek view that the earth was round. Columbus quoted Roger Bacon when he appealed to Isabella and Ferdinand of Spain for money to outfit a voyage west to reach the spices in the East.

In an imaginative leap unmatched in scientific predictions, Roger Bacon wrote, "Someday ships will move through the water without sails or oars. Chariots will speed over the land without horses. Boats will be built in which men will safely go to the bottom of the sea. Machines will fly with artificial wings. Little cars will take men up and down. And when we wish, things far off can be seen as near so that we can see grains of sand and small letters and suns and moons that are now hidden from us."

He conceived the idea of a hot air balloon. He believed if a container could be made light enough and filled with hot air, it would float in the air as many light objects do in water.

As Bacon studied more, he became convinced that the Bible was the only unfailing guide to his life. While in his 40s, he joined the Franciscans, a religious order that had been established only a few years before his birth. His family was wealthy, so poverty would not have led him to become a member of the order. His decision to become a Franciscan grew out of true piety and a belief in their work, which was preaching, charitable work, and devotion to learning.

The very highest church officials respected his ability. However, he did not deal well with local church authorities, who also ran the school systems. Bacon was critical of their teaching methods. His attitude did not endear him to the local authorities, who resisted change.

Bacon lived before the invention of the printing press, so it was easy to silence a critic by merely repressing his writing and putting him in prison. During most of the last 15 years of his life he was forbidden to teach, his writing was confiscated, and some of that time he spent in prison. His crime was "suspected novelties."

Although he was in constant trouble with his immediate superiors, high church officials encouraged him to continue his writing. Bacon wrote an encyclopedia of all science, *Opus Majus* ("Major Work"). Most scholars never saw the book because it was suppressed. When it did see print in 1733, its chief value was to confirm Roger Bacon's role as a bright light in the otherwise gloomy Dark Ages.

DANTE ALIGHIERI
1265–1321
ITALIAN POET, SPIRITUAL WRITER
MAJOR ACCOMPLISHMENT: AUTHOR OF *THE DIVINE COMEDY*

DURANTE ALIGHIERI IS UNIVERSALLY known by a shortened form of his first name, Dante. Until his time, classical literature was primarily pagan literature — Greek works such as the *Iliad* and *Odyssey* of Homer, or Roman works such as the *Aeneid* by Virgil. Dante's *Divine Comedy* showed that the Bible, rather than myths and legends, could serve as a model for powerful literature.

Dante came from an aristocratic family. His father was a lawyer but not a particularly prosperous one. Dante's mother died when he was a child, and his father died when Dante was 18 years old.

Dante grew up in Florence at a time when the Italian city-states were far ahead of other European cities in culture. Even so, living in Florence was one political crisis after another. The citizen who was unlucky enough to choose the wrong side in a political squabble could find himself in exile.

The city provided an adequate education, especially for a pupil so willing to learn. Dante studied philosophy and the ideas of Aristotle and St. Thomas. He may have also studied in Bologna. However, he returned to Florence, his favorite city.

Beatrice, the woman he loved, lived in Florence. What we know of her is revealed in his writings. When he chanced to meet her on the street, her smile was enough to keep him happy for a month. He admired her from afar. His love for her could not be given any greater expression because Beatrice was betrothed to another. Scholars believe she was Beatrice Portinari who married Simone de Bardi. She died in 1290.

Over the next three years, Dante composed a prose and verse memorial to her, *Vita Nuova* ("New Life"). He continued to write about her. Beatrice became one of the most celebrated women in literature because of the fascinating way Dante's perception of her changed over the years.

Dante married Gemma Donati in 1293. They had been betrothed since 1277. Gemma was a member of a prominent family, so Dante became active in the political life of Florence.

The city was a democracy and required those who voted in city matters to be a member of a guild. Dante joined the guild of physicians and apothecaries. In 1295, he became one of the elected officials that governed the city. It was a perilous time because of the conflicting view of church and state. The political parties split over the issue of who had final authority over the city — the emperor or church officials.

Dante was a moderate and tried to keep Florence independent of both. By 1302, his side had lost, and he went into exile. He spent some time in Verona and his last years in Ravenna, in northern Italy. He never returned to Florence where his wife and children lived. Three of his children — Pietro, Jacopo, and Beatrice — did come to his side in later years.

Dante devoted himself to writing. He had become increasingly convinced that the language of the future would be the language that the natives of a country spoke. At this time, scholars communicated in Latin. Dante called this language an "old sun that does not enlighten." He believed poetry and all learning would benefit from a wider audience by appealing to common people.

He took the daring step of composing his greatest work, *The Divine Comedy*, in Italian rather than Latin. The exciting and interesting story could be understood on a number of different levels. It appealed to both scholars and ordinary citizens.

Dante died in Ravenna in 1321. His son found the final pages of *The Divine Comedy* and the complete work was published. The book is called a comedy because it has a happy ending. After making his imaginary journey through Inferno (Hell), and Purgatory, Dante is given a tour of Paradise by his beloved Beatrice where he sees a vision of God.

The events take place during seven days starting on Good Friday in 1300. The story begins with Dante lost and disoriented. He asks a man for help and learns that the man is the Roman poet Virgil. Dante follows Virgil who conducts him through Hell, a vast funnel-shaped region under the surface of the earth. They come out on the opposite side of the earth at the foot of Mount Purgatory. They climb the mountain and find the early Paradise. There, Beatrice welcomes

Dante. She takes him upward, and he soars beyond the planets and is given a vision of the glory of God. In each region, he meets historical and fictional characters, each symbolic of a particular fault or virtue.

The richness of Dante's work is its many levels of interpretation. At one level it can be read as a literal, although fictional, account of Dante's wanderings through the three kingdoms. On another level, it is a moral story of overcoming sin and becoming right with God. On still another level, it is not about an individual, but is instead an allegory of life as a pilgrimage. Finally, the imagery has an enigmatic spiritual vision beyond complete human comprehension.

Within 100 years, Dante's *The Divine Comedy* had taken its place with the ancient works of the Greeks in university classrooms. The fact that Dante wrote it in Italian began the process of making literature and all learning, including the Bible, accessible to ordinary people.

JOHN WYCLIFFE
1330–1384
ENGLISH RELIGIOUS REFORMER

MAJOR ACCOMPLISHMENTS: FORERUNNER OF THE

PROTESTANT REFORMATION AND TRANSLATOR

OF THE BIBLE INTO ENGLISH

JOHN WYCLIFFE HAS BEEN called the "morning star of the Reformation" because his writings championed a direct, personal relationship with God 150 years before the start of the Reformation.

Wycliffe was educated at the University of Oxford. The people of England had begun to think of themselves as a distinct nation. England still had to answer to Rome on religious matters, and congregations could not appoint their own priests. King Edward III of England had been allowed to hold office only if the country paid heavy taxes to the church in Rome. Parliament balked at the payment, especially since the money sometimes supported armies hostile to England.

Wycliffe became the most brilliant scholar of his day. He said, "There cannot be two temporal sovereigns in one country; either Edward is king or Urban is king." He counseled members of Parliament to ignore church authority in civil matters.

Wycliffe rejected the abusive practices of church authorities. Rather than servants of the people, the priests had become princes of the church and lived in luxury while ordinary people struggled for existence. He urged the church to divest itself of excess wealth by giving it to the poor.

Wycliffe represented King Edward III at a meeting with representatives of the pope in Belgium. Church officials became furious that he supported the king rather than the pope. The Bishop of London ordered a trial. So many supporters showed up that entering the chapel was nearly impossible. Seeing the overwhelming public support, the bishop abandoned the trial.

Wycliffe had gone against the most powerful organization on earth — and won. For two years, Wycliffe enjoyed unprecedented influence. He boldly questioned the authority of the pope and the

Roman Catholic Church. He rejected a formal religion in favor of personal involvement. However, the church authorities were not idle. Armed with letters from the pope, an ecclesiastical court tried him a second time. This time he was branded a heretic, his writings were banned and he was expelled from Oxford.

Wycliffe retired to his parish of Lutterworth. He continued to preach. He developed a simple preaching style in which he read a Bible passage, explained its meaning and then applied the principle to the daily life of his congregation. He had been considering a step that would forever change the religious landscape. Until then, the priesthood had been placed between the Bible and the people. The Bible in use was Jerome's *Vulgate*. It was written in Latin, the language of scholars.

Wycliffe announced, "Believers should ascertain for themselves what are the true matters of their faith by having the Scriptures in a language which all may understand." He and others under his direction began a translation of the Latin Bible into English. A series of strokes left him weakened, although he continued to work on the project and preach. On December 29, 1384, he suffered a stroke while preaching and died two days later.

His followers released the new translation in 1388, and it became immensely popular. Wycliffe's Bible was the most extensive work in English, and it set the standard for English prose. The King James Version of the Bible was influenced by it. The first part of the Gospel of John is nearly identical in both translations. This was before the printing press, so the only copies were handwritten.

Church authorities began a determined effort to destroy all copies of the Wycliffe Bible. However, more than 170 handwritten copies still exist. Despite his being dead, church authorities decided to put Wycliffe on trial again. In 1415, a Church Council reconfirmed that he was a heretic, ordered that his body be disinterred, burned, and his ashes scattered.

JOHANNES GUTENBERG
1400–1468
GERMAN INVENTOR
MAJOR ACCOMPLISHMENT: INVENTOR OF THE
MOVEABLE TYPE PRINTING PROCESS

EXPERTS AGREE THAT Johannes Gutenberg's printing press has had a greater impact on the world during the last 1,000 years than any other invention. He was born in Germany about the year 1400. We know little about his early days. He earned a living at various times as a goldsmith and stonecutter.

Gutenberg grew up at a time when people made books by carefully copying them by hand. Those who copied the Bible took special precautions to guard against errors. As a final check, they counted every letter on a finished page. Each page had to have the same number of letters as the page in the original document. A person working alone needed about seven years to copy the complete Bible.

People also copied writing by carving a page on a block of wood and printing from it. They carved these wooden blocks exactly like the page, but with writings and drawings reversed. A few hundred sheets could be printed from one block. Ink would then soften the wood and cause blurred, messy pages.

Books were few in number and far too expensive for most people. Only governments, churches, and universities could have large libraries. The owner of a Bible or a dozen other books could be considered a rich person. Churches would put an open Bible on display. They would turn the page once a week so people could read it.

In 1436, Gutenberg began to think of using movable type to print books. Each letter would be on the end of a separate bar. He could assemble individual letters as a block of type for the page of a book and print the page time and again. Then he could rearrange the letters to make the next page. The process would give several hundred identical copies of a book.

Gutenberg worked for years to perfect the invention. His partners expected a quick return on their considerable investment. Gutenberg, on the other hand, preferred to perfect the printing press. Unsuccessful experiments took all of his and his partners' money.

Johannes Gutenberg

Gutenberg felt certain his idea would work. He needed money desperately. In 1450 he formed still another partnership with a businessman in Mainz, Germany.

He realized that printing involved several separate steps. He began fresh and worked on each part until he had it right — the type, printing press, ink, and writing surface all had to work together.

He began with the moveable type. The tiny metal letters had to all be the same size so he could interchange them with one another. They had to lock together evenly as a flat surface. They had to stand up to repeated impressions. He made the tiny letters from copper. This time the letters worked perfectly.

The press brought the paper into contact with the block of type. A handle turned a screw to flatten the paper firmly against the block of type. It gave an even impression across the entire sheet of paper.

He experimented with ink. It had to adhere to the metal type and then transfer to paper. He developed a new oil-based ink that he mixed himself.

Paper had come into use as a writing surface in Europe only a couple of hundred years before Gutenberg's time. Paper had a smooth surface that would accept ink. Paper was the only part of the printing process that he didn't invent himself. Even so, he sought out the best paper he could find.

Gutenberg's complete printing process was far superior to any other that had been tried. He now had a method to mass-produce books, all with identical pages.

In 1454, one of the greatest events of world history occurred. Gutenberg began to print the first book made by movable type. He put six presses in operation. He set type for his most monumental task: printing the entire Bible.

Gutenberg wanted the printed Bibles to be as beautiful as any handcopied one. He chose an attractive type design and took pains to make each page perfect. Gutenberg's Bible was not only the first book ever printed, but many people consider it the most beautiful book as well. Seldom does a new invention begin at its greatest point. His achievement has never been matched.

Each Bible had 1,282 pages, 42 lines on a page, divided into two columns. He printed 300 copes of each page and bound them together to make 300 identical Bibles. Of the 300 original books, only 45 complete copies are still in existence. Today, each is priceless. Loose sheets from incomplete Gutenberg Bibles sell for thousands of dollars.

Printing swept Europe. Within 50 years, more than nine million copies of books had been printed. Printers published Bibles in everyday languages such as German, English, and French. The price dropped so low even ordinary people could own a Bible.

Scientists, religious scholars, and thoughtful citizens could share their ideas easily and quickly. Gutenberg's invention started three separate revolutions. First, books by the founders of modern science such as Copernicus and Galileo spread the news about recent discoveries. This began the Scientific Revolution. At the same time, people read the Bible in their own language. This started a spiritual awakening that swept across Europe. Finally, ordinary citizens became informed about current events. They demanded a greater role in governing their day-to-day lives. This caused governments to be more democratic.

Why did Gutenberg succeed when many others tried the same task and failed? As his life drew to a close, Gutenberg stated the reason for his success. In a large dictionary published in 1460, he explained that his work had been under "the protection of the All-Highest, who often reveals to the humble what He conceals from the wise."

ALBRECHT DÜRER

1471–1528

GERMAN ARTIST

MAJOR ACCOMPLISHMENT: ARTISTIC PIONEER WHO
BROUGHT ART TO ORDINARY PEOPLE; ARTIST OF
THE *PRAYING HANDS*

ALBRECHT DÜRER GREW UP in the late 1400s as Europe struggled out of the Dark Ages. He was fortunate to be the son of a goldsmith who made enough money to keep his family fed. Young Dürer learned reading, writing, arithmetic, and a little Latin at the local grammar school.

On warm summer evenings, Dürer enjoyed taking long walks in the country. He sketched what he saw — squirrels, tree-covered hills, and flowers. Dürer wanted to be an artist. However, his older brother died, and it became Dürer's duty to learn the goldsmith's craft from his father. After two years, he summoned enough courage to ask to study art. His father agreed. Dürer received an apprenticeship to a master artist, Michael Wohlgemuth, who happened to live next door.

Dürer learned that his time as a goldsmith had not been wasted. Delicate muscle control was needed to etch intricate designs in gold. Making woodcuts required the same skill. The design was carved into the wood and dabbed with ink. Paper was pressed against the wood to pick up the ink. Several hundred identical designs could be printed from one wood block.

At age 19, Albrecht Dürer finished his art apprenticeship. He set out in search of success. He traveled to Frankfurt, which had a thriving book trade. Printing was a recent invention. The Bible and religious texts were the first to be printed. As the print shops competed for customers, they added illustrations to the books. Dürer earned an income carving woodcuts.

After two years in Frankfurt, Dürer continued his travels. Art at that time was usually of religious scenes to be put in churches or portraits of nobility to be hung in castles. Few artists drew nature scenes. Dürer was an exception. He painted watercolors of gentle valleys, cultivated fields, castles, and people going about their business. Dürer put hidden figures in his paintings to make them more interesting. He drew a mountain with a town at its base and a castle on its crest. He filled the scene with hidden faces.

He painted a young hare. The rabbit looked alive with twitching whiskers, ears held high, and eyes that examined the viewer. The rabbit's fur had a microscopic texture.

Traveling alone at that time was dangerous. Princes of cities made war with one another. Their armies marched through the countryside, burned homes, and trampled crops. They stole livestock and left villagers with nothing to eat. The poor country people of Germany suffered terribly. Then a plague swept through the country, striking down rich and poor alike. Some people feared that the year 1500 would bring even greater distress.

Albrecht Dürer was a Christian who knew that despite the possibility of hardships, God would take care of His people. When Dürer returned home, he worked for two years on 15 woodcuts that told the story of Revelation in the Bible. The final scene was one of triumph showing the apostle John looking at the heavenly city while an angel locked Satan away.

Dürer opened a workshop in Nuremberg, bought a printing press, hired assistants, and began printing the woodcuts. They were priced so ordinary people could buy them. Albrecht's mother often sat in a booth at the Nuremberg fair and sold her son's prints to travelers.

The prints made Dürer famous throughout Europe. A legend sprang up about one of his paintings, the *Praying Hands*. According to this story, he and his brother (some versions say a friend) could not both go to art school because they were too poor. Instead, they agreed that one would work in the mines to pay the other's tuition. Dürer was the first to learn to be an artist. He returned to pay his brother's way to school. The brother's hands had become twisted and stiff from the hard labor in the mines. He could no longer hold a brush. Dürer painted the hands as a tribute to his brother.

This story is a legend. The actual story of the praying hands is as interesting. For 13 months beginning in 1508, Dürer labored on an altarpiece for a church in Frankfort, Germany. He made detailed drawings of each part. One of the sketches was the praying hands of an apostle. He sealed the finished altarpiece with two coats of clear paint so the colors would not fade. He believed it would be his last-ing monument.

Later, fire destroyed the great painting. What survived was his preliminary drawing of the *Praying Hands*. It became his most fa-mous work. The praying hands may have been his own because he often used himself as a model and painted his own portrait.

One of Dürer's best-known self-portraits brings the viewers at-tention first to his eyes — the eyes of an artist. Then the viewer is drawn to his right hand with its long, delicate fingers — the hand of an artist. Finally, the face has a slight resemblance to many of the paintings of Jesus. It was Dürer's way of saying that he wanted to be like Jesus.

He took notes about his methods and wrote books about mak-ing scenes look real and the proper sizes of human figures. Albrecht Dürer died in 1528. By then, he had become Germany's greatest art-ist. In addition to influencing other artists, his reasonably priced woodcuts widened the audience for art to include people with lim-ited income.

NICOLAUS COPERNICUS
1473–1543
POLISH ASTRONOMER
MAJOR ACCOMPLISHMENT: DEVELOPED SUN-CENTERED
MODEL OF THE PLANETARY SYSTEM

NICOLAUS COPERNICUS WAS born in 1473 in Poland. His father was a successful merchant. Copernicus studied mathematics and astronomy at the University of Krakow in Poland. Then he traveled to Italy to study literature at Bologna, law at the University of Ferrara, and medicine at Padua.

Returning to Poland, he served as a private physician to his uncle, who was a bishop. He faithfully devoted most of his time to church work.

In his spare time, Copernicus applied mathematics to astronomy to calculate celestial events. One practical reason to study astronomy was to produce an accurate calendar and almanac. Farmers used almanacs to plan when to plant and harvest crops. Governments and church leaders relied on calendars and almanacs to mark off holidays and special events.

Copernicus, like other astronomers, used the sun, moon, and stars to calculate the important events. They recognized these objects as being put there by God: And God said, "Let there be lights in the expanse of the sky to separate the day from the night, and let them serve as signs to mark seasons and days and years" (Gen. 1:14).

At that time, the writings of the ancient Greeks, who lived almost 2,000 years earlier, were the final authority in academic scholarship. The Greek scholar Aristotle wrote about astronomy. He put a motionless earth at the very center of the universe.

Copernicus, like astronomers after Aristotle, noticed a puzzling change in the paths of the planets Mars, Jupiter, and Saturn. Every once in a while these planets slowed in their forward orbit. They stopped, made a backward loop, and then went forward again.

The Greek astronomer Ptolemy succeeded in explaining the backward loops of Mars, Jupiter, and Saturn. He used a combination of smaller circles looping around larger circles.

Astronomers, who worked without benefit of calculators, faced

Nicolaus Copernicus

a daunting task to track the seven known planets with Ptolemy's 70 circles. To simplify matters, Copernicus made two assumptions: the earth rotates on its axis every 24 hours, and the sun is at the center of the planetary system. This new model of the planetary system explained the backward loops of Mars, Jupiter, and Saturn. Those planets orbited further from the sun than the earth. As the earth overtook them, they fell behind. They seemed to travel in reverse.

Copernicus worked out his system in full mathematical detail. In 1530, he summarized his ideas in a short, handwritten manuscript. He sent it around to his friends and fellow scientists. His system was easier and more accurate. He noticed that it explained other observations, such as the changing brightness of Mars, better than the Greek system.

Copernicus spent 12 years gathering evidence for his sun-centered theory. He improved the original handwritten manuscript. He called the new book *On the Revolution of the Celestial Sphere.*

Copernicus hesitated to publish the book. Rulers did not encourage new ideas. Suppose astronomers removed the earth from its natural place as the center of the universe. People might think a king didn't belong on his throne at the center of the kingdom. New ideas led to unrest. Those in power punished authors of books that caused problems.

Finally, Copernicus took the dangerous step of sending his manuscript to a printer. The first copy of the book was delivered as he lay in bed desperately ill. A friend put the book in his hands. Copernicus died that same day.

The publication of *On the Revolution* began a revolution not only in astronomy but also in all science. Scientists often mark 1543, when it was published, as the start of modern science.

MARTIN LUTHER

1483–1546

GERMAN RELIGIOUS REFORMER

MAJOR ACCOMPLISHMENT: KEY FIGURE OF THE
PROTESTANT REFORMATION, BIBLE TRANSLATOR,
AND SONGWRITER

THE BEGINNING OF THE Reformation is usually marked as 1517 when Martin Luther published his 95 theses that questioned the excesses of the Roman Catholic Church.

Although from peasant stock, Martin Luther's father had risen to middle class status as the manager of a copper smelter. Martin Luther experienced a loving but strict childhood. It instilled in him the view that a father was stern and unforgiving. Luther's father encouraged him to attend college, and Martin received a master's degree in 1505. His father assumed his son was training to be a lawyer. He was aghast when Martin sold his possessions and began studying for the ministry.

Luther described a nearby lightning strike as the specific incident that caused him to reconsider his path. Faced with his mortality and an acute awareness of not being at peace with God, he joined an order that emphasized absolute obedience and self-denial. He was taught that in this way he could avoid the awful wrath of a vengeful God.

Although all students at the monastery were supposed to be treated alike, he found this not to be the case. There was a saying: "Rich students eat the king's fare; poor students are both hungry and bare." He slept on the floor in an unheated room and awoke during the dim light of early morning to begin the day with prayers, singing of hymns, and other duties. Martin didn't mind the hardships. Officials of the church taught that pious works would win the glory of heaven. They taught that a person could earn salvation through good deeds.

Luther was troubled by his inability to measure up to what he thought a wrathful God expected of him. He found new worries such as the command to honor father and mother. He had sold the law books his father had purchased and rejected his father's desires. His father had not spoken to him in two years, but Luther traveled home and managed reconciliation.

After receiving his doctor's degree in theology, he was selected to teach at the University of Wittenberg. Luther continued to be tormented by the conflicting demands of spiritual perfection and human failings. Despite this, his skill gained him additional duties, and by 1515 he was a supervisor of several monasteries.

Everywhere he diligently searched for copies of the Bible. Although monasteries had complete copies of the works of church leaders, few had complete Bibles. It seemed strange to him that a school dedicated to the study of Scriptures didn't even have a complete copy of the Bible. Students were told, "Leave the Bible alone. Read the church fathers. They are the experts in biblical matters. They have gone to the heart of the Bible."

Martin Luther became a serious student of the Bible. Luther's defining moment came as he read Romans 1:17: "The righteous will live by faith." His teachers had seldom talked about faith. Suddenly, he understood that faith was an essential principle of the gospel. Suddenly set free, he became a new, joyful Christian. He filled his preaching with hope and vitality. People responded, and he became an influential preacher.

As a reward for his church work, Luther was allowed to visit Rome. Rather than impressing him, the worldly pursuits of high church officials repelled him. He became appalled at one church practice — the sale of indulgences. The forgiveness of God was available at a price, or so church leaders claimed. A person could pay money in the present to avoid punishment for sin in the afterlife. A poem of the time said, "As soon as the coin in the strongbox rings, the soul from suffering springs!"

In 1517, Luther tacked his 95 theses on indulgences on the door of the castle church at Wittenberg. The theses were essentially debating points and were not intended for general circulation. However, someone translated the Latin document into German, and the printing press gave it wide circulation. Luther's ideas spread with knife-edge suddenness.

The 95 theses began a terrific debate. Luther had enemies, so they used this opportunity to bring the pope on their side of the controversy. What had started as a local call to discussion became a public controversy.

Luther believed the Bible was the final authority. Every idea was to be judged right or wrong according to what the Bible said.

Church leaders objected. Unlearned people might mistake the will of God. They needed someone to tell them what to do.

Luther was summoned to the Imperial Diet (religious assembly) at Worms in 1521 to answer the charges against him. After being presented with his writings, he was ordered to recant. Luther refused. His statement, "Here I stand, I cannot do otherwise," may be legendary, but it certainly typified how he felt.

Luther felt that Christianity was not an elaborate organization headed by the pope with priests controlling the worship. Luther believed every Christian had direct access to God.

The Diet declared Luther a heretic, banned his writings, and issued a death warrant. He was in danger of being burned at the stake. Before it could be carried out, Luther disappeared. A band of kidnappers (actually his friends) spirited him away to Wartburg Castle.

While in hiding, Luther began one of his greatest projects, a translation of the Bible from Greek into German. He believed a simple layman armed with the Scripture could find the will of God. Luther said, "Over the soul God can and will let no one rule except himself alone."

His translation was based on everyday language in common usage. He used words the people used. He explained, "You get the language from the mother in the home, the child in the street, the common man in the marketplace."

After some of his political enemies died, Luther returned to Wittenberg. In 1525, Luther married Katherine von Bora, a runaway nun. The 41-year-old Luther found that married life agreed with him. He and Katherine had six children. His family life became a source of comfort and support.

In addition to being a reformer, Luther was active in church music. About 12 of his songs are still in common use, including the awe inspiring "A Mighty Fortress is Our God."

During his time in hiding, Luther gained weight and his sedentary lifestyle did not help his health. He began to suffer digestive trouble. In 1546, he traveled to Mansfield, near where he had been born, to mediate a dispute between two German noblemen. On the way home, he fell sick and died.

Religious worship was the most tightly controlled activity of daily life in Germany. By championing individual religious liberty, changes in other areas of daily life followed. Advances in science, economy, and democracy had their roots in the Protestant Reformation.

AMBROISE PARÉ
1510–1590
FRENCH SURGEON

MAJOR ACCOMPLISHMENT: FOUNDED MODERN SURGERY
IN THE FACE OF DETERMINED OPPOSITION BY
MEDICAL AUTHORITIES

AMBROISE PARÉ WAS born to a poor family in Laval, France, in 1510. His education did not include Latin and Greek, the language of scientists and doctors. His parents did teach Paré about the love of God. At age 13, Paré became a barber's assistant. He learned how to cut hair and trim beards. The barbershop was the town's first-aid station. Barbers also pulled teeth and bandaged wounds. Even today, barber poles are striped with red for blood and with white for bandages.

Ambroise Paré grew interested in the medical side of his barber profession. He decided to become a doctor. He told his parents, "The best medical schools are in Paris. I'll study there."

The medical schools turned him away. He could not pass their entrance examinations because they were in Latin and Greek, languages that he had not learned. Paré found a job as a barber-surgeon at the Hotel-Dieu, a charity hospital. For three years, Paré gained experience taking care of the sick and suffering at the hospital.

In 1537, France went to war. Paré worked on the injured men as bullets flew around him. Doctors taught that powder burns from gunshots

Ambroise Paré

were poisonous. According to them, the poison had to be driven out by pouring boiling oil in the wound. Otherwise, the gunpowder poison would prove fatal. This terrible remedy was horribly painful.

One day during a fierce battle, Paré ran out of oil. In desperation, he made an ointment of egg yolk, oil of roses, and turpentine. He rubbed the cool ointment into the wounds. He hardly slept during the night because of worry about the injured men. He expected many of the young soldiers to die of the powder burn poison. The next morning he made the rounds. To his great relief, he discovered that the men who had received soothing ointment were alive, doing well, and feeling little pain. The ointment proved far better for his patients than boiling oil.

He reported, "Those treated with boiling oil ran a high fever. Their wounds were inflamed, swollen, and painful. I resolved within myself never so cruelly to burn poor wounded men."

Paré, always humble, never claimed credit for his success. He kept a record of his treatment for each patient. When a patient recovered, he wrote, "I dressed him. God healed him."

Paré's most difficult duty came when musket shot destroyed the bone in a soldier's arm or leg. Paré had no choice but to remove the damaged limb. Otherwise, infection would bring on certain death. After removing the limb, Paré had but two and a half minutes to stop the bleeding. He followed the advice of doctors to sear the stump with a red-hot iron. This sealed the blood vessels and prevented the victim from bleeding to death.

Seeing the pain on a patient's face was almost more than he could endure. Paré tried to think of a less painful way to stop the bleeding.

During one battle, a young French soldier suffered a bullet wound that shattered his left leg beyond repair. After Paré amputated the limb, his assistant handed him the hot iron.

"Not this time," Paré said. Instead, he removed from his medical bag a spool of silk thread. Working rapidly, he tied closed the blood vessels. Bleeding stopped. Other surgeons could not work as quickly as Paré. They had no choice but to continue using the technique of searing the blood vessels closed. A few years later, the invention of the tourniquet to stop temporarily the flow of blood gave them time to close the blood vessels with thread.

Paré became popular with soldiers. Despite being poorly paid, the soldiers filled a helmet with silver and gold coins to reward their battlefield surgeon.

In Paris, however, doctors in medical schools resented his success. He still had no medical degree, yet he dared to improve the healing arts. Paré closed wounds with a needle and thread like a common housewife mending a tear in cloth. Dr. Gourmelen, one of France's best-known doctors said, "To tie the blood vessels after amputation is a new remedy; therefore, it should not be used."

Paré decided to write about his medical discoveries. Although he had learned Latin, he chose to write in French so common barber-surgeons could benefit from his discoveries. His manuscript, *Method of Treating Wounds*, was easy to read and filled with practical surgical advice.

However, doctors blocked its publication. They were the experts, they believed, and Paré only a backward barber. An old law was found and used against Paré. No medical book could be published unless a committee of doctors from the medical schools of Paris approved it. Dr. Gourmelen headed the committee. For four years, he blocked publication of the book.

Finally, Paré obtained the necessary approval. His book became an immediate success. It marked the beginning of modern surgery.

Some people expressed surprise that he shared his medical knowledge so freely. His livelihood came from the medical facts he put to work each day. Paré answered, "The light of a candle will not diminish no matter how many may come to light their torches by it."

Paré's faith, humble nature, and proven success triumphed over the opposition. King Henry II of France employed him as his personal surgeon.

This humble barber-surgeon is ranked as the founder of modern surgery. The people of France raised a statue in his honor. Inscribed on it is his simple statement: "I dressed him; God healed him."

JOHN KNOX
1513–1572
SCOTTISH PROTESTANT REFORMER
MAJOR ACCOMPLISHMENT: FOUNDER OF THE
REFORMATION IN SCOTLAND

JOHN KNOX WAS ONE of the most effective religious reformers of the 1500s, although he did not set out in that role. He was born in Scotland and educated at the University of Glasgow. He studied church law at a time when church and state were one. He worked first as a notary in preparing official church documents. Then, because of his Protestant leanings, he became the tutor of the sons of Protestant noblemen.

The climate became dangerous for religious nonconformists when a Scottish reformer, George Wishart, was executed for heresy at St. Andrews in 1546. Knox traveled under the name John Sinclair (his mother's maiden name) to avoid arrest. He intended to escape to Lutheran Germany, but the boys' fathers ordered him to the castle at St. Andrews, which had been retaken by the Protestants.

During his three months at the castle, he preached sermons and acted as spokesman for the reformers. The Scottish governor received help from France to quell the uprising. The garrison at St. Andrews castle fell. Knox was taken prisoner and sentenced to hard labor in the galley of a French ship.

After 19 months, the king of England interceded for Knox and gained his release. The power in England was Edward Seymour, the protector of 12-year-old Edward VI. Both the king and protector strongly favored the principles of the Reformation. They consulted Knox in preparing the first *Book of Common Prayer* for the administration of the rites of the church in England.

Edward VI was the son of Henry VIII and Jane Seymour. When Edward VI died in 1553, Mary Tudor, daughter of Henry VIII by Catherine of Aragón, ascended to the throne. She immediately swept the religious reforms from the church and purged the reformers from the country. She earned the title "Bloody Mary" because she sentenced more than 300 Protestants to their deaths.

At the same time, French-born Mary of Guise ruled Scotland as the regent for her daughter Mary, Queen of Scots. Mary of Guise began a determined persecution of Protestants.

John Knox managed to escape to Europe. Mary I of England, Mary of Guise of Scotland, and Catherine de Médicis (who ruled for her sickly son Frances II) of France were Catholics and persecuted Protestants. Knox wrote *First Blast of the Trumpet Against the Monstrous Regiment of Women*. The book opposed rule by women, especially those three. It also made a powerful statement against a country's religion being at the whim of a sovereign.

The book was published the year Mary I died. Her half-sister, Elizabeth I, daughter of Henry VIII and Anne Boleyn, became queen. Elizabeth I slowly restored England to Protestantism. However, she took the *Monstrous Regiment* personally and refused to let John Knox on English soil.

John Knox lived in Geneva as minister to English exiles. Those were the happiest years of his life. He had gotten married. Knox met Marjorie Bowes while ministering in the north of England in the early 1550s. During his exile in Geneva, he managed to make a furtive return to Scotland in 1555. John Knox and Marjorie Bowes were married, and she returned to Geneva with him. They had two sons before she died in 1560.

The city was in peace and filled with people who respected him and agreed with his religious views. Because of its freedom, Geneva became his favorite city. He said Geneva was the "most perfect school of Christ that ever was in the earth since the days of the Apostles."

While in Geneva, John Knox met John Calvin who influenced him, although Knox never embraced the unbending predestination that Calvin taught. Knox encouraged people to study and discuss the Bible during family worship at home and in the assembly.

In 1559, Protestants in Scotland rebelled against Mary of Guise and took Edinburgh Castle. John Knox returned to Scotland. The French supported Mary of Guise, and it was only a matter of time before Edinburgh fell. However, Knox's tenacious resolution held the defenders together until they managed to enlist the aid of Elizabeth I of England.

Despite their personal differences, Knox and Elizabeth I needed one another. She realized that if the French conquered Scotland, England would be in peril. She sent 10,000 English troops to defend

Edinburgh. The French withdrew and Scottish noblemen managed to gain control of the government and restore Protestantism.

Knox became a minister of St. Giles Cathedral in Edinburgh. His preaching style was passionate logic, a mixture of reason and emotion. He opposed ritual, ceremony, and the adoration of relics. Knox was not considered a theologian, nor did he claim to be a deep religious thinker. Instead, he worked for a practical application of religion to society. He helped establish Presbyterianism in which lay people had a prominent role in managing the church.

Mary Stuart became queen in 1561. Mary Stuart was also known as Mary, Queen of Scots. She was a Catholic but could never gain enough support to turn the country back to her religion. She and Knox had several meetings. He lectured her on religion. She was reduced to tears of frustration at not being able to rid her realm of him.

John Knox opened Parliament with prayers that galvanized the noblemen to support the reforms. Mary said, "I fear John Knox's prayers more than any army of 10,000 men."

Knox's wife had died in 1560. Four years later, he married Margaret Stuart. She was 17 years old and he was 51. They had three daughters. Knox's young wife was related to the husband of Mary, Queen of Scots, a fact that did not endear Knox to the queen.

In 1567, Mary, Queen of Scots was forced to abdicate the throne in favor of her infant son, James VI. Knox gave the sermon at his coronation. Knox was one of his counselors, and James became a staunch Protestant. Years later, he ruled England as James I.

John Knox wrote *History of the Reformation in Scotland*. As a history written while the events were still fresh, it was unusual for its time. The impact of Knox's religious reforms was immense, both in Scotland and beyond its borders.

FRANCIS BACON

1561–1626

ENGLISH POLITICIAN AND PHILOSOPHER

MAJOR ACCOMPLISHMENT: PROMOTED SCIENCE AS AN
INDUCTIVE PROCESS AND IDENTIFIED HINDRANCES
TO LOGICAL THOUGHT

FRANCIS BACON LIVED at the same time as Shakespeare and served his country under Elizabeth I and James I. Although an important politician, he is remembered today primarily for his writings about the methods of scientific research.

Francis Bacon was born in London to an affluent family. His father was a government official under Queen Elizabeth I. At age 12, he entered Cambridge University. He dropped out without graduating because the professors were merely parroting the teachings of Aristotle without adding anything new. While still a teenager, he served as a member of the British ambassador's staff in Paris.

He was called home when his father died suddenly. He learned that the family fortune no longer existed. For the rest of his life, he lived on a public servant's salary. Bacon tended to spend more than he made, so he was always in need of money.

Bacon was elected to the House of Commons. Unfortunately, he won the ire of Queen Elizabeth by opposing her tax measures. He practiced politics at a time when those on the losing side could end up in prison or worse. From this experience, he soon developed an uncanny skill at politics.

Bacon developed an alliance with James VI of Scotland who became James I of Britain in 1603 upon the death of Queen Elizabeth. Bacon was knighted — Sir Francis Bacon — and began advancing in government.

In addition to political papers for James I, Bacon wrote *Advancement of Learning* in 1605. His key point was that science should deal with the actual world that was apparent to the senses.

He did not feel that this idea was contrary to Scripture. He was a devout believer in the Bible. He wrote, "There are two books laid before us to study, to prevent our falling into error: first, the volume of the Scriptures, which reveal the will of God; then the volume of the Creation, which expresses His power."

In 1620, he published *Novum Organum* ("New Instrument"). Because of the success of Euclid's *Elements of Geometry*, which was based on the deductive logic of Aristotle, scientists thought all of nature could be deduced from a few basic principles. Bacon argued otherwise. He believed that scientists should first collect data by careful observations and experimentation. Then they could draw conclusions by inductive reasoning. He developed procedures to strengthen inductive conclusions. For instance, he pointed out that a large body of data that agrees with a theory could be nullified by a single contrary fact.

Another important contribution was his four human "idols" or errors that prevented logic from arriving at a correct conclusion.

The first error was the tendency toward more simplicity than actually existed. He argued against building a conclusion from a single, isolated event. Aristotle, who observed smoke rising and leaves fluttering to the ground, concluded that each object has a natural place. Additional experiments, as Galileo conducted, would have shown a more thorough description of falling bodies.

The second error was the problems caused by individual differences. For instance, one person may concentrate on how objects are different — solid, liquid, or gas — while another person may see similarities — solid water (ice), liquid water, or gaseous water (steam).

The third error comes from inadequate communication. Words often have multiple meanings. Some people use words loosely while others use them with more precision. A whale was often called a fish because it lived in the sea. However, naturalists knew that whales were warm blooded and air breathers, which gave them traits common to beasts of the field.

The fourth error was the belief in faultless authority. Throughout the Middle Ages, the ancient Greek writers were the final authority in most academic matters. Until their hold on learning was broken, progress was slow and painful.

In his book *The New Atlantis*, Bacon described a modern research institution where scientists met and exchanged the latest information. His fictional academy had libraries, laboratories, and printing presses. Scientists who read the description set about to make his fictional institution become a reality.

Oddly, Francis Bacon was not a scientist himself. He did no research and discovered no scientific laws. However, he was well respected and wrote with conviction. He succeeded in making the scientific method respectable. He effectively promoted the idea that science could strengthen a nation and improve the daily lives of ordinary citizens.

Bacon received high government posts: attorney general in 1613 and Lord Chancellor in 1618. By 1621, Francis Bacon was at the high point of his life. In that year, he was accused of taking bribes from litigants who came before him. He frankly admitted that he had received the "gifts" but claimed that they did not cloud his judgment in the court cases.

At the trial Bacon expressed his penitence and threw himself on the mercy of the court. He received a harsh sentence including a heavy fine and imprisonment in the Tower of London. However, the king released him from jail and remitted the fine. He was still excluded from coming within 12 miles of the center of London. This restriction kept him away from the libraries he so fervently wished to patronize.

His public career was ended. Bacon continued to write, primarily on political matters. He died five years later of bronchitis.

GALILEO GALILEI
1564–1642
ITALIAN PHYSICIST AND ASTRONOMER
MAJOR ACCOMPLISHMENT: CHIEF SCIENTIST OF THE
SCIENTIFIC REVOLUTION; WEAKENED THE
INFLUENCE OF GREEK DOGMA ON SCIENTIFIC
RESEARCH

GALILEO IS BEST KNOWN for his discoveries with a telescope. Less well known, but as important, was his analysis of motions of objects on earth. His approach to research emphasized experimentation and helped establish the scientific revolution.

In 1581, Galileo began his career at the medical school in Pisa. The professors stood before the classes and read from books written by ancient Greek writers. Nobody questioned the ancient books or put their statements to the test. Discoveries of modern scientists such as Copernicus were ignored.

One morning after Galileo said his prayers in the chapel, he arose to watch a lamplighter light the candles in a lamp, hanging 30 feet from the high ceiling. Lighting the candles caused the lamp to move in a slow back and forth motion. Galileo timed the chandelier swing with his pulse. As its motion died down, it seemed to take as long to make a small swing as a large one.

He returned to his room to try other pendulums. A string was fixed firmly at the top and carried a weight on the bottom that could swing freely. Galileo discovered that only by making the string longer could he lengthen the time needed to make one back and forth swing. The weight at the bottom could be glass, metal or some other material. It did not matter. The size of the arc, small or large, did not matter. Galileo's discovery, the principle of the pendulum, would later be used for making the first accurate clocks.

The ancient Greeks had been willing to observe and reason, but not experiment. As a mere 17 year old armed with the experimental method, he had worked out a new scientific law that had been completely overlooked by the greatest minds of the ancient world.

He became known as "The Wrangler" because he challenged his professors and their blind belief in the accuracy of Aristotle. When Galileo asked for a scholarship to complete his schooling, the professors were glad to deny it. He had to leave without receiving a medical degree. He earned a living as a tutor and returned to the university as a professor of mathematics in 1589.

Galileo Galilei

Aristotle stated that composition and weight determined how fast objects fell. Teachers at Pisa repeated this claim. Galileo's pendulum experiments convinced him that the composition and weight did not matter. A rumor sprang up that Galileo embarrassed the entire Pisa faculty by dropping different size iron balls from the Tower of Pisa. Both the heavy and the light iron balls struck the ground at the same time.

The professors, however, made his life so miserable he moved to the University of Padua. For almost 20 years he worked in relative obscurity, although he did make many important discoveries. He measured the speed and acceleration of balls rolling down nearly frictionless inclined tracks. He measured the acceleration of gravity (32 ft/sec per sec). He made the statement, later proven correct, that a feather and lump of lead would fall at the same speed were it not for air resistance. He established the law of inertia, which became Newton's first law of motion — a body changes speed or direction only if acted upon by an outside force.

In 1609, Galileo learned of a "magnifying tube" invented by a lens grinder in Holland. The magnifying tube, or telescope, had the power to make distant things appear near at hand. Despite never having seen one, he figured out its principle and built one that magnified 32 times. He was the first person to turn the new scientific tool to the heavens.

Galileo saw mountains, craters, plains, and deep valleys on the moon. It was as rocky and uneven as the earth itself. He found dark spots on the sun (and suffered eye damage in later life because of his lack of caution). He looked at the star group called the Pleiades. A sharp-eyed person could see 7 stars with the unaided eyes. With his telescope, Galileo counted 43. He saw that the Milky Way is a faint spray of dim stars. Aristotle had earlier taught that heavenly bodies were smooth and perfect. The moon was a smooth ball, the sun an unblemished sphere. The number of stars was fixed, with the Milky Way a cloudy body. In every aspect, Aristotle was wrong.

Galileo wrote a book about his discoveries, *The Starry Messenger*, in 1610.

His discoveries supported Copernicus's sun-centered planetary system. For instance, he reported that the planet Venus had phases like the moon, an indication that the planet orbits the sun and not the earth. Critics contended that the earth would run away from the moon if the earth orbited the sun. His discovery of four satellites orbiting Jupiter showed that a planet could move without leaving its moons behind.

Galileo's success infuriated the teachers at Padua who resisted new ideas. They began a campaign to discredit him. When the grand duke of Tuscany offered him a private appointment, Galileo was happy to leave the school.

The professors continued their opposition. They claimed he secretly spoke against the Bible. Galileo wrote letters to everyone protesting the lies. He traveled to Rome and begged church leaders to leave a way open for change. He asked, "What will it do to people's souls to find proof of a fact they had been told it was a sin to believe?"

He demonstrated his telescope in Rome and received a warm reception. However, after six years of trying, his enemies convinced church authorities to silence Galileo. In 1616, he was informed that he could not speak nor write about the Copernican theory. Galileo remained silent on the subject until 1632 when he published *Dialogue Concerning the Two Chief World Systems*. Although it presented both the old and new planetary systems, the best arguments were reserved for the Copernican system.

Jealous professors tried to discredit him. They said, "Galileo is trying to prove the Bible is wrong."

The charge was groundless. Galileo was a deeply religious person. Despite his conflict with church authorities, he never rejected religion or his Christian beliefs. Galileo's problems were not with the Bible but with the established authorities of his day who gave as much reverence to the works of ancient Greek writers as they did to the Word of God.

The next year, in 1633, the 70-year-old Galileo was brought to trial for heresy anyway. The verdict was life imprisonment, but because of his age (and the fact that some of the higher church authorities did not agree with the judgment), his sentence was changed to house arrest. Galileo died in 1642 at his villa in Arcetri. By then, he was recognized as the world's foremost scientist.

JAMES I

1566–1625

KING OF ENGLAND AND SCOTLAND

MAJOR ACCOMPLISHMENTS: AUTHORIZED ENGLISH LANGUAGE KING JAMES TRANSLATION OF THE BIBLE

JAMES CHARLES STUART WAS BORN in Edinburgh Castle in Scotland. His father was assassinated soon after his birth. His mother, Mary, Queen of Scots, could not control the religious division in her country. She was forced to give up her throne in favor of her son. She escaped to England but found no support there. She was held in an English prison for 19 years before being executed by Queen Elizabeth I.

James was crowned King James VI of Scotland at the age of 13 months when his mother fled the country. He never saw her again and grew up with no memory of his mother or father. Regents ruled the kingdom until James was 15 years old when he began to take an active role. Overall, the regents had the best interests of the new king at heart and prepared him for his rule with unusual vigor. He was given an exceptional education and was allowed to pursue his interest in classical literature and theology.

During his 37 years as king of Scotland, James became an effective monarch. He spoke fluent Greek, Latin, French, English, Scottish, and had learned a smattering of Italian and Spanish. He could conduct business with other heads of state without the need of a translator.

James married Anne of Denmark. It was apparently a happy marriage. He wrote poetry to her and together they had nine children. Concerned that he might die by assassination before his young son Prince Henry could benefit from his council, James wrote a private guide, *Basilikon Doron* ("Kingly Gift").

In the book, he advised his son to study the Word of God: "Diligently read his word . . . The worship of God is wholly grounded upon the Scripture, quickened by faith." And, "Now faith . . . must be nourished by prayer, which is nothing else but a friendly talking to God." When he released the book for general circulation, it became a best seller. In fact, his books generally outsold those by other writers.

Elizabeth I of England had guarded against Mary, Queen of Scots, taking over the throne. However, the childless Elizabeth realized that when she died James would be her successor. She authorized her advisors to pave the way for his ascension without turmoil.

In 1603, Queen Elizabeth I died and the monarchy fell to James. He kept the title of James VI of Scotland and ascended to the throne of England as James I. He had 36 years experience as a king before coming to London. However, England and Scotland were separate countries whose people distrusted each other. As a Scotsman ruling over the English and a Presbyterian ruling a country divided along religious lines (Catholic, Church of England, and nonconformist Protestants), he faced a daunting task.

James made reforms to strengthen the Protestants, but tried to maintain tolerance for the Catholics, a step that did not endear him to either side. While in Scotland, he had been kidnapped by a group of Protestant noblemen and held prisoner for a year before he escaped. As the king of England, he was the target of the infamous Gunpowder Plot in which Guy Fawkes, a Catholic, plotted to blow up the Parliament building on the day James and other high government officials were to be present.

James did succeed in establishing an uneasy truce among the moderates on all sides. He began a determined effort to unite Scotland, England, and Ireland and promote the growth of the American colonies. He was the first to use the term "Great" Britain. During his reign, colonies were established in Nova Scotia (New Scotland), Massachusetts, and Virginia. Jamestown was named after him. Its chief export was tobacco that provided tax revenue to England. However, James I opposed the use of tobacco products and did so publicly in his pamphlet *A Counterblaste to Tobacco*.

Few monarchs have been depicted in such contrasting terms. To some historians, he was the greatest monarch from the time of William the Conqueror (1066) to Queen Victoria (1837). To others, he inherited a stable government from Elizabeth I and let the seeds of the English Civil War grow during his reign.

His greatest failing was to misjudge the importance of the English Parliament as a representative body. In Scotland, the noblemen and not Parliament had been the key players. In England, he disregarded Parliament and suffered from their irritation at being ignored. His reign was weakened by his inability to fully engage Parliament in the reforms he sought.

His greatest achievement began one year after he became King of England. James appointed 54 scholars to make a new translation of the Bible into English. The scholars labored in three locations — Oxford, Cambridge, and Westminster — for seven years to render into English what became known as the Authorized King James Version of the Bible. The words were chosen to reflect the common English language spoken at that time. The King James Version was published in 1611, and for 300 years it remained the standard of English translations. The KJV, as it is often abbreviated, continues to hold the record as the best-selling book of all time.

Authorizing the translation did incur risks. Had his rivals who opposed the translation gained power, he could have lost his head because of his support for the project.

Despite being a sickly man and the target of several assassination plots, King James lived to be 59 years old. He died in bed while peace reigned at home and abroad.

JOHANNES KEPLER
1571–1630
GERMAN ASTRONOMER
MAJOR ACCOMPLISHMENT: DISCOVERED THE THREE
LAWS OF PLANETARY MOTION

JOHANNES KEPLER WAS A giant of science and faith. He believed
in a harmony in the universe put there according to God's design. He
traced out that harmony as three laws of planetary motion that became the foundation of the law of gravity. Kepler lived when superstition and fear about the night sky gripped the hearts of common
people and learned scholars as well. He began the process that replaced superstition with reason. All of the astronomers who came
after Kepler built upon his discoveries.

Johannes Kepler was born in Weil der Stadt, Germany. He studied theology at the University of Tübingen and prepared to be a minister of the gospel. Shortly before he graduated in 1593, the Seminary at Graz, Austria, had an unexpected vacancy for a mathematics
teacher. The university selected Kepler as the replacement.

As part of his duties, Kepler composed a yearly calendar and
almanac. An almanac helped farmers and travelers by predicting time
of sunrise, sunset, full moon, and other events. Kepler knew that
God had given the sun, moon, stars, and planets as natural clocks
and calendars.

Kepler also practiced astrology, a false science that tries to predict the future. During his time, astrology was deeply entrenched. At
first, the signs in the sky were believed to portend major events for
an entire nation or its leader. As time passed, people began to think
they could see the future of everyday events in the stars.

Kepler's careful records of his own predictions caused him to
doubt astrology. Before his life drew to a close, he said, "I fear astrology is nothing but a dreadful superstition, so unlike astronomy which
is a true science."

Several years earlier, Copernicus had proposed that the sun
and not the earth was the center of the planetary system. Few
astronomers took Copernicus's idea seriously although it did make

Johannes Kepler

calculations easier. Kepler began using the sun-centered planetary system. In 1596, he published *Cosmic Mystery*. The book was very much a throwback to the Greek idea of music of the spheres. Much of it Kepler himself later proved to be in error. However, in the book he became the first well-known scientist to publicly support Copernicus. He did so 20 years before Galileo.

Kepler noticed persistent errors in the calculations of planetary positions. He worked with old data about the planets' positions. The only person who could supply Kepler with better information was Tycho Brahe. Tycho had spent a lifetime measuring the exact positions of the planets against the background of stars. Unfortunately, the great astronomer lived far away in Denmark and had not yet published his data.

In 1600, Kepler fled Germany because of religious persecution. He sold his home and furnishings at great loss. He settled in Prague.

Unknown to Kepler, the great Tycho Brahe had moved to that same city. Tycho asked the young mathematician to be his chief assistant. "My chief calculator has been working on the orbit of Mars for months. He has reached a dead end. Can you do it?"

Kepler said, "I'll have the orbit of Mars finished before the month is out, eight days. But I'll need access to your observations."

Tycho considered his observations his treasure. He guarded them more closely than crown jewels. Slowly Tycho nodded. "You shall have them," he agreed.

Kepler began his calculations based on the assumption that Mars traveled at constant speed along a circular orbit centered on the sun. At the end of the month, he had no solution. A year passed and then two. Tycho died, but left his precious tables of data in Kepler's hands.

The tedious hand calculations filled over nine hundred pages. Kepler's best orbit misplaced Mars from the observations by only eight minutes of arc, about the width of a pea held at arm's length. Kepler tossed out his original assumption. He realized Mars did not travel at a constant speed, the orbit did not center on the sun, and it was not circular.

He solved the orbit of Mars not after eight days as he had boasted, but after six years. His solution showed that Mars traveled in an elliptical orbit. Other planets also followed elliptical orbits. This discovery became the first law of planetary motion. The other two laws related the position of a planet to its speed in orbit. Kepler published his findings in 1609 in the book *The New Astronomy*.

Kepler's laws of planetary motion became the foundation of modern astronomy. Isaac Newton would later say, "If I have seen farther it is because I have stood on the shoulders of giants." Johannes Kepler was one of the giants.

Johannes Kepler believed in a harmony in the universe put there according to God's design. He wrote, "Thus God himself was too kind to remain idle, and began to play the game of signatures, signing his likeness into the world." In 1619, he wrote another book about his many astronomical discoveries. In the book, *Harmony of the Worlds*, he wrote, "Great is God our Lord. Great is His power and there is no end to His wisdom."

Johannes Kepler enjoyed great fame during his lifetime. His fame has not diminished with time. On any list of the great scientists, he is usually in the top ten.

SQUANTO (ALSO KNOWN AS TISQUANTUM)
1585–1622
NATIVE AMERICAN
MAJOR ACCOMPLISHMENT: INTERPRETER AND GUIDE TO PLYMOUTH COLONY

THE FIRST YEAR IN THE New World was a bleak and disastrous winter for the Pilgrims and crew of the *Mayflower*. Cold, famine, and disease struck the people at Plymouth. They had been inactive, poorly fed, and in the gloom and cold aboard the *Mayflower*. Worn-out and feeble, they fell to disease. The first house built ended up being used as a hospital.

The next spring the Pilgrims struggled to plant crops, fish, and hunt game. Many foods grew wild, but they did not know which berries were good to eat and which ones might be poisonous.

One day a Native American walked into the village. The people were astonished to hear him speak perfect English. His name was Squanto. He decided to stay with the Pilgrims. He helped them in many ways. He showed them how to fish with traps, stalk game, plant Indian corn and ensure the seeds would grow.

Squanto had been born in what is now Massachusetts. At some point, the exact date is unclear, Captain George Weymouth, an English sailor who searched for the Northwest Passage, took him to England. Squanto spent at least three years there. In 1614, he met Captain John Smith who had returned to England after being badly burned in an accident. When Smith sailed back to America, Squanto accompanied him. The Native American proved invaluable as Smith explored and mapped the coast of New England.

Squanto was apparently released after his service to Smith, but taken prisoner by another exploring party who sold him into slavery in Málaga, Spain. Catholic priests purchased his freedom and he escaped to England.

He gained passage for the return voyage to North America in 1619. He found that his tribe had been wiped out by disease. Everyone had died, including his mother and father, and the village had been abandoned.

Two years later, when he revisited the site, he was astonished to see English buildings in the place he had once called home. Squanto asked to stay with the Pilgrims. With his help, it became clear the colony would survive. Governor William Bradford declared a three-day thanksgiving celebration. The Plymouth settlement owed much of its success to Squanto.

While living with the Puritans, Squanto became a Christian. The Native American spoke excellent English. In 1621, he acted as interpreter for the Pilgrim representative negotiating a treaty with Massasoit, chief of the Wampanoags. Squanto died one year later at age 37 while guiding a party around Cape Cod. The peace treaty he helped negotiate, built on trust on both sides, lasted for more than 40 years.

POCAHONTAS (REBECCA ROLFE)
1595–1617
NATIVE AMERICAN
MAJOR ACCOMPLISHMENT: PUT A CIVILIZED, HUMAN
FACE TO A PEOPLE THAT WERE TOO OFTEN VIEWED
BY EUROPEANS AS SAVAGES

POCAHONTAS WAS THE daughter of Powhatan, a powerful tribal chieftain of the Algonquians in what is now Virginia. She was given the name Matoaka at birth but her personality earned the familiar nickname Pocahontas, meaning "playful one."

She first saw European settlers at about age 12. According to the well-known story, she threw herself upon Captain John Smith to prevent him from being clubbed to death by her father's warriors. Although John Smith wrote about his rescue in a book published 20 years later, many historians doubt the story because he did not mention the incident in his earlier letters. Another explanation is that the episode occurred as a symbolic ceremony, and Pocahontas participated as part of the ritual.

Pocahontas became friends with John Smith and visited the settlement at Jamestown. The colony had nearly failed until Captain John Smith took over with his strict leadership. Some of the settlers were gentry who were not used to working. John Smith ordered, "He that will not work shall not eat."

Pocahontas learned to speak English and became a messenger for trade between the Native Americans and the colonists. The Algonquians exchanged fur and food for hatchets, iron tools, necklaces, and other adornments.

In 1609, John Smith was badly burned by an accidental gunpowder explosion and left for England to recover. When Pocahontas asked about him, she was told that he had died.

With John Smith away, some of the colonists looked for an easier way to obtain food. Captain Samuel Argall conspired with a Native American to lure Pocahontas to Argall's ship. He kidnapped her and demanded a ransom of food from her father. Although treated well, she remained a captive for several years. Finally, a partial payment of her ransom allowed her greater freedom at a new settlement under the leadership of Sir Thomas Dale. She became interested in the Christian faith and eventually embraced it. She met John Rolfe, a successful tobacco farmer, in 1613.

Her captivity continued to create friction that broke into armed conflict. Pocahontas sent word to her father that she was being well treated. She devised a solution to the problem — she asked to marry John Rolfe.

Both Chief Powhatan and Governor Thomas Dale gave their blessings to the peace-making marriage, although John Rolfe was reluctant at first. His main objection was that he would be marrying a non-Christian. However, Pocahontas had accepted Christianity and was baptized. She celebrated her new birth by taking the name Rebecca. They were married in the spring of 1614.

Immigration to the New World had slowed because of tales of Indian cruelty. Governor Dale realized the charming Pocahontas would ease those fears. She, her husband, and their young son Thomas accompanied Governor Dale back to England. There she met John Smith and was speechless to learn he was still alive.

Pocahontas was presented to King James I and the royal family. She was labeled an Indian princess and treated as visiting royalty herself. After a year in England, Rolfe made plans to return to Virgina. Pocahontas boarded the ship but was taken ashore when it became clear she was too weak for the demanding voyage. The exact cause of her distress was not identified, being variously reported as pneumonia or smallpox. She died and was buried at a chapel in the port city of Gravesend, England.

Although manipulated by others for their own advantages, Pocahontas nevertheless was a person of strong character who came honestly to her Christianity. Her last words are reported to have been, "All must die. 'Tis enough that the child liveth." She referred to her son Thomas, who was educated in England and returned to Virginia. Thomas Jefferson was a descendent of Pocahontas through Thomas Rolfe.

Many towns and other locations are named in honor of her. For instance, one of the earlier settlements in Arkansas was named Powhatan, after her father, while a nearby county seat was named Pocahontas. Her wit, strength of character, and compassion provided a bright moment in the turbulent relationships between Native Americans and Europeans.

PRISCILLA MULLINS
1602–1682
COLONIAL AMERICAN
MAJOR ACCOMPLISH: PREMIERE EXAMPLE OF THE
PIONEER SPIRIT OF AMERICAN WOMEN

IN ENGLAND DURING the early 1600s, Christians had to worship as the ruler directed or face arrest. In addition, poor people worked on farms that they did not own. To ensure a brighter future for their children, a group of Christians decided to voyage to the New World. Although called Separatists in their day, they later became known as Pilgrims.

Two ships, the *Mayflower* and *Speedwell*, set out because it was dangerous to make the Atlantic crossing in a single vessel. However, the *Speedwell*, sprang a leak and had to turn back. Some of the passengers transferred to the *Mayflower*. The 102 passengers and 25 crew members occupied a space of about 2,500 square feet — hardly more room than in a good-sized, single-family dwelling.

Priscilla Mullins at age 17 was the oldest of the 11 girls aboard the ship. She traveled with her father, mother, and younger brother Joseph. Her father was a shoe cobbler.

In October a fierce storm struck. The rain and ocean spray drenched everyone with icy water. Their clothes, food, and bedding became soaked. The rolling made it too dangerous to start a fire to cook food. For 30 days, everyone had to eat cold hardtack biscuits and salt pork.

The storm blew the ship off course. Instead of the warmer climate of Virginia, the ship landed far north at Cape Cod. Rather than returning to the stormy Atlantic, the Pilgrims decided to begin their settlement in that area.

The settlers at Plymouth suffered through an unusually harsh winter. Worn out and feeble, they fell to disease. Every member of three families died. The first governor, John Carver, died. Priscilla Mullins lost not only her mother and father but also her brother Joseph. Like Priscilla, two other girls, Mary Chilton and Elizabeth Tilly, also lost every member of their families. Priscilla took a lead in caring for the children who had lost their parents.

Two of the girls, Ellen More, age eight and her sister Mary, age four, were there because of divorce. Earlier in England, having found that his children were actually those of another man, Samuel More divorced his wife, gained custody of the children, and then punished his wife by arranging for her children to be sent away to America. Without mother, without father, little Ellen and Mary died the first winter.

Captain Christopher Jones of the *Mayflower* anchored in Plymouth harbor for the winter so his ship could be used as shelter. In March, he announced he was leaving for England. He offered passage to any Pilgrims who wanted to return. None accepted his offer.

John Alden (?–1687), one of the crew, chose to stay with the Pilgrims. He was the cooper, or barrel maker. Almost everything was shipped in barrels because in an age when human muscles did much of the work, it was easier to roll a barrel than lift a box. Alden came from a wealthy family, and as a young man he had studied for the law. However, he became interested in woodworking when a garden house was built on his uncle's estate. He dropped out of school to learn carpentry. His job on the *Mayflower* was his first as a cooper.

John Alden was the youngest unmarried man in the crew, and Priscilla Mullins was the oldest unmarried girl. Later events suggest that the 18-year-old girl was the reason for his decision to stay in Plymouth rather than return to England.

The Pilgrims who remained struggled to plant crops, fish, and hunt game. In the fall of 1621, they had reason to be thankful. Seven houses, a meeting building, and a watchtower were finished. The new governor, William Bradford, said, "Our wheat did prove well, and, God be praised, we had a good increase of Indian corn." He declared the harvest feast that became the first Thanksgiving.

The next year, John Alden asked to marry Priscilla Mullins. She had no father, so he asked permission of the other men in the village for her hand. At the wedding, she wore one of her mother's dresses and a pair of shoes her father had made.

The young couple stayed in Plymouth for a few years and then moved to a farm near Duxbury, a town John and his friend Miles Standish founded. He and Priscilla built a home on their property and raised 11 children. Their descendents include two presidents (John Adams and his son, John Quincy Adams) and one vice president (Dan Quayle).

Another famous descendent was the American poet Henry Wadsworth Longfellow. In 1858, Longfellow embellished a family story and published *The Courtship of Miles Standish*. In Longfellow's poem, John Alden acted as an intermediary for his friend Miles Standish to ask for the hand of Priscilla. Instead, she responded, "Pray thee, why don't you speak for yourself, John?"

John Alden served as a surveyor of highways, assistant to the governor of Massachusetts, and twice served as deputy governor. When he died in 1687, he was the last surviving signer of America's first freedom document, the *Mayflower Compact*.

Priscilla demonstrated strength of character at a pivotal moment in American history. Despite concerns that the young women would face a greater risk of death during the voyage and first year in the New World, Priscilla and the other girls proved their resilience. Proportionally they suffered fewer deaths than any other group. Only the two More girls died.

The Pilgrims were profoundly religious. Despite the urgency of building homes and planting crops, they took time to worship God. Each week one of the men blew a horn from the roof of the meeting house. It called the people to worship. All day Sunday, the Pilgrims would put aside their work for worship.

JOHN MILTON
1608–1674
ENGLISH POLITICAL WRITER AND POET

MAJOR ACCOMPLISHMENT: AUTHOR OF *PARADISE LOST*

JOHN MILTON WAS BORN in London, educated at Cambridge, and was preparing to be a clergyman but broke with the teachings of the Church of England. He retired to his father's country home and immersed himself in reading the classics. He practiced poetry by making rhymed paraphrases of the Psalms. He toured Europe and upon his return settled in London.

Although he wrote some religious tracts at this stage of his career, his major efforts were supporting the parliamentary cause against the royalists. He argued forcefully that Parliament and Cromwell were just in beheading Charles I (son of James I).

His first marriage was to Mary Powell, the daughter of a Royalist. After the honeymoon, his wife visited her family. When war began, she decided to stay with her family rather than return to Milton. Later, he would write a tract defending incompatibility as an acceptable cause for divorce. However, the couple did not divorce. After her family's fortune was lost in the fighting, Mary and her entire family moved in with Milton. They had three daughters before she died in 1652.

John Milton's most important document at this time was an attack on censorship and an appeal for freedom of the press. He had met Galileo while in Italy and was appalled that the great scientist was under house arrest for publishing his *Dialogue Concerning the Two Chief World Systems.*

With the restoration of the monarchy in 1660, Milton went into hiding. His friends, including Robert Boyle, worked behind the scenes to negotiate his surrender. Charles II, the son of the beheaded king, was more interested in restoring England than seeking revenge, so he agreed to a light sentence. Milton turned himself in, was fined, and served a short term in prison.

Milton composed most of *Paradise Lost* after becoming totally blind in 1652. The story is of Satan's rebellion against God and expulsion from heaven, the temptation of Adam and Eve and the "paradise lost" of the Garden of Eden. The book, written in unrhymed blank verse, is not for the faint of heart. Although written in a noble style as if organ music were playing in the background, many people find the syntax, vocabulary, and complex arrangement impenetrable in places. Other readers criticize it because they interpret his portrayal of Satan as a sympathetic figure.

Regardless of the controversy, *Paradise Lost* is considered one of the greatest poems in world literature.

BLAISE PASCAL

1623–1662

FRENCH PHILOSOPHER AND SCIENTIST

MAJOR ACCOMPLISHMENTS: PASSIONATE CHRISTIAN
WRITER, DISCOVERED PASCAL'S LAW, AND
CO-INVENTED THE MATHEMATICS OF PROBABILITY

BLAISE PASCAL'S FATHER WAS a member of nobility and a rich merchant who had an interest in science. Blaise's father was a tax collector for Upper Normandy, a position that involved the drudgery of repetitive calculations. To ease the burden for his father, Blaise built one of the first mechanical adding machines. He continued to improve the calculator for the next three years.

He was distracted from his calculating machine when he became interested in measuring air pressure using the recently invented barometer. In one of his simplest experiments, Pascal measured the air pressure at the bottom of Puy-de-Dôme Mountain and again one mile higher in elevation. He proved that the atmosphere becomes less dense with height.

By 1648, he had established Pascal's principle: a fluid in a container transmits pressure equally in all directions and acts at right angles to the surfaces it contacts. From these studies he invented the hydraulic press, the first simple machine that used liquid to gain a mechanical advantage.

In 1654, Pierre de Fermat, a French lawyer and amateur mathematician,

Blaise Pascal

wrote to him about a problem in probability. The two men exchanged a flurry of letters, and in the process developed the modern science of probability. Probability became an essential part of insurance mortality tables. In physics probability is used for dealing with huge numbers of particles, and in industry as a method of quality control. Manufacturers tested the quality of products by taking samples from the production line. Probability allowed the company to calculate quality of the entire production based on the few samples that were tested.

Another of his discoveries was a simple triangular number pattern in which each number was the sum of two numbers in the row above it. The arrangement, known as Pascal's triangle, provides the coefficients of the binomial expansion, combinations used in probability, and other number series.

At age 32, he had a frightening accident. While riding in a carriage, the horses bolted. The carriage was left hanging over a bridge. He was rescued, but the accident changed the direction of his life. From then on, he devoted himself almost full-time to religious matters. He became one of the most important writers in Christian literature. He wrote, "Man needs a Savior if the world is to make sense." He found that Savior to be Jesus Christ.

His writings are noted for their logic and passion. One of his famous sayings is, "This letter is longer than usual, because I lack the time to make it short." Pascal's most important work in philosophy was a collection of personal thoughts on faith and human suffering. His best known work is *Provincial Letters*, written in 1656.

One of his statements has caused never-ending discussion among religious groups. Known as Pascal's wager, he based the argument on expected value — the probability of an event occurring compared to the value of the event. Pascal argued that the value of a faithful Christian life and eternity in Heaven was far greater than the loss would be should faith be in vain.

In his short life, Blaise Pascal made a difference in science, mathematics, and Christian thought. After his death at age 39, a servant found a prayer that Pascal had sown into the lining of his coat. "Almighty God. . . . Mercifully grant to us thy servants, according to our several callings, gifts of excellence in body, mind, and will, and the grace to use them diligently and to thy glory, through Jesus Christ our Lord, who liveth and reigneth with thee and the Holy Spirit, one God, now and for ever."

THOMAS SYDENHAM
1624–1689
ENGLISH PHYSICIAN

MAJOR ACCOMPLISHMENTS: FOUNDED MEDICAL
TREATMENT BASED ON DIRECT OBSERVATION OF
PATIENTS, INTRODUCED THE USE OF LAUDANUM TO
TREAT PAIN AND PERFECTED THE USE OF QUININE
TO TREAT MALARIA

THOMAS SYDENHAM WAS from a class of English landowners rank-
ing just below the nobility. He enjoyed a good education at Oxford
with the intention of qualifying for a medical degree. However, those
plans were put aside with the outbreak of the English Civil War. His
family supported Parliament and Cromwell. Two of his brothers were
killed during the fighting, and he had at least one narrow escape.

At the end of the war in 1648, he received his medical degree.
However, he took an active role in government under Lord Protector
Cromwell. When Charles II returned to power after the fall of the
Commonwealth, Sydenham decided to keep a lower profile by open-
ing a medical practice in London.

Sydenham developed the concept of clinical medicine — detailed observations of patients and maintenance of accurate records
of their treatments. Until his day, patients were treated based on a
few general principles without much regard to their specific symp-
toms. His new method of treating disease led to several successes.

For instance, quinine, a derivative of the bark of the cinchona
tree, had been used without much success to treat malaria. Quinine
proved toxic in too many cases. Sydenham's careful records revealed
the proper moment in the cycle of the disease to administer the drug.
He championed the use of laudanum (a mixture of alcohol and opium)
to reduce pain and allow patients to rest more easily. He also recognized iron as a treatment for anemia.

In 1666, he wrote a book on fevers and identified scarlet fever,
which he named, as different from measles. His methods drew from
experimental science. One of his friends was Robert Boyle, the great
English experimental scientist who also lived in London. They had

much in common, including a strong Christian faith and recognition of the importance of communication among scientists. Sydenham and Boyle were charter members of the Royal Society.

Other doctors and scholars in medical schools at first dismissed his work because he did not base his treatment upon underlying principles espoused by the ancient Greeks. However, his methods led to success after success, and before he died he had gained the title "the English Hippocrates." His books on medicine, especially *Observationes Medicae* (1676), remained the best available for almost two hundred years.

One of his beliefs was that God had designed nature so that a cure was possible with natural factors. The role of the physician was to help nature achieve the cure. He spoke of the "remedies which it has pleased Almighty God to give to man to relieve his suffering."

ROBERT BOYLE

1627–1691

ENGLISH CHEMIST

MAJOR ACCOMPLISHMENT: FOUNDER OF MODERN
    CHEMISTRY; ONE OF THE TOP TEN SCIENTISTS OF
    ALL TIME

ROBERT BOYLE LIVED IN the home of an Irish peasant family during the first four years of his life. He was the seventh son of the Great Earl of Cork, one of the richest men in the world. However, his father did not want to spoil his children, so he sent them to live with poor families as they grew up.

After returning home, Boyle received private tutoring and then attended Eton in England. After a long tour of Europe, he settled at Oxford. Although he did not attend school there, he met each week with a group of experimental scientists and discussed the latest discoveries. Robert called the group his invisible college.

With his brilliant assistant, Robert Hooke, he built an improved air pump. He showed that it could be as useful a scientific invention as a telescope or microscope. Together they proved that sound does not carry in a vacuum. They confirmed Galileo's claim that without air resistance a feather and a lump of lead would fall at the same speed.

Robert Boyle

Until then, people thought of air as a mysterious substance that didn't follow natural laws. Boyle measured the volume of a sample of air at different pressures. He found pressure and volume were inversely related — doubling pressure reduced volume to half. Boyle's law, announced in his book *Touching the Spring of the Air,* was the first scientific law that applied to a gas.

Boyle next turned to chemistry. The false science of alchemy hindered progress in the true science of chemistry. Alchemists searched for a way to combine two ordinary substances and make gold. He believed gold to be an element that could not be made from simpler substances. Most chemists date the start of modern chemistry from 1661 when Boyle published *The Skeptical Chemist* that contained his definition of an element. An element, he wrote, was a substance that could not be separated into simpler substances by chemical means.

Boyle discovered the element phosphorus. It glowed in the dark and the heat of friction would set it afire. He used it to make the first match. Later, he learned that others had discovered phosphorus but kept the discovery to themselves. He had no patience with secrecy. He urged scientists to quickly report their discoveries. In this way, one scientist could build on the work of others.

How could useful information be spread more quickly? Boyle and his fellow scientists petitioned Charles II for a royal charter to begin a formal scientific organization. The Royal Society of London, which still meets today, became the first group of scientists to hold regular meetings. Its motto was the same as Boyle's: "Nothing by mere authority." The Royal Society hired Boyle's assistant Robert Hooke to test all new scientific claims by public experiments at their weekly meetings.

Although Boyle became famous, he remained a humble Christian. The Great Fire of 1666 left a hundred thousand people homeless in London. Boyle saw to it that they received food, clothing, and shelter. Most people never learned who had helped them.

Early in life he developed the habit of reading from the Bible each morning and having a time of prayer. His interest in religion grew as time passed. He learned Latin, Greek, Hebrew, and other biblical languages to better understand the Word of God. His missionary enthusiasm led him to pay for Bible translations into foreign languages. He gave away thousands of Bibles at his own expense.

His book of devotions, *Occasional Reflections*, became so popular that it became a target of a satire by Jonathan Swift.

Robert Boyle's friends were a roll call of the famous: Christopher Wren, Samuel Pepys, John Milton, Thomas Sydenham, Isaac Newton, and many others. Yet, during his life, Boyle towered over all of them. The King of England repeatedly offered Boyle high government posts and titles. He preferred to be known as simply "Mr. Robert Boyle, a Christian gentleman."

Boyle died on December 30, 1691. In his will, he provided for a series of lectures on the defense of Christianity against unbelievers. These sermons are known as the Boyle Lectures.

JOHN RAY

1627–1705

ENGLISH NATURALIST

MAJOR ACCOMPLISHMENTS: FOUNDER OF NATURAL
HISTORY IN BRITAIN; PIONEERED THE CLASSIFICATION
OF LIVING THINGS, ESPECIALLY PLANTS

RAY'S FATHER WAS A village blacksmith of limited means. However, Ray won a scholarship to Cambridge and earned a master's degree in 1650. University officials asked him to stay on as a lecturer.

Botany became his passion. Books about plants were printed mainly to show those that were believed to promote healing. The books identified plants by the organs of the body they were supposed to help. The information often had little scientific value. Ray collected different plants, and his garden became a living museum of interesting plant specimens. In 1660, he published his *Catalogue of Cambridge Plants* describing the plants he had found in the area.

Ray searched for a natural system of classification that would reflect the order given by God when he created plants and animals. He noticed that some flowering plants had single seed leaves and others had double seed leaves. This separated the flowering plants into two distinct classes, still known today as monocotyledons and dicotyledons.

In addition to his scientific studies, Ray became a clergyman in the Church of England. He often gave the daily devotion during the chapel service at Cambridge. After the collapse of the Commonwealth under Cromwell's son, Parliament invited Charles II to return and restore order. The new monarch insisted that all clergymen sign the Act of Uniformity that renounced the religious changes instituted by Cromwell.

Ray refused to sign because of his religious beliefs. He was dismissed from Cambridge. He could not use the college library. His garden of 700 plants that he had worked on for 10 years grew on school property, so he lost that, too.

With the support of a wealthy former student, Ray thoroughly explored England, Scotland, and Wales and traveled in Europe. He collected information about plants and animals. In 1667, he published *Catalogue of British Plants*. People who studied plants quickly accepted the book as a reliable guide. They answered his call to send corrections and samples of plants he had not described. He said, "The bounds of science are not fixed. The treasures of nature are inexhaustible."

By 1685, a persistent infection in his legs prevented him from long travels. He turned to a study of insects. Over the years, he wrote more books. He wrote a book on fish, another on insects, and his most important work, *Historia Planarum* ("History of Plants"). It contained detailed information on 18,600 different plant species.

He also pondered the difficult question of fossils, rock-like remains of what appeared to be ancient life. Ray lent his support to the idea that fossils were the remains of once-living organisms. Although he agreed that some fossils of sea life could have been washed ashore during the biblical flood, he offered other explanations including the idea that the sea may have once covered what is now dry land.

Some fossils did not look like any known plant or animal. Ray lived when much of the earth remained unexplored. He suggested that the strange forms might live elsewhere on earth in hidden places. At that time both scientists and Bible scholars agreed that no species had become extinct. As friends continued to send him samples of unusual fossils, he began to think it possible that species could die out.

Everywhere he looked, he saw evidence of God the Creator. He wrote a book titled *Wisdom of God Manifested in the Works of the Creation*. The book was a persuasive argument for studying God's creation. He wrote in a simple, straightforward style that engaged the readers, far different from the pompous and complex style of other scholars.

Unfortunately, printers faced heavy fines if they printed religious books by nonconformists. Ray's religious writings were banned. He could publish scientific books but not religious ones. This changed after William and Mary became joint rulers of England in 1689. For the first time in 30 years, Ray found a printer for his religious books. *Wisdom of God* was published in 1691. Other books followed, including *Persuasive to a Holy Life*.

Today, John Ray is called the "founder of English natural history." What did he think of his work? Ray said, "I predict that our descendants will reach such heights in the sciences that our proudest discoveries will seem slight, obvious, and almost worthless."

His work has proven to be far from worthless. In addition to solid scientific content, John Ray's many books emphasize the doctrine that the wisdom and power of God can be seen through His creation.

JOHN BUNYAN

1628–1688

English writer and Puritan minister

Major accomplishment: author of *Pilgrim's Progress*

JOHN BUNYAN GREW UP near the farming community of Bedford, England. His early education consisted of a minimum of reading and writing. He dropped out of school to learn his father's trade as a tinker. Tinkers, itinerant travelers who mended pots and pans, were not held in high regard. Bunyan's father had managed to make his living in a permanent residence and ply his trade without traveling.

John Bunyan was an athletic, redheaded boy who preferred games on the village green to attending school or listening to Sunday sermons. His favorite game was tipcat, played with a bat and wooden peg rather than a ball. He also began to read popular adventure stories sold in cheap editions hawked at the annual Stourbridge fair in Cambridge.

At age 17, his mother died. A few months later, he was mustered into Oliver Cromwell's army to oppose the royalists in the English Civil War. He saw no action, but once a fellow soldier switched sentry assignments with him, and the man who took his place was killed by a sniper's bullet. During his military service, he met Quakers and others who questioned religious authority.

After the war, the 20-year-old Bunyan returned home and married. His wife, Mary, was poor, too. They had to borrow dishes and cutlery to set up housekeeping. Mary's entire dowry consisted of two religious books: *Plain Man's Pathway to Heaven* and *Practice of Piety*. To please his wife, Bunyan listened as she read aloud from the books and from the Bible. She persuaded him to attend church with her.

He chose to continue enjoying his pleasures and managed to stifle his growing feelings of guilt. He became miserable because of the conflict between what he wanted to do and what he knew he should do.

Finally, he began to drop one by one his favorite Sunday sports and managed to put off the swearing he had picked up as a young man. He was baptized as an adult in the River Ouse. Yet, he lacked peace and suffered an inner struggle that plunged him into despair. He felt he could never be good enough to deserve God's love. Only after reading Luther's commentary on Galatians and understanding salvation by God's grace did his outlook become positive.

John and Mary had two daughters and two sons. The first daughter, Mary, was born blind. His wife died in 1654. The religious freedom that separatists enjoyed under the Commonwealth ended with the restoration of the monarchy in 1660.

Bunyan worked by day mending pots and spent his nights and Sundays preaching in barns, shops, and open fields. He began to attract large crowds and thus came to the notice of the sheriff of Bedford. Rabble-rousers who incited riots against authority often resorted to harangues in open fields. The sheriff arrested him on the charge of conducting a meeting without the permission of the state church.

After three months the sheriff offered release, provided Bunyan would promise to preach only with permission of the established church. Bunyan knew that such permission would not be given. One church official had already asked, "What right does a tinker have to preach?" John Bunyan said, "If I were out of prison today, I would preach the gospel again tomorrow." The sheriff refused to release him.

Bunyan had married again shortly before his arrest. His second wife, Elizabeth, fully supported his decision and took on the responsibility of raising his children. Bunyan struggled to provide for his family while incarcerated. He made bootlaces that were put in the hands of street merchants who sold them throughout the area. He also wrote books that earned some money. While in prison, he had limited access to books for research, so he wrote about subjects he knew best — his own sermons and fiction he created out of his imagination.

After six years, England suffered a terrible outbreak of the Black Death. Bunyan was released from jail during this emergency. While out of jail, he published his spiritual autobiography *Grace Abounding*. However, freedom was short-lived, and he was returned to prison where he spent another six years.

Bunyan's second release came about because of a quirk in the way Charles II freed his supporters who were Catholic. They, too, had been put in prison for being in disagreement with the Church of

England. Charles II annulled the laws against the Catholics but doing so also released the separatists, including Bunyan.

During the 12 years in jail, Bunyan wrote about 12 books. His greatest book, Pilgrim's Progress, had not yet been written. He may have been thinking about it, but when he was released, he devoted his full time to preaching the gospel.

After three years, Charles II revoked the release of separatists, and Bunyan went to prison again. He was no longer a little-known tinker and itinerant preacher. He had become recognized as a leading Puritan minister and writer. This time Elizabeth enlisted the support of his friends in high places, and he was released in six months.

During the six months in jail, John Bunyan composed the first part of Pilgrim's Progress. He wrote it on the brown paper that wrapped the food his wife brought to him. The 50-year-old Bunyan published the book in 1678. Bunyan continued with additions and improvements to the book through eight editions before it reached its final form.

In the allegory, the central character, Christian, leaves the City of Destruction and travels toward the Celestial City. Along the way, he meets people with names that reflect their character — Faithful, Talkative, Ignorance. Bunyan named his characters so they would "stick in your memory like burrs." The book combined stirring action, telling details and highly symbolic elements but maintained an authentic feel of real life.

Although he had little formal education, John Bunyan became the most popular religious writer in the English language. Pilgrim's Progress became the most widely circulated Christian book other than the Bible. Those who dismissed him as an uneducated tinker now sought to be seen in his presence.

Bunyan continued to write and preach. He died ten years after the publication of Pilgrim's Progress.

CHRISTIAAN HUYGENS
1629–1695
DUTCH SCIENTIST
MAJOR ACCOMPLISHMENTS: INVENTED THE PENDULUM
CLOCK, DEVELOPED WAVE THEORY OF LIGHT

CHRISTIAAN HUYGENS WAS BORN in 1629 at The Hague, Netherlands. Christiaan was educated at home by private tutors and his father, who was an official in the Dutch government. Later, Christiaan attended the University of Leiden.

Although talented in mathematics and physics, astronomy captured his interest. He developed a better way to fashion telescope lenses and learned a way to reduce chromatic aberration, a distracting color fringe due to the lens acting as a prism. With his improved telescope, he made a series of discoveries including a large moon of Saturn that he named Titan. His telescope also revealed the true nature of the rings of Saturn.

To time astronomical events, Huygens built the first accurate clock in 1658. He used the regular back and forth motion of a swinging pendulum. Clocks of his design became known as grandfather clocks.

He became a well-known scientist, and England's Royal Society elected him a member in 1663. France's King Louis XIV invited Huygens to start a French version of the Royal Society. Huygens was the first president of the Royal Academy of Science. His friends included René Descartes, Blaise Pascal, and Gottfried Wilhelm Leibniz.

In 1684, Louis XIV closed all the Protestant churches. The king believed that most people would stay in France and worship the way he directed. Instead, more than 200,000 Christians left the country. Many were intelligent, hard-working people, and their loss was a blow to the economy of France.

Christiaan Huygens held very strong Protestant religious beliefs. He saw the changes coming, and in 1681 he left Paris for The Hague where he could worship God freely. He gave up his privileged position and many of the scientific instruments that he had designed.

Although science was important to him, he did not hesitate to put service to God first.

He continued to make important contributions to science, including a theory of light as wave motion. He developed the concept, Huygens' principle, that each point of a light wave becomes the source of new waves. Years after his death, scientists realized light did have a wave nature, and his work became as important as that of Newton's.

CHRISTOPHER WREN

1632–1723

ENGLISH ARCHITECT

MAJOR ACCOMPLISHMENT: BUILT LONDON'S ST. PAUL'S
CATHEDRAL

CHRISTOPHER WREN WAS THE son of a minister. He studied astronomy and mathematics at Oxford and earned a master's degree in 1653. Oxford had experienced authoritarian scholarship for years, but Parliament had replaced entrenched scholars with professors who were more interested in truth than ancient authority. Wren was one of the first generation of students to enjoy the benefits of the scientific revolution.

Wren became instructor of astronomy at Gresham College in London. While looking for an area in which his mathematical skills could make a difference, he learned that the progress in architecture had come to a standstill in England. The last great architect, Inigo Jones, had died ten years earlier and no one had risen to take his place.

Wren realized that people wanted to take part in the proceedings in churches and public buildings. The gothic style of architecture allowed large buildings, but support pillars often obscured the audience's view. Wren applied mathematics to design buildings that had large open spaces but were structurally sound.

In 1665, Wren was given the assignment to restore Old St. Paul's. Before he could develop a plan, the Black Death (bubonic plague) struck London. He escaped the threat by making a tour of Europe to study the design of great buildings. He saw the nearly completed Louvre and the remodeled Palace of Versailles. He returned to London to learn that the Great Fire had destroyed Old St. Paul's beyond repair.

Before he could start on a new building, Charles II gave Wren the title of surveyor of the royal works, a position that carried with it the responsibility of all public buildings in Britain. His duties included supervising the rebuilding of London. Wren replaced the 87 parish churches that had been destroyed with 51 new buildings. He also designed the Greenwich Observatory. For his work in rebuilding London, Wren was knighted.

Wren was 40 years old when construction began on St. Paul's. Twenty years later, Londoners could see the dome begin to rise over nearby buildings. It was still unfinished when they heralded the new century. Finally, in January 1711, Wren's son Christopher acted for him to install the cross on top of the great dome.

Wren had seen the building through to its finish. He had made his first sketch at age 33 and saw the final stone put in place when he was 79 years old. Most remarkable of all, Wren never became obsessed with his project. He still had time for a happy home life, meeting with scientific friends and worshiping each week. He remained cheerful and polite despite the stress of being daily involved in one of the most difficult construction projects of all time.

After its completion, Wren went to St. Paul's each day for a time of devotion. One day after returning home, the 91-year-old Wren fell asleep in his favorite chair by the fire. A servant came to wake him and found he had died. He was buried inside St. Paul's in a simple crypt topped with black marble. Later, his son placed a plaque on a wall nearby that became one of the most famous of all inscriptions: "Reader, if you seek his monument, look around you."

Wren's architecture style influenced England and Colonial American architecture for a hundred years. The U.S. Capitol in Washington D.C. is modeled after the dome of St. Paul's.

ANTON VAN LEEUWENHOEK

1632–1723

AMATEUR SCIENTIST

MAJOR ACCOMPLISHMENTS: FIRST TO REPORT THE
EXISTENCE OF MICROORGANISMS INVISIBLE TO THE
UNAIDED EYE

ANTON VAN LEEUWENHOEK ATTENDED grammar school in his
hometown of Delft, Holland. At age 21, he opened a drapery shop
and sold cloth and sewing supplies. He also served as chief steward
in charge of the Delft City Hall.

He devoted his spare time to making microscopes and viewing
small objects through them. Along with patience and keen eyesight,
Leeuwenhoek possessed a never-ending curiosity. He peered at hair,
skin, cork, ivory, blood, eyes and wings of insects, scales and fins of
fish, muscle tissue, and everything else he could fit under the lens.

At this time, prominent scientists readily accepted the idea of
spontaneous generation. They believed vermin such as ants, weevils,
and other small life could spring into existence from non-living matter. Leeuwenhoek traced out the life cycle of insects and showed that
weevils were really grubs hatched from eggs deposited by adult insects. The eggs were often so tiny as to go unnoticed. Leeuwenhoek
rejected the idea of spontaneous generation.

In another investigation, he examined the fine network of blood
vessels in a rabbit's ear. He observed red blood cells flowing from
arteries into smaller and smaller capillaries and then coming out on
the other side in veins. He saw similar structures in the webbed feet
of frogs. He confirmed the existence of capillaries connecting arteries
and veins, and was the first to give an accurate description of red
blood cells.

Starting in 1673, he described the world his lens revealed in letters to the Royal Society in London. The letters, written in Dutch, were
informal and chatty. The Royal Society could have dismissed his work,
but some of its members showed their true greatness. They encour-

aged him to keep them informed about his discoveries.

He examined insects and noticed that some of the eyes were complex with 4,000 individual lenses. His study of the underside of leaves revealed tiny openings, stomata, for the passage of air. Leeuwenhoek's microscope revealed that living tissue was far more complex than anyone had imagined.

Anton van Leeuwenhoek

In 1674, Anton made his most important discovery. He found single-celled animals, protozoa, living in a drop of canal water. The small life moved, ate, grew, and reproduced by splitting. The one-celled life seemed to be everywhere — in rain barrels, ponds, and even inside his own mouth.

The English writer Jonathan Swift summed up Leewenhoek's discovery in a humorous poem:

> So, naturalists observe, a flea
> Hath smaller fleas that on them prey;
> And these have smaller still to bite 'em
> And so proceed ad infinitum.

Leeuwenhoek made hundreds of microscopes so he could keep favorite specimens permanently mounted for later study. Although he reported his findings, he did not detail how he fashioned the lenses. One of Leeuwenhoek's lenses magnified 270 times, far greater than any other microscope then in use. That magnification also caused the object being viewed to become 270 times dimmer. Additional illumination had to be focused on the subject. Exactly how he accomplished this is unknown.

At the very limit of his most powerful microscope, he saw rod-like and ball-like bacteria. He drew pictures of what he saw and sent the drawings to the Royal Society. One hundred years passed before another scientist succeeded in seeing them. Another century passed before scientists learned that bacteria were the cause of many diseases. For a single individual working alone, to make a discovery of this importance seldom occurs in science.

Leeuwenhoek died in 1723 at the age of 90. By then he had become known throughout the world. Despite his great fame, he remained a humble person who only wanted to learn more about God's creation. His greatest skill was in his single-minded determination to present exactly what he observed.

ROBERT HOOKE

1635–1703

ENGLISH SCIENTIST

MAJOR ACCOMPLISHMENT: FIRST PERSON TO EARN AN
INCOME ENTIRELY AS AN EXPERIMENTAL RESEARCH
SCIENTIST

ROBERT HOOKE'S FATHER WAS a clergyman in Freshwater, a town on the Isle of Wight. Robert suffered smallpox as a child and became an orphan at age 13. He attended Oxford University and paid his tuition by waiting tables and serving wealthy students and professors.

While at Oxford, Hooke became the laboratory assistant to Robert Boyle. Together, they built an improved air pump. The two scientists made a series of discoveries such as the role of air in combustion and breathing, the fact that sound could not be transmitted through a vacuum, and that a feather and a lump of lead fell at the same speed without air resistance.

In 1662, the newly formed Royal Society employed Hooke to demonstrate three or four interesting new experiments each week. He held this position of curator of experiments for 41 years. He became the first scientist to earn an income entirely by research. As the years passed, his tireless efforts extended scientific discovery into many areas.

He improved upon the barometer, designed a rain gauge, and built a device for measuring humidity in the air. For the first time, scientists had the tools they needed to begin a study of weather and make weather forecasts. He invented the balance wheel hairspring that made small watches possible. His drawings of the planet Mars were so detailed they were used later to measure how rapidly the planet rotated.

Hooke designed an improved microscope. He was the first to examine petrified wood with a microscope and notice the similarity between the fossil wood and living specimens. While viewing a thin slice of cork through his microscope, he noticed a series of honeycomb-like pores. He gave the name "cell" ("small room") to the smallest structural unit that makes all living organisms.

His microscopic studies were published in 1665 in *Micrographia*. In addition to his written descriptions, the book contained detailed drawings of small living things. He made the drawings himself and pioneered the method of changing focus to render each section of the insect in focus. Even the invention of photography two hundred years later could not improve upon his drawings. His portrait of a flea is often reproduced.

Shortly after the publication of his book, a disastrous fire destroyed the center of London. Ten thousand buildings — homes, churches, public buildings, and shops — were consumed in a four-square-mile area. When Christropher Wren was given the task of rebuilding the city, he chose Hooke as his chief assistant. Hooke held the official title of Surveyor of London and was the architect for the College of Physicians building and Bethlehem Hospital.

He continued his duties at the Royal Society. Unfortunately, almost every discovery was a shared one because he either completed the work of others or had to move on to other matters before concluding his own studies. He stated, but could not prove, that gravity follows the inverse-square law, which became part of Newton's law of gravity. However, one law in physics is clearly his alone. Hooke's law relates the amount a solid object bends is proportional to the force that acts on it. Spring scales for weighing produce in supermarkets make use of this discovery.

Robert Hooke did have his critics who labeled him a quarrelsome individual. Those who knew him well, such as Robert Boyle and Christopher Wren, had nothing but praise for his fortitude. Intense headaches and pain in his arms and legs from childhood diseases wracked his body. Sometimes Hooke visibly shook from pain even during his sleep. His Christian character has never been called into doubt.

In any other age, Robert Hooke would have been the premiere scientist. He had the misfortune of living in the shadow of the greater intellect of Isaac Newton. The only portrait of Hooke was lost shortly after his death. Recently, a small park in his honor was built across from a chapel he designed.

NICOLAUS STENO

1638–1686

DANISH ANATOMIST AND GEOLOGIST

MAJOR ACCOMPLISHMENT: FOUNDER OF SCIENTIFIC GEOLOGY

NILS STENNSEN WAS BORN on New Year's Day 1638, in Denmark. His life was filled with abrupt transitions. He studied to be a physician, but made key discoveries in geology. He changed his name from Nils Stennsen to the Latin form of Nicolaus Steno. At age 30 he abandoned a successful career in science to devote himself full time to religious matters. Even his birthday has changed from January 1 (Julian calendar) to January 11 (Gregorian calendar.)

During his training as a physician, Steno studied anatomy in Amsterdam. He discovered a gland at the angle of the jaw. This duct supplies the mouth with most of the saliva for digestion. He pointed it out to a professor who dismissed the discovery as a botched dissection. Later, the professor published a book that described the gland and claimed to have discovered it. However, Steno had written about that gland, tear ducts, and other glands with an insight that went beyond mere description. The salivary gland is still referred to as the duct of Steno.

His skill at medicine earned him a position as the court physician to the grand duke Ferdinand II in Florence, Italy. During his travels accompanying the duke, he studied rock formations in the region. His discoveries about the rocks and minerals established him as the founder of three physical sciences: crystallography, scientific geology, and paleontology.

He studied crystals and set forth the first law of crystallography: Crystals of a specific substance all have the same angles between corresponding faces. For instance, although quartz crystals differed in size, color, and where they were found, angles between corresponding faces were always the same.

Steno published a book on geology and noted the key principle of geology: The superposition of rock strata — layers of rock are deposited horizontally with older material at the bottom and newer layers at the top. Each layer contains a record of past events. He studied fossils and concluded that they were the remains of actual plants and animals of ages past. Geologists at that time believed that fossils were stones made either by God as He practiced making creation or by the devil to lead people astray. Nicolaus Steno in Italy and Robert Hooke in England gave convincing evidence that fossils had a natural cause.

All of these discoveries were made while Steno was in his twenties.

From his childhood, Steno had an interest in religion. Unfortunately, as he grew up, his Protestant friends were always in heated and contradictory arguments about their beliefs. In later life as his mind turned more to God, his friends among the Roman Catholics in Florence engaged in no such controversy. Although it took more than a year for him to make the decision, at age 30, he abandoned science entirely and threw himself wholeheartedly into his new faith as a Roman Catholic.

He wrote numerous theological works that focused on Christian duty to provide the spiritual needs of individuals, especially the poor.

Steno had a talent for languages. He could speak Danish, German, Dutch, French, Italian, and Latin. He had learned to read Greek, Hebrew, and Arabic. He became a bishop after ten years and was assigned to Hanover, Germany. It had a large number of people from other countries, and he became popular with the foreigners because he delivered sermons in their languages.

Gottfried Wilhelm Leibniz, the German mathematician and philosopher, came to hear his sermons and may have visited him at home. Steno welcomed visitors to dine with him because it gave him an opportunity to give a devotion from the Gospels or from a devotional book. His favorite was the simple and uncomplicated *Imitation of Christ*, usually credited to Thomas à Kempis (1379–1471).

When Steno died at the relatively young age of 48, his last words were "Jesus, be my Jesus [Savior]."

NEHEMIAH GREW

1641–1712

English botanist

Major accomplishment: co-founder (with Marcello Malpighi) of plant anatomy

NEHEMIAH GREW'S FATHER was a nonconformist clergyman. His father served as the vicar of a church in Coventry during the Commonwealth. However, when Charles II was restored, his father refused to sign the Act of Uniformity and, like John Ray, lost his position. Grew was studying medicine at Cambridge but with the reversal of the family fortunes, his studies ended before he qualified as a doctor.

The details of Grew's life during the next ten years are unclear. He may have practiced medicine in his hometown of Coventry where his father had started a grammar school. After ten years, his finances improved enough for a trip to the medical school at Leyden in the Netherlands. There he took the examinations that qualified him as a doctor.

Henry Sampson, Grew's half-brother was a doctor, for the nonconformists in London. Sampson introduced Grew to members of the Royal Society who encouraged Grew to move to London. A position as lecturer was made for him at Gresham College.

For seven years Grew had been working on a manuscript, *Anatomy of Vegetation*, which he sent to the Royal Society. Much to his dismay, he learned that the more experienced and better-known Italian scientist Marcello Malpighi had delivered a similar manuscript to the Royal Society. Rather than enter a scientific squabble about priority, Grew frankly admitted that the work was similar and deferred to Malpighi. The Royal Society, however, published his book and encouraged him to continue his studies. Malpighi also showed the spirit of a true scientist and began to correspond with Grew. Their cooperative effort established the new science of plant anatomy.

Robert Hooke supplied Grew with an improved microscope and instructed him in its use. In 1682, he completed the manuscript *Anatomy of Plants*. It included many three-dimensional microscopic drawings of plant tissues and details of flowers. He was the first person to identify the male and female parts of flowers.

Publishing books on scientific subjects was an expensive business. Because of a lack of funds, the Royal Society could not publish *Anatomy of Plants*. Grew, who was not a wealthy person, devised an unusual way to pay for the book — public subscription. He pre-sold the book so the printer knew that the cost of printing would be covered. It was a new way to finance the publication of scientific books.

Grew was the first to describe the friction ridges that today are better known as fingerprints. As a doctor, he made a study of chemicals used to treat disease. He obtained magnesium sulfate from a spring outside the town of Epsom. The chemical, which he named Epsom salt, was used to treat scratches and upset stomachs as a mild antacid.

Like his father, Grew was a strong Christian believer. He invented the term "comparative anatomy" and noticed repeated designs in nature. He pointed to this as evidence that plants and animals "were therefore the contrivances of the same wisdom." In his study of the walking stick insect, he said that its design far surpassed the most elaborate human needlework ever made.

ISAAC NEWTON
1642–1727
ENGLISH PHYSICIST AND MATHEMATICIAN
MAJOR ACCOMPLISHMENT: FORMULATED THE LAW OF
GRAVITY

ISAAC NEWTON WAS BORN on Christmas Day on a farm in England. His father had died before he was born. When Newton proved inept as a farmer, his uncle, a preacher of the gospel, enrolled him in a school at Grantham (the same school that English Prime Minister Margaret Thatcher would attend nearly four hundred years later.) He showed no particular promise as a student, either, although his best grades were in religion. His mother had remarried and lived with her husband, who was the minister in a town near her farm. When his stepfather died, Newton inherited a large library of religious texts. Throughout his life, Newton devoted more time to studying Bible subjects than he did to mathematics or science.

Like Robert Hooke at Oxford, Newton worked his way through Cambridge. He studied theology and mathematics, but appeared to be an ordinary student. He began study for a graduate degree in 1665, the year Black Death struck. The school sent students home for 18 months. Newton spent the time on his mother's farm. With the freedom to study on his own, he made the preliminary discoveries that would fuel his researches for the rest of his scientific career. In England, the time became known as the Plague Year, but to Newton it was his *Annus Mirabilis* — "marvelous year."

Newton's discoveries in physics, optics, astronomy, and mathematics rank him as the greatest scientific intellect of all time. He proved that white light from the sun is actually a mixture of all the colors, invented the reflecting telescope, developed the powerful mathematical tool of calculus, and stated the three laws of motion.

His greatest achievement was his formulation of the law of universal gravitation. It consists of two principles: the inverse square law states that gravity grows weaker with the square of the distance; and the second part states that objects attract according to the product of their masses and along the straight lines connecting their centers. The story, apparently true, is that the fall of an apple prompted Newton to begin thinking about gravity. He wondered why it fell straight down but the moon and planets followed nearly circular orbits.

Scientists believed that the sun produced a whirlpool effect that pushed along the planets. The understanding that gravity acted along the imaginary line connecting a planet and the sun came from Newton's study of the Bible. In addition to his well-worn King James Version of the Bible in English, Newton had earlier translations in Latin and Hebrew, which he could read. From descriptions in the Bible, he made a detailed floor plan of the temple that Solomon built. In the center was a fire for offering sacrifices. Visualizing people being attracted to the fire gave him the idea that the sun attracted the planets along a line connecting their centers.

Edmund Halley visited Newton with a question about gravity and learned that Newton had completed his gravity studies years earlier without publishing them. Working as Newton's editor and publisher, Halley encouraged Newton to write *Principia Mathematica*. The book was published in 1687, and established Newton's reputation as the leading mind of his, or any other, generation. In the second edition, Newton wrote, "This most beautiful System of the Sun, Planets and Comets could only proceed from the counsel and dominion of an intelligent and powerful Being."

Five years after the publication of *Principia*, the 50-year-old Newton grew weary of his scientific pursuits. Newton had served a short time as a member of Parliament in London and occasionally he attended Royal Society meetings. He found that he enjoyed contact with Robert Boyle, Edmund Halley, Christopher Wren, and the other great minds of his age. He sought a government post and became Warden of the Mint. He rose to Master of the Mint and oversaw England's re-coinage, a difficult task that required a person of absolute honesty because the effort involved vast amounts of silver and gold.

Newton did have his flaws. In his early years, he was very much a loner with poor social graces and a tendency toward secrecy. As an only child raised by two doting women (mother and grandmother), he had his way in most things and found it difficult to realize the other person's point of view. These rough edges to his personality were smoothed by his years in London.

Isaac Newton

Newton was elected president of the Royal Society, an office he held for 24 years. In 1707, Queen Anne knighted him. To show that it was for his scientific achievements, the ceremony was held at Cambridge. When he died, Newton was buried at Westminster Abby.

Newton wrote two books on biblical subjects, *Chronology of Ancient Kingdoms* and the *Observations upon the Prophecies of Daniel*. He said, "I find more sure marks of authenticity in the Bible than in any profane history whatsoever."

As a young man, he had tried his hand at poetry. Although untitled, the following religious poem by Newton could be called *Three Crowns*:

> A secret art my soul requires to try,
> If prayers can give me, what the wars deny.
> Three crowns distinguish'd here in order do
> Present their objects to my knowing view.
> Earth's crown, thus at my feet, I can disdain,
> Which heavy is, and, at the best, but vain.
> But now a crown of thorns I gladly greet,
> Sharp is this crown, but not so sharp as sweet.
> A crown of glory that I yonder see
> Is full of bliss and of eternity.

JOHN FLAMSTEED
1646–1719
ENGLISH ASTRONOMER

MAJOR ACCOMPLISHMENT: FIRST ASTRONOMER ROYAL
OF GREAT BRITAIN

JOHN FLAMSTEED FOUNDED THE Greenwich Observatory, made the first star catalog based on telescopic observations, and established Greenwich as the starting point for the prime meridian.

Flamsteed's father was a maker of malt. The young Flamsteed's formal education ended before he completed grammar school. His father took him out of school and cited the boy's poor health as the reason. Later in life, Flamsteed suspected his education ended so he could help his father at home.

Flamsteed studied astronomy on his own and built his own telescope. He began corresponding with members of the Royal Society. One of the great problems facing the seafaring British Empire was an accurate way to determine position of ships in the middle of the ocean. The only method then available measured the position of the moon against the background of stars.

Tests by Flamsteed showed that star charts were woefully inadequate. His solution was to build an observatory dedicated solely to finding the positions of the stars accurately enough for navigation. The Royal Society agreed and pressed Charles II to establish a royal observatory and hire Flamsteed as the Astronomer Royal.

In 1675, Charles II authorized building the observatory at Greenwich. Because it would not do for the royal astronomer to be without a college degree, he issued a special warrant authorizing Cambridge University to grant an M.A. degree to Flamsteed. At the same time, Flamsteed became a minister in the Anglican Church. He served a parish near the Greenwich observatory.

Although Flamsteed had a title and observatory building, he had no equipment and only a small salary. He managed to borrow some instruments and build others. He tutored students for money to buy the rest.

Observations of even the most careful observers were filled with errors introduced by telescope mounts, timing irregularities, and observer bias. Removing the errors, a process known as reduction, required hours of tedious computations. He ran the Royal Observatory without assistants. He performed all of the calculations himself.

The final step was to adjust all the stars to a best fit to the network. Data released piecemeal would not be up to his standards of accuracy. However, Isaac Newton and Edmund Halley, as well as other astronomers, needed data for their projects. Flamsteed did provide preliminary data for Newton to complete his research on the orbit of the moon. Edmund Halley, Newton's friend, published Flamsteed's preliminary data in 1712. Flamsteed was furious that his uncorrected data had been released without his permission. He managed to buy 300 of the 400 books and destroy them.

Flamsteed's life did not outlast his perfectionism. He died before the tables were complete. Edmund Halley became the second Astronomer Royal and finally published Flamsteed's star catalog in 1725. It contained precise positions of 3,000 stars and remained the best available star catalog for nearly 100 years.

Stars' positions were given in right ascension and declination, measurements that were similar to latitude and longitude. Flamsteed measured the east and west positions from Greenwich. British chartmakers used it as the prime meridian for British charts. In 1884, the Greenwich meridian became the worldwide standard by international agreement.

GOTTFRIED WILHELM LEIBNIZ

1646–1716

GERMAN PHILOSOPHER, MATHEMATICIAN, AND
POLITICAL WRITER

MAJOR ACCOMPLISHMENT: DEVELOPED THE PRINCIPLE
OF SUFFICIENT REASON AS AN ARGUMENT FOR THE
EXISTENCE OF GOD

GOTTFRIED WILHELM LEIBNIZ WAS a universal genius who mastered mathematics, philosophy, theology, and law at an early age. He completed his legal studies at age 20 at the university in his hometown of Leipzig, Germany. Authorities refused to give him a doctor of law degree. They rejected him because of his age rather than his knowledge.

Leibniz left Leipzig and never returned to the town. Nuremberg granted a law degree immediately, and he found employment as political advisor to Prince Johann Phipp von Schönborn in Mainz. The prince tried to ally himself with France but found it difficult because of Louis XIV's aggressive attitude. In addition, refugees were flowing into Germany because of Louis XIV's intolerance toward Protestants.

Schönborn sent Leibniz as his diplomat to find a way to stave off war. The plan was to divert Louis XIV's conquest elsewhere such as into Africa, but to do it in such a way that the king was not aware of being manipulated. Leibniz traveled with science research as a cover for his covert mission. Although his primary objective failed, Leibniz did meet the leading scientists throughout Europe.

In France, conversations with Christiaan Huygens awakened in Leibniz an interest in geometry and mathematics. Leibniz recognized the advantages of representing numbers with 1 and 0 alone and developed the binary number system. Three hundred years later, binary notation became important as the simple on or off code for digital computers.

Leibniz visited London in 1673, where he met Robert Boyle and other scientists. Leibniz showed a mechanical calculating machine he had built. His machine could multiply, divide, and extract square roots as well as add and subtract. The invention was superior to Pascal's machine and gained him membership in the Royal Society.

When Leibniz returned to Germany, Schönborn had died. Leibniz received an appointment with the powerful Brunswick family as librarian. He moved to Hanover and remained at that post for the rest of his life.

Leibniz is credited as co-inventor of calculus, but the recognition came with controversy. Today, most historians agree that Newton developed calculus first and used it in handwritten documents that circulated to a few scientists. However, Leibniz developed his version independently and published it first in 1684. Newton did not make a public showing of his discovery until 1687.

The English claimed that Leibniz had gotten an inkling of Newton's idea from letters he had seen addressed by Newton to other scientists. Both Newton and Leibniz tried to stay out of the fray. Leibniz employed a vastly superior notation for working with calculus that won out in competition with Newton's cumbersome symbols.

Leibniz gained recognition as a philosopher. His theory of philosophy required several books to formulate and cannot be easily summarized without becoming overly simplistic. However, one of his chief points is known as the causation argument for the existence of God, or the principle of sufficient reason. Certain things exist for which there is no reason for them to exist other than the free choice of God. In 1697, he published a book that identified God as the ultimate origin of things. In a later book, he arrived at the conclusion that human beings live in the "best of all possible worlds," a phrase that Voltaire satirized in *Candide*.

Leibniz championed reconciliation among Christian groups. During his travels and in his writing, he worked tirelessly to persuade Christians to stop fighting one another. The persecution of the Counter-Reformation caused Protestants to leave Catholic countries. At Leibniz's suggestion, Frederick I of Prussia invited the refugees to resettle in his country. Prussia gained some of the best minds in Europe and remained a well-educated and powerful country throughout the 1700s and 1800s.

In 1707, Leibniz convinced Frederick I to establish a society of scientists modeled after the Royal Society. Leibniz drew up the charter and the Academy of Sciences in Berlin became an important meeting place for European scientists.

Unlike some people who become a jack-of-all-trades and master of none, Leibniz was master of them all. Unfortunately, that too hindered his influence on later generations. Few people could keep up with his quicksilver mind, and he had no cadre of disciples to carry on his philosophy.

His books encompassed mathematics, physics, philosophy, theology, and diplomacy. Only he and a few other people understood his deep insights into a variety of fields. Biographers of his life faced the daunting task of summarizing achievements in areas that no one person is likely to have mastered. For those reasons, accounts of Leibniz's life tend to focus on one particular aspect at the expense of others.

Although recognized as a universal genius, his appeal faded in later life. His reversal of fortune began in 1698, when the leadership of the Brunswick family in Hanover fell to George Louis, who would later become George I of England. Even Leibniz's personal charm and skill as a diplomat could not conceal his evident dislike of the uneducated prince. In turn, George I made Leibniz's life miserable and when he rose to the throne in England, he refused to let Leibniz visit the country.

During his last years, Leibniz became a lonely figure traveling from city to city and preaching a message of Christian reconciliation that no one heeded. His friendships faded; his appearances in court grew less frequent, and without a family — he had never married and had no children — he became nearly forgotten. When he died in Hanover in 1716 only his secretary attended the funeral.

EDMUND HALLEY
1656–1742
ENGLISH ASTRONOMER
MAJOR ACCOMPLISHMENT: DISCOVERED HALLEY'S
COMET

EDMUND HALLEY ATTENDED Oxford, but left without a degree because of a unique opportunity to make a major contribution to astronomy. Only a portion of stars in the Southern Hemisphere could be seen from London or from other northern observatories. Stars on southern charts had inaccurate positions. Halley decided to remedy the situation. A British ship delivered Halley and his telescope to St. Helena, an island in the South Atlantic Ocean about 1,200 miles from the nearest land. (Years later, Napoleon was exiled on the island and died there.)

Ships visited the place only about once every six months, so Halley was undisturbed and in two years collected accurate positions of 341 stars. When he returned to London, his work received high praise. The Royal Society welcomed him as a member.

Halley became a friend of Christopher Wren and Robert Hooke. After the weekly meetings of the Royal Society, they discussed the unsolved problems of science. One question was whether gravity growing weaker by the square of the distance would explain why the planets followed Kepler's three laws. Neither Hooke nor Halley could solve this problem, but Halley took it to Cambridge for Isaac Newton's opinion.

Halley was aghast to learn that Newton had proven the inverse square law for gravity years earlier but chose not to publish it. Newton did not want to deal with the tedious task of having a book printed. Halley encouraged Newton to write about all of his discoveries and promised to arrange for illustrations, proofreading the document, and paying to have it published. After 18 months, Newton's book, the *Principia Mathematica*, was published. It is generally considered the greatest book on science ever written.

Halley gathered information about comets and calculated their orbits. He noticed that a comet he tracked in 1682 had an orbit similar to the bright comets of 1607 (Kepler had reported on this one) and 1531. Until then, astronomers did not think comets followed the same laws as the planets, but Isaac Newton's law of gravity applied to all objects in the solar system. Halley realized that the three bright comets were the same one on return visits about 76 years apart. He predicted his comet would again be seen in 1758. Halley's comet did return as predicted.

Edmund Halley

Throughout his life, Halley collected old star charts. While studying one made by the ancient Greeks, he found that the bright star Sirius had been displaced about the width of the full moon. Rather than an error, Halley proved that the so-called fixed stars actually moved.

Halley became Astronomer Royal in 1720. One of his goals was to observe the complete orbit of the moon through its complex 18-year cycle. He completed the work in 1738, four years before he died.

In a poem, Edmund Halley correctly pointed out that God had created the laws that governed the movement of planets, moon, and comets:

> Divine! Here ponder too the Laws which God,
> Framing the universe, set not aside
> But made the fixed foundations of His work.

WILLIAM WHISTON

1667–1752

ENGLISH MINISTER AND MATHEMATICIAN

MAJOR ACHIEVEMENT: PROVIDED SCIENTIFIC
EXPLANATIONS FOR CATACLYSMIC EVENTS IN THE
OLD TESTAMENT

WILLIAM WHISTON HAD but two years of formal education before he entered Cambridge. He studied for the ministry, although he also attended Newton's lectures and became an accomplished mathematician. He was ordained in the Church of England in 1693. While serving as a private chaplain, he wrote *A New Theory of the Earth* that he dedicated to Isaac Newton. The book attempted to explain events in the Old Testament by means of Newtonian physics.

When Newton left the university for London, he recommended Whiston to fill his position. Whiston succeeded Newton as professor of mathematics at Cambridge in 1703.

Whiston was a clergyman in the Church of England, but a non-juror — he refused to take the oaths of allegiance that were required each time a new king came into power. This along with his view on the Trinity caused him to lose his position at Cambridge in 1710.

He was not a wealthy man, but he managed to survive by two methods that had never been tried before. He became a freelance science lecturer and writer. He lectured in the coffeehouses of London. He also wrote a flyer about solar eclipses, a pamphlet about the weather, and translated a new edition of Euclid's *Geometry* for use in schools. Few people depended on writing as a source of income — most books lost money and a wealthy patron had to sponsor them. However, Whiston was groundbreaking in this regard because his self-published books did earn money. His most enduring work was a translation of the works of Josephus. His edition of the Jewish historian's treatise is readily available today in reprint.

In 1714, Parliament passed the Longitude Act that offered a 20,000-pound cash prize for a way to measure longitude at sea.

Whiston had been instrumental in convincing Parliament to encourage efforts in this area. He developed many ingenious solutions, including using sounding rockets, a dip compass, and a special telescope to observe eclipses of Jupiter's moon aboard rolling ships. But all fell short of the accuracy required. Many people tried to solve the problem and all failed until John Harrison invented a clock in 1763 that could keep accurate time during long sea voyages.

After leaving the Church of England, Whiston organized a society for the revival of primitive Christianity. Near the end of his life, he joined the Baptists.

ISAAC WATTS

1674–1748

ENGLISH PASTOR AND HYMNWRITER

MAJOR ACCOMPLISHMENT: AUTHOR OF MORE THAN 600 HYMNS

ISAAC WATTS WAS THE oldest of nine children. His mother was a Huguenot (French Protestant) and his father served jail time as a dissenter. The terms "dissenter," "nonconformist," and "Puritan" were applied to believers who did not accept the teachings of the Church of England.

Watts's education began at home. He enjoyed reading and languages. He learned Latin, Greek, Hebrew, and his mother's language of French. Watts was especially skilled at writing verse, and often fell into a rhyming pattern in his speech. Once during a time of devotion, Watts watched as a mouse climbed a rope to the bell tower. His father asked his young son why he was distracted. Watts responded, "A mouse for want of better stairs, ran up a rope to say his prayers."

His father found the constant rhyming tiresome and warned his son against it. When the rhyming persisted and his father decided to apply discipline, Watts could not resist saying, "O father, do some pity take, and I will no more verses make."

Watts showed such promise as a scholar, a local doctor offered to pay for his education at Cambridge or Oxford. However, to do so Watts would have to embrace the teachings of the Church of England, something he could not bring himself to do. He instead studied at the Dissenting Academy at Stoke Newington, London. He graduated in 1694.

Isaac Watts returned home without any particular prospects for employment. For two years he wrote the majority of the hymns that would make his first songbook. At that time, leaders of Protestant churches believed that the Bible alone could serve as a songbook. They cautioned against the introduction of hymns outside the Word of God. They used songbooks that contained the Psalms of David composed in poetic meter.

Watts did not agree with this view. He believed that a song could be spiritual without being a paraphrase of a Bible passage. He pointed out that prayers were uttered in worship without being based on a Bible verse, so songs could extol the glory of God without reference to Scripture.

He found employment as a tutor for the sons of a wealthy Puritan and delivered his first sermon in the chapel of his employer. He preached at other locations, and in 1702 he became the minister at Mark Lane, London, a congregation of independents (still another name that described those not affiliated with the Church of England).

Watts distributed handwritten copies of his songs and he heard them sung in worship for the first time. He published *Hymns and Spiritual Songs* in 1707. One of the songs was "When I Survey the Wondrous Cross."

The collection was not an immediate success because of the reluctance of congregations to sing words from sources other than the Bible. Isaac Watts then began writing hymns that overcame this objection. He translated the concepts of the Old Testament Psalms into the language of the New Testament. He emphasized faith over fear and the Savior over sin. The New Testament sacrifice of the Lamb of God replaced the Old Testament sacrifice of bulls and goats. Watts used the New Testament blessings of grace, glory, and life eternal in place of the Old Testament rewards of wealth, honor, and long life.

He published this collection as *The Psalms of David Imitated in the Language of the New Testament* in 1719. Songs in it include "Jesus Shall Reign" from Psalm 72, "Our God, Our Help in Ages Past" from Psalm 90, and "Joy to the World" from Psalm 98.

Almost as soon as Watts became a full-time pastor, he had to relinquish most of his duties to a co-pastor because of illness. He had never enjoyed the best of health, and in 1712 he became violently ill with a fever. Sir Thomas Abney took him into his house to recover. Watts had planned to stay only a week or so. However, he lived in the home of Abney for the next 36 years.

Physically, he was but five feet tall with the head of a much larger person. His slight build, pale complexion, and hooked nose gave him an appearance far different from the powerful and soaring songs for which he was known. He never married, although one woman imagined herself in love with him after they became acquainted through correspondence. Unfortunately, when she came to visit, the frail man who greeted her at the door was nothing like what she had imagined. They remained friends, but she quickly put marriage aside.

In addition to his hymns, Watts wrote more than 50 books on a variety of subjects including astronomy, geography, grammar, theology, ethics, and logic. His book on logic, published in 1725, was used as a textbook on the subject for more than a hundred years.

Watts's songs enjoyed great success in the American colonies. The American printer Benjamin Franklin published his *Psalms of David* in 1729. Watts saw his other books gain favor during the Great Awakening in the 1740s. Jonathan Edwards and George Whitefield realized the moving imagery of Watts's songs would augment their preaching styles and began singing them.

Isaac Watts survived the "three score ten" by two years. By then, he was recognized as the father of English hymnody. He was buried at Bunhill Fields Cemetery where John Bunyan had been buried. As a dissenter, Watts was not eligible to be buried in Westminster Abby, but a monument was erected to him in the building.

STEPHEN HALES
1677–1761
ENGLISH CLERGYMAN, BOTANIST, AND CHEMIST
MAJOR ACHIEVEMENT: BROUGHT SCIENTIFIC
MEASUREMENTS TO BIOLOGY

THE SCIENTIFIC REVOLUTION began in the physical sciences because subjects such as astronomy and physics readily lent themselves to measurements. Biology had remained a descriptive science until Stephen Hales developed ways to measure such quantities as the pressure of sap running in trees and the pressure of blood in the arteries of the human body.

Hales had been born to a wealthy and well-known English family. He attended Cambridge University to study for the ministry. While there, he also took courses in chemistry and botany. Although sympathetic to the ideas of the Puritans, he became a clergyman in the Church of England.

After graduation, he received a teaching position at Cambridge University. In 1709, he moved to the parish at Teddington. The small country town about 12 miles from London attracted retired Londoners who came for its rustic seclusion.

Although his duties as a clergyman were his primary activities, his scientific researches gained him admission to the Royal Society. The French Academy of Sciences elected him as one of the only eight foreign members. He came to the attention of the scientific world with his book *Vegetables Staticks* (1727). The book demonstrated his preference for experiments and measurements over vague theories.

In one experiment, he placed a plant in a closed container and weighed the soil, plant, water, and amount of air as the plant grew. He gave specific weights and percentages and established that a plant absorbed air through its leaves.

In another experiment, Hales pruned a grapevine so the sap began to run. He placed a bladder over the exposed limb and it filled with sap. The bulge of the membrane measured the pressure of the sap. The plant leaves exhaled water vapor, which caused the circulation of sap up from the roots.

In 1733, a second book made the first major contribution to human blood flow since the work of William Harvey in 1628. Hales succeeded in measuring blood pressure by inserting a small glass tube into an artery and noting how high the blood was driven.

His work was far-ranging. He championed the benefits of fresh air and invented ventilators for use in prisons and aboard ships. He studied reflex action and concluded that the sudden movement had to be initiated by the spinal column and not the brain. He developed ways to preserve beef (inject brine into the arteries) and keep weevils out of grain (fumigate with sulfur dioxide).

However, Hales's scientific achievements did not overshadow his primary mission, preaching the gospel of Christ. In 1698, Thomas Bray had founded the Society for the Promotion of Christian Knowledge. Hales was active in this work and in another that brought the gospel to the black slaves in the West Indies. He also wrote *A Friendly Admonition to the Drinkers of Brandy and Other Distilled Spirit.*

Stephen Hales was well-known in royal circles. Frederick, the Prince of Wales and father of King George III, shared his interest in botany. Frederick and his wife, Augusta, had established a botanical garden at Kew. Hales designed a ventilated greenhouse that was built on the estate. In 1751, the year her husband died, the princess appointed Hales her chaplain. When Hales died at the age of 84, the princess arranged for a monument to be erected to him in Westminster Abby.

In 1927, the American Society of Plant Biologists decided to issue a biannual prize for work in plant biology. They named it the Stephen Hales Award.

JOHN BARTRAM

1699–1777

AMERICAN BOTANIST

MAJOR ACHIEVEMENT: FOUNDER OF BOTANICAL STUDY
IN AMERICA

JOHN BARTRAM WAS THE first scientist born in America who became well-known in Europe. For his botanical studies, Bartram explored extensively throughout the American colonies from Lake Ontario in the north to St. Augustine in the south. He collected seeds, bulbs, and cuttings to ship to England. King George III appointed Bartram as his botanist in America. In addition, Bartram supplied plants to European scientists including Carolus Linnaeus, the Swedish botanist.

John Bartram was born in Darby, Pennsylvania. He was orphaned at the age of 13 and worked as a field hand. His interest in botany began as he wondered about the wildflowers that his plow uprooted. In his spare time, he managed to teach himself botany and the medical uses of herbs.

When he was 28 years old, he inherited a small farm from his uncle. An epidemic had taken his first wife. When he remarried, he decided to sell the farm and move closer to Philadelphia, the intellectual center of the United States at that time. He purchased a small farm about three miles outside of town and as his fortunes increased, added more acreage. In addition to wheat, oats, corn, flax, and livestock, he and his wife also raised eight children.

On a five-acre plot, Bartram began a botanical garden that became the best (if not the first) in North America. His experiments included growing hybrid flowering plants by cross-pollination, another first for the colonies.

Bartram was a Quaker and through his religious contacts, he began a 36-year association with Peter Collinson, a Quaker businessman who lived in London. Collinson, who had an interest in botany, asked Bartram to send him seeds, bulbs, and cuttings of American plants. Bartram's religious beliefs kept him from being a slave owner, and he could only make plant-collecting trips after harvest. However,

Collinson offered to pay for the samples and act as his agent in England. With plant collecting a moneymaking operation, Bartram could justify spending more time at it. Collinson managed to interest more than 50 other scientists in buying the plants. In some cases, Bartram accepted payment in books on nature that were hard to find in America.

Bartram became friends with other scientists in Philadelphia. He tried to start a scientific organization similar to the Royal Society. He had nearly given up when Benjamin Franklin revived the idea as the American Philosophical Society. Franklin and Bartram were the first two names on the charter.

In 1765, the 66-year-old Bartram became King George III's botanist in America. The position carried an annual salary and freed Bartram from his other duties. With his son William, Bartram explored as far south as the St. Johns River in Florida.

One of Bartram's last acts before he died was to ensure that the advancing British forces during the American Revolutionary War did not destroy his botanical garden. It did survive and still exists as a public park in Philadelphia. His son William became the lead botanist on the Lewis and Clark expedition of 1803. William earned the distinction, once held by his father, as the person who made the most extensive scientific explorations of North America.

JONATHAN EDWARDS

1703–1758

AMERICAN CLERGYMAN

MAJOR ACHIEVEMENT: WITH GEORGE WHITEFIELD,
LAUNCHED THE GREAT AWAKENING IN AMERICA

JONATHAN EDWARDS ATTENDED Yale to become a minister like his father and grandfather. He entered at age 13 and graduated at age 17. After preaching in a Presbyterian Church in New York for four years, he returned to Yale to earn a graduate degree. In 1727, he became associate minister in his grandfather's Congregational Church at Northampton, Massachusetts. With 600 members, the congregation was the largest in New England outside of Boston.

His personal acceptance of Christianity did not come easily. He had difficulty with the prevalent Puritan view of predestination, what he called a "horrible doctrine." He came to embrace predestination, but also accepted optimism in the sovereignty of God.

Upon the death of his grandfather, Edwards became pastor. His tenure marked a rising concern that the people in New England had fallen into self-sufficiency and moral arrogance. Some congregations believed that morality alone was the essence of religion. While in Boston in 1731, he preached the sermon "God Glorified in Man's Dependence" that rejected human self-sufficiency.

In 1734 he returned to a strict interpretation of Calvinism in a series of sermons delivered at his church. His spellbinding oratory style resulted in several conversions. The number of responses increased each week as the series continued. In the space of two years, the number of believers increased by 300.

His most dramatic sermon during this period, and the one for which he is remembered, was the fiery "Sinners in the Hands of an Angry God." Rather than merely stirring his audience, he electrified them: "The God that holds you over the pit of hell, much as one holds a spider, or some loathsome insect over the fire, abhors you, and is dreadfully provoked: His wrath towards you burns like fire; He looks upon you as worthy of nothing else, but to be cast into the fire."

This and other sermons had a profound effect on the listeners. Women fainted and men bolted from the pews. People cried, moaned, and responded with a religious frenzy. Edwards usually preached his most intense sermons while visiting other congregations. The "Angry God" sermon was preached at Enfield, Connecticut.

In 1740, George Whitefield, who had worked with John and Charles Wesley in England, came to New England and visited Edwards. Together, they started a revival movement known as the Great Awakening. Although Edwards acknowledged the intense emotional response to his sermons, he defended the revival because lives were permanently changed.

Edwards had 11 children. One of his daughters, Jerusha, became engaged to David Brainerd, a Presbyterian missionary to the Seneca and Delaware Native American tribes. David Brainerd contracted tuberculosis and spent four months at the Edwards's home before he died at the age of 29. Edwards inherited his journals and published them as *The Life and Diary of David Brainerd*. The book was an exciting account of a young man who became the pioneer of modern missionary work.

Throughout the 1740s, Edwards became sterner in his interpretation of acceptable religious service. He banned children in the congregation from reading certain books. He tried to reverse some of the long-standing policies established years earlier by his grandfather. He limited church membership and excluded others from receiving communion because he questioned their conversions.

The people he tried to expel from worship were the very ones who could vote to retain him as a preacher. When they had to choose between leaving the congregation themselves or turning him out, they decided that he was the one who should go. He was dismissed in 1750.

His admiration of the work of David Brainerd motivated him to move to Stockbridge on the frontier. He became a missionary to the Native Americans and the 12 white families in the village. In his isolation, Edwards wrote some of his most important books, including *Freedom of Will* (1754.) The book established him as a significant American theologian.

In 1752, another of Edwards's daughters, Esther, married Aaron Burr (father of Aaron Burr, of political fame). Aaron Burr Sr. had become president of the College of New Jersey shortly after it was formed. The school was poorly funded and Burr weakened his health in his efforts at fundraising. He died in 1757.

Jonathan Edwards was invited to be the new president of the college. (It would later become Princeton University.) He declined at first because he had come to enjoy the lighter duties at Stockbridge. However, a committee of ministers appealed to his sense of duty and he relented. He took office in January 1758 but died five weeks later of smallpox.

Although Jonathan Edwards had written several influential books, none of his followers maintained a distinct version of his theological ideas. Edwards's influence declined even more as Calvinism lost favor in the late 1800s.

CAROLUS LINNAEUS

1707–1778

SWEDISH BOTANIST

MAJOR ACHIEVEMENT: DEVELOPED THE BINOMIAL
NOMENCLATURE FOR GIVING SCIENTIFIC NAMES TO
PLANTS AND ANIMALS

CARL LINNAEUS WAS BORN into a religious family in a small town in rural Sweden. His father, a pastor, was interested in nature and kept a large garden. Linnaeus showed curiosity about plants, too, and earned the nickname "the little botanist."

Linnaeus was attracted to the medical profession because university courses for doctors emphasized the uses of herbs to treat diseases. However, the garden at Lund where he first attended college was neglected, and professors seldom lectured on the subject. He transferred to Uppsala, which had a better garden and much larger library. He became assistant to Professor Olaf Celsius. The professor taught religion and needed help in writing a book about plants in the Bible.

Although he had not received a degree, Linnaeus stayed on at Uppsala and lectured on botany to overflow classes. However, after two years he left the school to make a 4,600-mile trip through northern Scandinavia to collect plants. He also visited the Netherlands, where he stayed long enough to earn a medical degree.

He found it difficult to decide if the plants he had collected were new discoveries or ones already known under a different name. Other biologists faced this problem, too. For three hundred years, the Age of Exploration had opened the vast biological storehouse of the world to scientists. The rich harvest of new plants far outstripped the biologists' ability to place them in a named category.

Linnaeus concluded, "If you don't know the name, you waste the knowledge of a thing." In 1735 he published *System of Nature*, a book that detailed his method of naming plants. He gave the modern names for most of the parts of a flower, and used those parts to distinguish one flowering plant from another.

A short stay in Stockholm gained him recognition as a doctor — his patients included members of the royal family — and a wife.

Then it was back to Uppsala where he wrote his most influential book, *Philosophia Botanica,* published in 1751. In *Botanica,* he explained his binomial nomenclature of two Latinized words. He gave each plant a species name and collected similar species into a larger group, or genus.

The naming rules he developed were so reasonable that scientists adopted them instantly. His books were internationally agreed upon as the starting point for naming flowering plants. Naturalists applied his naming convention to animals, too. For instance, the common domestic cat is *Felis domesticus*, meaning household cat, while the mountain lion is *Felis concolor*, meaning cat of one color.

Grouping plants by similarities and going from broad categories to ones that are more specific gave the appearance of a tree of life. Linnaeus believed his classification system derived from the original creation plan of God. He strongly opposed the idea of evolution.

Linnaeus gained many honors during his life and enjoyed a warm family life. He had many pets, including a parrot that would remind him to eat lunch with "Twelve o'clock, Mr. Carl." His dog Pompey accompanied him to church and would sit under the pew. Linnaeus was so steadfast in his worship that on those occasions when he could not attend, the dog would go anyway and sit under the pew until the service ended.

LEONHARD EULER
1707–1783
SWISS MATHEMATICIAN
MAJOR ACCOMPLISHMENT: DEVELOPED ALGORITHMIC
APPROACH TO PROBLEM SOLVING

IN HIS LONG AND productive career as a mathematician, Leonhard Euler tackled the most complex unsolved problems of science. Euler was the first to apply Newton's three laws of motion to liquids and gases. He invented the science of hydrodynamics with equations to predict the flow, turbulence, and pressure of water going around an obstacle. His equations applied to all fluids including air. Much of the science of air flight makes use of Euler's work.

As another example, no one had been able to calculate fully the gravitational tug of earth, moon, and sun upon one another. This was known as the three-body problem. Isaac Newton said it was the only problem that made his head hurt. It had a real-world application because until the invention of accurate clocks, navigators used the moon's position to calculate longitude. Euler's solution to the three-body problem remained the best available for two hundred years, although even today it has not been fully solved.

Euler attended the University of Basel in Switzerland to become a minister, the same profession as his father. At the university, he excelled at theology and Hebrew, but showed even more promise in mathematics. Euler's professors urged his father to let him become a mathematician.

After graduation, Catherine I of Russia invited him to St. Petersburg as a teacher of applied mathematics. To provide a salary, she gave him a commission in the Russian navy with a rank of lieutenant, although he had no sea-faring experience. He stayed in Russia for 11 years and then moved to Germany. However, his work was so important that both countries continued to pay him a salary, and occasionally Britain would reward him for work useful to that country.

His training as a minister served him well because of his large family. At one time, 18 family members lived in his household. He

Leonhard Euler

conducted the family devotions and preached sermons. He was a devoted father who loved to have his children around him, even as he worked. Sometimes he would rock a baby to sleep as he wrote his research papers.

Euler did not enjoy court life, so he took on extra assignments as a reason to be excused from appearances at the palace. He oversaw reform of Russia's weights and measures, designed water pumps for fire engines, and wrote mathematics textbooks for elementary schools. He supervised the making of Russian maps.

Mathematicians hold him in high regard for his pure research, the study of numbers without any direct applications. For instance, he did the first studies of topography. He solved the famous Königsburg Bridge problem (can a single path go across the seven bridges in the city without crossing the same one twice.) Later, this work became useful in network design. He also developed algorithms for solving problems. His algorithms allowed people with ordinary abilities to arrive at answers to difficult problems. This was the forerunner of the systematic procedures used in computer programming. What appeared to be pure mathematics in the 1700s became applied mathematics in the 2000s.

Euler lost vision in one eye because of an infection when he was 31 years old. Later, he lost sight in the other eye because of cataracts. Despite total blindness, his phenomenal memory and assistance of one of his sons, Johann, allowed him to continue to work. He accomplished more in the 17 years he was totally blind than he did in the same period when he could see. Work on the three-body problem came after he lost his sight.

Leonhard Euler wrote 800 research papers and 31 books. His backlog of research papers continued to be published for 50 years after his death.

CHARLES WESLEY
1707–1788
ENGLISH CLERGYMAN AND HYMNWRITER
MAJOR ACCOMPLISHMENT: CO-FOUNDER OF THE
METHODIST MOVEMENT

CHARLES WESLEY, WITH HIS brother John and their friend George
Whitefield, were the co-founders of Methodism. The "method" referred to a way of worshiping that emphasized faith, worship, study,
and Christian service.

Charles entered Oxford in 1728, the year his brother graduated.
Charles and some other classmates met each night to read the Bible
and pray. They set a definite schedule for religious activities, including fasting on Wednesday and Friday and helping prisoners and the
poor. Other students referred to them derisively as the Holy Club.
When John returned to Oxford as a graduate student, he became the
leader of the group. One of the new members was George Whitefield.

Charles, like his brother, became a clergyman in the Church of
England. In 1735, they sailed for Georgia, the last of the 13 original
colonies to be established. The Wesleys were missionaries sent out
by the Society for the Propagation of the Gospel. Their privileged
and sheltered lives had not prepared them for the rugged and primitive conditions of the frontier. After four months, Charles became
sick and dispirited. He returned home shattered from the experience. His faith was shaken, and he began to question what he believed. He had sailed to Georgia with 26 German Moravians. Their
beliefs included a reliance upon faith rather than works, a rejection
of Calvinism, and a simple, uncomplicated approach to Christianity.

While in London, Charles met with other Christians who held
views similar to the Moravians. Charles became persuaded that his
previous religious commitment lacked the faith that marked true
Christianity. He also searched for a more natural expression of religious worship. For instance, the hymn singing of the Moravians had
impressed both brothers. Charles became convinced that hymns could
be used as a way to teach Christianity.

John Wesley, who was still in Georgia, published a book that
contained some of the new hymns of Isaac Watts. He was charged

with introducing unauthorized hymns into the church. John decided to return home to England rather than stay around for the trial.

In May 1738, Charles read Psalm 40:3 and was deeply affected by the keywords "new song" and "trust." In celebration of having his faith restored, Charles began writing hymns. His first one contained the words "learning through song." He certainly made that his goal because he wrote two or three songs a week for the rest of his life. About 4,500 were published and another 3,000 exist in manuscript form. His songs include "Hark! The Herald Angels Sing", "Jesus, Lover of My Soul", "Soldiers of Christ, Arise" and "Love Divine, All Love Excelling."

His preaching style changed, too. Before then, clergymen were admonished to write out their sermons and embed their thoughts in rigorous logic. For the first time, Charles followed the example of George Whitefield and preached in a more flexible style. He watched his audience and changed his delivery to keep his listeners involved.

Although John Wesley was considered the organizer, George Whitefield the preacher, and Charles the songwriter, all three were preachers of the first rank. Charles and John found themselves preaching to large audiences in open fields, which brought them renewed criticism. Church authorities believed Christianity should be confined to church buildings.

Church leaders also leaned heavily toward Calvinism in which God predestinated certain individuals to eternal punishment. Because the leaders considered their wealthy friends blessed by God, they left the impression that the weak, poor, untitled, and non-land owners would reap God's wrath. Many Church of England clergymen made only token attempts to bring religion to the poor.

The Wesleys, however, gave hope to hard-working poor people and welcomed them to religious services. Some historians have stated that the work of the Wesleys helped prevent in England a bloody rebellion of lower classes that took place in the 1700s in other countries such as France.

In 1749, Charles married Sarah Gwynne. His brother John officiated. Charles preferred a home life and songwriting to iterate preaching, so he settled in London. He remained a clergyman in the Church of England. He had been keeping a daily journal, but he stopped with the arrival of his children, so his last days were not as well documented as his earlier life. It is known that his dying words were a song that he dictated to his wife.

JOHN NEWTON
1725–1807
English sailor, minister, and songwriter
Major accomplishment: writer of the hymn "Amazing Grace"

JOHN NEWTON WAS AN only child. His parents were devout Christians and dissenters from the Church of England. His early education and spiritual training came by his mother's efforts, but ended at her death when he was six years old. His father captained a merchant ship that sailed to European ports along the Mediterranean Sea. After a time in boarding schools, Newton's 11th birthday was celebrated by going to sea with his father. Newton later reported that he was always in awe and fear of his father.

Two years later he was pressed into service aboard the man-of-war *HMS Harwich*. By then he had become a rebellious youngster and an insubordinate seaman. He managed to alienate not only his captain but also his fellow crew members. He deserted but was captured, flogged, and demoted from officer-in-training (midshipman) to seaman. Newton suggested to his captain that he be allowed to sail on another ship. His captain readily agreed to rid himself of a troublemaker.

One of the passengers on Newton's new ship was a slave trader who had a plantation in Africa. Newton became his apprentice and worked on his plantation near the Gambia River in western Africa. The man went away on business but Newton stayed behind because of illness. He came under the control of the man's wife, who was African. She treated him as a slave and in his weakened state he could not escape. He suffered indignities of being locked in a shed and being fed scraps from her table. Local people came to see the black woman who had a white slave.

Later, Newton was traded to another slave owner who treated him much better. He was rescued by the captain of a sailing vessel who knew his father. Eventually, Newton made it back to England. One of his goals was to visit Mary Catlett, a childhood friend whom he wished to marry. To earn money he became the captain of a slave-trading ship. At that time, he thought of his chosen career as an honorable profession.

Considering the difficulties he had already faced, and the new dangers he encountered, one wonders why Newton remained a sailor. Even the normally lucrative slave trade did not make him wealthy.

In 1748, his ship, *The Greyhound,* encountered a fierce Atlantic storm. The wind shredded the sails, waves pounded the ship, and timbers were shattered. Waves swept over the deck, and Newton had to be lashed in place to stay at the helm. The ship began taking on water. Until then he had recognized Christian faith as necessary to please God, but he loved sin more than salvation. The 12 hours at the helm being soaked with cold water while this crew desperately manned the pumps gave him time to think about his sinful condition.

He returned to his spiritual roots and stocked his library aboard ship with a Bible and religious books. Like Nicolaus Steno, one of his favorite writings was *Imitation of Christ* by Thomas à Kempis.

Two years later, in 1750, he and Mary Catlett were married. He wanted to stay with her, but he could find no employment on shore and continued as a slave trader for four more years. In 1754, he was 29 years old and had begun to pray for a way out of the slave trade. Nothing opened for him, but he could not bring himself to go back to sea.

Finally, after six months of unemployment, he found a job as Surveyor of Tides in Liverpool. He began to study for the ministry in earnest. He became friends with George Whitefield and John Wesley. Both men were considered evangelists, an activity that the hierarchy of the Church of England frowned upon.

After nearly ten years of study, Newton felt he was ready for the ministry. However, church authorities viewed the record of his parents as dissenters and his association with evangelists as marks against him. Finally, he was appointed pastor in Olney, England. It was a poor, rural area with an influx of immigrants — a backwater parish suitable for a preacher with no college education and no prospects to amount to anything.

Newton loaded his days with service to his parishioners — two sermons on Sunday, a Tuesday evening prayer service, and activities for the young people. He also wrote extensively and for years wrote a new song nearly every week to accompany the theme of his Sunday sermons.

One of his songs, "Faith's Review and Expectations," so impressed the poet William Cowper (pronounced "Cooper") that he moved to Olney and bought a house next door to Newton. Cowper and Newton published a songbook, the *Olney Hymns*. It contained 280 songs by Newton and 68 by Cowper. The songs became as popular as those by Isaac Watts 50 years earlier.

After 16 years in Olney, Newton became principle clergyman for the St. Mary Woolnoth parish in London. In 1806, a year before he died, Parliament considered laws against slavery and Newton wrote about its evils and testified before a royal commission. Newton died in 1807, the year that Parliament passed the first laws against the transport of slaves.

John Newton's song "Faith's Review and Expectations" told the story of his life. Under the alternate title, it became the best-known hymn ever written: "Amazing Grace."

WILLIAM HERSCHEL
1738–1822
ENGLISH ASTRONOMER
MAJOR ACCOMPLISHMENT: DISCOVERED THE PLANET
URANUS

AMATEURS HAVE A LONG history of making important discoveries in science. In astronomy, one of the greatest amateurs was William Herschel. He was a professional musician who did not look through a telescope until he was 40 years old. His greatest discovery came while astronomy was still his hobby.

William Herschel was born as Friedrich Wilhelm Herschel in Hanover, Germany. His family was piously Protestant — great-grandfather Abraham Herschel, grandfather Isaac, and father Jacob. At age 12, Herschel began playing drums in a military band. The Hanover ruler was George II who also was king of England. When fighting came to Hanover, Herschel decided he could serve George II as easily in England as in war-torn Germany. At the age of 19 years, he escaped to England and changed his name from Wilhelm to William.

He studied his chosen profession and became a successful musician. In 1766, he moved to the resort town of Bath on the Avon River. There he composed music and taught as many as 35 students a week. He played the organ, led the choir of the famous Octagon Chapel, and eventually became the leader of the orchestra.

His study of music led him to an understanding of the mathematics of harmonics, physics of organ pipes, and science in general, including astronomy. When he read about the wonders of the solar system, he developed an intense interest in seeing with his own eyes the objects described in the books.

He rented a telescope for three months. Neighbors saw a remarkable sight on nights when he conducted the orchestra. During intermission, he would race out the back and jump the hedge. He would run down the cobblestone street to his house. Still dressed in his conductor's clothes, he would peer into the telescope set up in his garden. After a few minutes, he would hurry back to finish the concert.

When the three-month rental was up, Herschel had not yet viewed all the wonders of the night sky. He had to have a telescope of his own, but the cost was prohibitive, so he decided to build one. His design was a modified version of the Newtonian reflecting telescope with simple but sturdy mounting. He used what he learned after making the first one to build improved models. The tube of his largest telescope towered over his house.

He selected a research project for his telescope. He began a survey of every star visible in his telescope. Rather than moving the tube to follow stars, he let the rotation of the earth carry them into view. During the four-year sky survey and others that followed, he found more than 800 double stars. Over the years, it became clear that many double stars circled one another. Herschel calculated their orbits with Newton's law of gravity. It was the first time that anyone proved the law worked so far from the sun.

On Tuesday night, March 13, 1781, his sky survey took him into the constellation of Taurus the Bull. He found a faint spot of light. His star chart showed no object in that location. He used a more powerful eyepiece. The higher magnification revealed a definite disk quite unlike the pinpoint light of stars. The object, which he thought might be a comet at first, moved from night to night but had an orbit beyond that of Saturn. Only a planet could be visible at such a great distance.

The new planet received the name Uranus. William Herschel came back to his planet often. In 1787, he discovered two moons of Uranus that he named Titania and Oberon from characters in Shakespeare's play *A Midsummer Night's Dream.*

King George III named William Herschel his royal astronomer. The position came with a yearly salary. He gave up his musical duties. He married a wealthy widow who lived next door. They had a son, John Herschel, who became a great astronomer and scientist, too. With the blessing of his wife (and some of her money), William Herschel built the largest telescope in the world, a 48-inch reflector. He made the first attempt to measure the size and shape of the Milky Way Galaxy. He also proved that the sun was in motion and was carrying its planets, including the earth, toward the constellation of Hercules.

In 1816, King George III conferred upon William Herschel the title of knight – *Sir* William Herschel. William Herschel was a simple

Christian, devout and humble. He believed the heavens revealed the work of God. He once said, "The astronomer who isn't devout must be insane."

Herschel's sister, Caroline Herschel, was also an astronomer of note — his son John Herschel mapped the stars in the Southern Hemisphere and became one of the leading scientists in the 1800s. William Herschel is remembered today for his discovery of Uranus. The discovery of a new planet revitalized science, and his star surveys opened deep space to scientific inquiry.

CAROLINE LUCRETIA HERSCHEL

1750–1848

BRITISH ASTRONOMER

MAJOR ACCOMPLISHMENT: FIRST WOMAN ASTRONOMER
OF INTERNATIONAL REPUTATION

CAROLINE HERSCHEL WAS THE sister of the English astronomer William Herschel. A re-evaluation of her contributions to astronomy on the 250ᵗʰ anniversary of her birth revealed that she had an important role in his success. The reduction of her brother's observations (a difficult mathematical task to eliminate systematic errors) was her work alone. Indeed, it could be reasonably argued that she co-discovered the planet Uranus.

Caroline was born in Hanover, Germany. As a youth, she appeared small and weak because of a bout with typhoid fever. Her father encouraged her to develop her intellect because only in that way, he said, would she attract a man. However, she never married.

After her brother William had established himself as a musician in Bath, he invited her to England. She trained as a singer and performed professionally. She believed in service to others as an important part of her Christian duties. In addition to running her brother's household and performing as a singer, she also assisted him from the first in his astronomy efforts.

When William began making a telescope, she was at his side. Caroline read aloud to him as he worked, and she learned as much about astronomy as he did. When his arms grew tired, she would take over for him. Their telescopes rivaled those in the best observatories. In recalling these days, she said, "Can you imagine the thrill of turning it to some new corner of the heavens to see something never before seen from earth?"

Each day Caroline planned the daily observation schedule and shared the night watches with her brother. He observed through the eyepiece high up on the tube and described the stars as the earth's rotation brought them into view. She recorded the time of the observation (necessary to calculate an accurate position of the star), classified the star from his description, and verified the object against a star chart. Later, she reduced the observations for publication.

On Tuesday night, March 13, 1781, Caroline sang out to her brother that the object he had seen was not on the star chart, and she plotted its position. It was a sixth magnitude object at the limit of visibility with the unaided eyes. In the telescope it showed a fuzzy disk and looked more like a comet than the pinpoint light of a star.

Although William Herschel cautiously called it a comet, Caroline Herschel realized its slow motion from night to night placed it beyond the orbit of Saturn, the most distant known planet. Astronomers hailed it as a new planet — the first one discovered in modern times — and gave it the name Uranus.

The discovery of Uranus was a happy event for the king of England. George III had lost the American colonies to the Revolutionary War, but Caroline and William had given him a whole new world. He created the post of royal astronomer for Herschel. Caroline's work was recognized, too. The king granted her an annual payment of 50 pounds, sufficient to support her full time as an astronomer.

Caroline and William gave a farewell musical performance at Bath in 1782. She was 32 years old.

In 1788 her brother married Mary Pitt, a wealthy widow who lived next door. Perhaps Caroline was not entirely pleased with her brother's marriage because the pages for the ten days after the event have been ripped from her diary. However, William's wife took over managing the house, so Caroline had more time for her astronomy. She was the first woman to discover a comet, and in a ten-year period starting in 1786, she discovered eight new comets. In this, she surpassed her brother for he found none.

Caroline was a careful worker. She corrected star catalogs in use, and made it possible for William to measure slight shifts in the position of stars because of the motion of the sun. He proved that the sun traveled in space and carried the earth and the other planets toward the constellation of Hercules.

With the financial support of his wife, William built a telescope with a mirror four feet in diameter. It was the largest in the world. When William had to travel to London to attend Royal Society meetings, Caroline used the occasion to be the chief astronomer with the big telescope. She said, "I actually like that he is busy with the Royal Society, for when I finish my other work I can spend all night sweeping the heavens."

She worked, it seems, night and day. When not at the telescope with her brother, she was correcting his paperwork and that of other astronomers. In 1798, she completed the cataloging of 2,500 nebulas and star clusters. In 1828, the Royal Astronomical Society awarded her the gold medal for this work and for editing the star catalogs of her brother and of the British astronomer John Flamsteed. Her records were so accurate that they remained in common use until the 1900s.

Caroline felt she had been summoned by God to her scientific work with the same fervor that sent others to the missionary field. When asked about her diligent efforts, she replied, "However long we live, life is short, so I work."

After William Herschel's death, Caroline returned to her family in Hanover. On her 98th birthday, she greeted visitors by singing hymns. She died later that year. One of her predictions turned out to be incorrect: "As for my name, it will also be forgotten."

JOHN DALTON
1766–1844
BRITISH CHEMIST

MAJOR ACCOMPLISHMENT: ESTABLISHED THE ATOMIC
THEORY OF MATTER

JOHN DALTON WAS A HUMBLE schoolteacher of limited scientific education who succeeded in establishing the single most important principle in chemistry — that matter is made of small particles, atoms, that are unchanged by chemical reactions.

Dalton received his early education from his father who was a weaver. He attended a Quaker grammar school, completed his studies there at age 11, and returned the next year as a teacher. Later, he became a teacher of mathematics and science at a Presbyterian school in Manchester, England. The school had been opened because Cambridge and Oxford Universities would only admit members of the Church of England.

The first scientific subject that interested Dalton was weather. He built his own weather gages and kept a daily weather journal. In 1787, at age 21, he wrote *Meteorological Observations and Essays*, one of the first scientific books on weather. He showed that clouds release their burden of rain because of falling temperature and not because of changing atmospheric pressure. During the next 57 years he recorded about 200,000 weather observations.

John Dalton

Both John Dalton and his brother were color-blind. He wrote the first scientific paper about this condition.

Dalton made a series of discoveries about gases. He found that the weights of each element in a gas never varied regardless of the chemical reaction that produced the gas. Another discovery, known as Dalton's law, states that each gas in a mixture exerts a pressure independent of the others and the total pressure equals the sum of the individual pressures.

Dalton's most important contribution to science was his atomic theory. He proposed that individual particles that could not be divided by chemical reactions composed all matter. Atoms of the same element were identical and had the same weight. Atoms of different elements were different in their properties, especially their weights. He found that atoms always combined in simple ratios by weight.

Scientists of his day often developed general theories as a starting point for argument. However, Dalton's atomic theory was not based upon idle speculation but upon a wealth of experimental evidence. He said, "Having been often misled by taking for granted the results of others, I have determined to write but what I can attest by my own experience."

Dalton announced his atomic theory in 1803. The great English scientist Humphry Davy rejected it. He thought it could not be proven because atoms were too small to be seen. When Davy reviewed Dalton's data, it removed all of his concerns. The atomic theory was quickly accepted, and Davy nominated Dalton to the Royal Society.

Although Dalton continued as a teacher and tutor, people recognized him as a great scientist. His friends arranged an audience before William IV, king of England. As a Quaker, Dalton could not wear the expensive garments and a sword required for court appearances. He declined the invitation.

In 1832, Oxford University gave him a doctor's degree. It was the same university that 48 years earlier would have denied him admission. As part of the ceremony, the university provided him with a cap and robe. Although bright scarlet, Dalton in his color-blindness saw it as a dull gray. The university robe could be substituted for court dress, so William IV received him after all.

Upon retirement, he had no money and no source of income. Because of his contributions to England, the government gave him a retirement pension of 150 pounds. It was sufficient for his simple needs as a humble Christian.

His documents, including his weather journals that he kept for nearly six decades, were stored at a museum in Manchester, England. They were destroyed during the bombing of World War II.

GEORGES CUVIER
1769–1832
FRENCH ANATOMIST
MAJOR ACCOMPLISHMENT: SCIENTIFIC
RECONSTRUCTION OF EXTINCT ANIMALS

GEORGES CUVIER'S FAMILY fled France because of persecution directed at Protestants. Although they settled in Switzerland, Cuvier found himself back in France without moving a step. In 1793, his birthplace was annexed to France, and he became a French citizen.

While a tutor to a wealthy Protestant family, he became interested in science and wrote papers that came to the attention of the Museum of Natural History in Paris. He began as assistant professor of animal anatomy. He had a phenomenal memory and had all but memorized the contents of his personal library of 20,000 books.

As the years passed, he became a professor at the College of France and eventually rose to high government posts. He also had administrative and economic abilities, so he managed to stay in favor with the country's rulers despite the rapidly changing political times. While serving under Napoleon, he refused to accompany him on his Egyptian campaign but remained on good terms with the emperor. In 1808, Napoleon put Cuvier in charge of improving both secondary and higher education in France. Cuvier also served under Louis XVIII after the restoration of the monarchy. He eventually became head of the Interior Department.

Cuvier was one of the first scientists to write about the structural order in the animal kingdom. He said the teeth and claws of an animal could be used to identify what kind of food it ate. One night, one of Cuvier's students dressed in a devil's costume. With his friends waiting at the door, the student sneaked into the professor's room and whispered, "Cuvier, wake up. I have come to eat you!" Cuvier opened one eye, looked at the devil's horns and said, "Creatures with horns and hooves eat grass. You can't eat me."

Fossils that he exposed in deeper and presumably older layers of rocks were not identical to fossils in the uppermost layers or to living animals. Deeper fossils had greater differences. Cuvier believed animals had been created to perfectly match their environment and could not change. Some animals could not survive when the environment changed and they became extinct. He believed the earth had been subjected to a series of major disasters, or catastrophes, that caused mass extinction of animals. According to Cuvier, the last catastrophe was the biblical flood.

Cuvier believed the organs of animals had been perfectly created to do efficiently a specific task. He opposed the idea that the organs that worked so well in one environment could be modified to do something else. He said, "If the species have changed by degrees, we should find some traces of these graduation modifications."

His understanding of anatomy allowed him to reconstruct ancient forms of life from a limited number of fossil fragments. He recreated many of the great animals of the past, including a giant sloth. In 1812, he exhibited an ancient flying reptile that he named a pterodactyl. His work in the museum was both scientifically sound and impressive to the public. He became one of the best-known scientists in Europe. He, like many ordinary citizens and world famous individuals, fell victim and died of the disastrous cholera epidemic that struck Paris in 1832.

LUKE HOWARD
1772–1864
ENGLISH BUSINESSMAN AND AMATEUR METEOROLOGIST
MAJOR ACCOMPLISHMENT: NAMED TYPES OF CLOUDS

LUKE HOWARD WAS BORN in London. His parents were devoted Christians who taught him to respect and serve God. He attended a Christian school near Oxford. In 1783, a volcano in Iceland erupted and spread dust and ash high in the atmosphere. The violent eruption gave England and the rest of Europe a dreadful lemon-colored sky. On August 18, the 11-year-old Luke Howard climbed to the top of a nearby hill for a better view of the sunset.

The sun showed through the haze with an eerie copper glow. As the sun sank below the horizon, the sky became lighted with a remarkable array of colors. Along the western horizon, the sky turned a shimmering green. The light fanned out as it extended upward and colored the clouds pink. Directly overhead, the dark sky became a deep violet.

Slowly the fantastic colors faded. A sizzling streak of light from a fireball flashed across the sky. It was one of the brightest shooting stars on record. Along the northern horizon, the northern lights began a vivid display. Curtains of crimson weaved back and forth.

In one night, Howard saw sights that many people never see in a lifetime. The vivid light show captured his attention. He became a regular observer of the sky. He kept detailed weather records for several decades.

He studied the clouds and sketched what he saw. Most scientists believed it senseless to study clouds. Clouds came and went, changed shape, and disappeared, all without any obvious reason. He became convinced that clouds, like all aspects of nature, followed set rules. Would the God of order make a disorderly sky?

During the long London winters, Howard met once every two weeks with scientific-minded friends. Membership in the meetings required each person to read a report on some subject or pay a fine. Members listened to each other's work and encouraged one another.

In 1802, Howard presented a paper on the naming of clouds. He chose Latin names based on the shapes of the clouds. Scientists from England, France, Italy, and other countries communicated in Latin, a language they all understood.

He described four main types of clouds: stratus ("layers"), cumulus ("heap," like fleecy puffballs), cirrus ("hairlike"), and nimbus ("rain"). These categories became the foundation for naming clouds.

Howard's work made a lasting impression on those who study the atmosphere. The Royal Society of London, England's greatest organization of scientists, elected him a member. Even artists used his ideas. Their paintings of clouds became more realistic.

Howard was the first to realize that burning coal and other human activities could change the weather. His temperature readings showed that London was warmer than the surrounding countryside. Moisture condensed around particles spewed into the air by smokestacks and gave rise to what he called city fog. Today the combination of fog and smoke is called smog.

Despite the honor of being elected to the Royal Society, Howard never claimed to be a scientist. He continued to be a dedicated Christian who gave his time unselfishly to the congregation where he worshiped. He had a warm family life and raised a family. He earned a living as a businessman. His company, Howard and Sons, manufactured chemicals for use by druggists.

Today Luke Howard is remembered as the man who named the clouds.

CHARLES BELL

1774–1842

SCOTTISH SURGEON

MAJOR ACHIEVEMENT: FIRST TO ESTABLISH THE EXISTENCE OF SEPARATE MOTOR AND SENSORY NERVES

CHARLES BELL WAS a Scottish surgeon who did groundbreaking work in understanding the brain and nervous system. Bell was born in Edinburgh, Scotland. His father, who died when Charles was five, was a minister in the Church of England. Responsibility for Charles' education fell to his mother, who gave him a strong grounding in the Christian faith. She was an artist, and with her help Bell developed an artistic talent that he used to illustrate his medical books.

Charles Bell's older brother was an established surgeon who lectured on anatomy at the University of Edinburgh. Charles Bell took advantage of his brother's extensive personal medical library. Charles was well prepared for medical school. While still a student at the University of Edinburgh, he wrote the first of his books on anatomy and illustrated it with his own drawings.

Bell graduated in 1799. No position was available for him at the university except as his brother's assistant in the anatomy class. During this time, he prepared additional texts on the anatomy of the human body. He also wrote a textbook especially for artists, *Essays on the Anatomy of Expression in Painting*.

In 1804, he moved to London as a surgeon. London became the treatment center for soldiers injured during England's struggles against Napoleon. Bell saw firsthand how damage to the spinal cord and nerves could affect the physical ability of soldiers. In 1811 he summarized what he had learned in *New Idea of Anatomy of the Brain*. It is considered the foundation of modern neurology.

Charles Bell was present on June 18, 1815, at Wellington's decisive defeat of Napoleon at the Battle of Waterloo. It was one of the bloodiest battles in history. About 45,000 soldiers lay dead or wounded in an area of three square miles. Bell worked tirelessly in their treatment. His coat became stiff with blood, and he only stepped aside when the prolonged exertion left his arms and hands incapable of functioning.

With the coming of peace, he became professor of anatomy and surgery at the College of Surgeons in London. He had time for research and made the key discovery that nerves are one-way streets. Some nerves carry impulses toward the brain, while others carry impulses away from the brain. Those nerves that conduct information to the central nervous system he called sensory nerves. Those that convey instruction from the brain to the organs he called motor nerves.

He tested reflex action and became convinced that some sensory information is interpreted at the spinal cord for immediate response without going to the brain. He summarized 30 years of research in *The Nervous System of the Human Body* (1830).

The groundbreaking nature of the book earned him an award from the Royal Society and knighthood from King William in 1831. Despite the honors in England, the 61-year-old surgeon returned to Scotland. He stated that London was a good place to work, but not to retire. He did not retire, although he found more time for fly-fishing. He became professor of surgery at the University of Edinburgh.

Bell had been invited to deliver a Bridgewater treatise by the Royal Society, and he did so in 1836. The Earl of Bridgewater set aside 8,000 pounds to print and distribute works "On the Power, Wisdom and Goodness of God as Manifested in the Creation."

The president of the Royal Society discussed the selection of eight individuals for the project with the Archbishop of Canterbury and with the Bishop of London. Bell was one of the eight selected because he had infused even his scientific writings with a religious overtone.

Bell's subject was "The Hand, as Evincing Design." His approach, known as natural theology, argued that unique features in human beings revealed the existence of a Creator. Bell's influence in surgery, neurology, and theology lasted throughout the 1800s. During most of the century, natural theology essays were required reading at Cambridge University and other schools.

The Sir Charles Bell Society, established in 1992, was named in his honor. It is an international organization dedicated to exchanging ideas relating to the facial nerves.

JOHN CHAPMAN (JOHNNY APPLESEED)

1774–1845

AMERICAN FOLK HERO AND ITINERANT PREACHER

MAJOR ACCOMPLISHMENT: EXEMPLAR OF THE PIONEER SPIRIT OF INDEPENDENCE, HUMBLE CHRISTIAN NATURE, AND WILLINGNESS TO HELP THOSE LESS FORTUNATE.

JOHN CHAPMAN GREW UP on a farm in Massachusetts. Each fall, he picked apples from the orchard around the farmhouse. Apples were easy to keep throughout winter. They could be sliced and dried or cooked to make apple butter. Their juice made apple cider and vinegar.

In 1794, John Chapman decided to strike out on his own. Pioneer families had begun moving west. He planned to advance ahead of them and plant apple seeds. Rather than a bleak wilderness, they would find apple orchards.

Chapman traveled over the rugged mountains of the Alleghenies into western Pennsylvania. He collected seeds from the cider presses. He walked west with his bag of seeds until the last large settlement was a hundred miles behind him. He looked for fertile soil, the right amount of sunlight, and moisture. After planting the seeds, Chapman constructed an enclosure of brush and limbs to keep out the deer.

He hiked alone and carried no gun, hunting knife, or traps to take animals for food. He ate cornmeal mush with wild foods such as herbs, fruits, nuts, and berries. In good weather, he enjoyed sleeping in the open. If the weather was miserable, he quickly built a lean-to shelter from fallen logs, tree branches, and leaves.

Chapman wore whatever clothes he could find. They were usually cast-off shirts and trousers with holes in them. For a cloak he cut head and arm holes in a coffee sack. Because of his small stature, it covered him from shoulders to knees. At first, he wore his mush pot upside down as a hat. It had no bill to shade his eyes from the relentless sun. Chapman pasted together cardboard to make a cap with a bill to keep the glare of the sun from his eyes.

One day near sundown, a pioneer family heard a happy song: "The Lord is good to me. And so I thank the Lord for giving me the sun and the rain and apple tree. And some day there'll be apples there, for everyone in the world to share."

The settlers knew the legendary Johnny Appleseed was coming. John Chapman had earned that name after his years in the wilderness.

He gave the girls calico ribbons for their hair. He told the boys stories of his adventures. Pioneer women welcomed him, too. He brought news about other families who lived miles away. He was a welcome sight to the farmer who needed to start an orchard but had no money. Chapman would provide seedlings in exchange for clothing or cornmeal.

In the log cabin, Chapman took none of the food that was offered until he saw that everyone else had been fed. He drank milk with fresh bread. After he finished, Chapman said, "I have some news right fresh from heaven." He read the Beatitudes from Matthew (Matt. 5:3–12.) He always carried his Bible with him.

With the meager income from the sale of his trees, Chapman bought books on nature, history, and the Bible. When he finished a book, he left it in the care of a pioneer family. The next time he passed through, he retrieved the book and left another in its place. People were eager for learning.

In 1834, he pushed beyond Ohio and traveled into Indiana and Illinois. He kept a chain of orchards in various stages of development spread along three hundred miles. Each year he walked more than a thousand miles.

Most of his plots were small, only one to five acres. He charged about seven cents for one of his trees. If his customers were poor, they could pay with clothing or cornmeal.

Despite his simple ways, Chapman had become a successful businessman. He owned land in several states, and his annual income would have rivaled any stay-at-home nursery operator. However, he kept none of the money but gave it to worthy causes such as medical help for sick farmers.

He also had a soft heart for worn-out domestic animals. Often unthinking families released old or injured horses at the start of winter. Chapman searched for these strays. He took care of them until spring and gave them to a farmer. If the animals were too old and lame to work, he paid for their care until they died of old age.

Fifty years after he started, Chapman's original goal had become a reality. The fragrance of apple blossoms greeted each new spring throughout western Pennsylvania, Ohio, northwestern Virginia, Indiana, Kentucky, and Illinois. Despite his age, his hair flowed jet black, his eyes sparkled, and he walked with vigorous intensity.

The fathers and mothers who greeted him in Indiana recalled being entertained by his stories when they were children in Ohio. Some of the women showed him the calico ribbon he'd given them as young girls.

In March of 1845, Chapman sang as he walked along the trail near Fort Wayne, Indiana. "The Lord is good to me. So I thank the Lord for giving me the sun and the rain and the apple tree."

The weather turned cold, night fell, and he became chilled. The William Worth family insisted he spend the night with them. By the evening of the next day, he had died of pneumonia. It was the only time he had ever gotten sick. He was buried with a simple headstone that read "He lived for others."

Chapman's gentle nature and generous personality had a lasting impact on American life. Pioneer families modeled their independence, humble Christian nature, and willingness to help one another after his example. Much of the pioneer spirit came from John Chapman.

HUMPHRY DAVY
1778–1829
ENGLISH CHEMIST
MAJOR ACCOMPLISHMENT: DISCOVERED SODIUM,
POTASSIUM, AND OTHER METALLIC ELEMENTS

HUMPHRY DAVY MOVED chemistry into the modern era by introducing electricity as a way to refine metals from their ores.

Although he came from a middle-class family that could afford to send him to school, Davy did not do well as a student. He enjoyed fishing and exploring the countryside more than class work. His father died and left the family in debt. Because of their Christian beliefs, Davy and his mother were determined to repay the debt, and eventually succeeded in doing so.

Davy took a job in the shop of a druggist. He became fascinated with chemicals but mixed them without regard for his safety. The owner of the shop dismissed him before he blew up the business.

Davy next took a job at a clinic that tested the medical uses of new gases. During the previous 25 years, chemists had found that the atmosphere was made of gases, including oxygen. The new gases were thought to have a health benefit. Doctors opened clinics to treat patients by having them inhale the gases. Davy nearly suffocated himself while testing a mixture of hydrogen and carbon monoxide.

Davy discovered nitrous oxide, which became known as laughing gas. He suggested its use as a painkiller. Although the gas did not render a person completely insensitive to pain, it did find a role in dentistry and is still sometimes used for that purpose today.

In 1800, Davy lectured on science at the Royal Institution in London. He was a natural showman, and his lectures became popular. He stayed on as a chemist at the Royal Institution.

Twelve years earlier, the French chemist Antoine Lavoisier had drawn up a list of substances that he believed contained new metals. These substances included soda ash and potash. Metals were usually freed by heating the ore in a blast furnace with carbon. Soda ash and potash resisted such treatment. Something was needed to pry the metal away from the oxygen that was bound with it. Davy found the more powerful force in electricity.

Humphry Davy

Davy built the most powerful batteries then in existence and sent the current through molten potash. A silvery metal collected at one of the electrodes. He called the new metal "potassium." In the next few days he separated a metal from soda ash and called it "sodium." He quickly discovered five other metals including barium and calcium.

The triumph made him famous. In 1812, he was knighted, got married, but also nearly killed himself while trying to make nitrogen trichloride. The unstable chemical had a hair-trigger temperament and could explode without warning. It did explode and left him blinded for a time. Davy was fortunate to find the young and brilliant Michael Faraday as his assistant. At first Faraday read to him, but later began taking a greater role in their work.

Like Faraday, Davy was a Christian and especially generous. One of his important inventions was the miner's safety lantern. The industrial revolution was in full swing with coal as the primary fuel. Coal mines took an annual toll of lives because of explosions of coal dust. Davy designed a safety lantern that reduced the possibility of explosions. He released it for use without patenting it. He also took up the chemistry of agriculture and became a popular lecturer on the subject in farming communities.

In 1820, Davy became president of the Royal Society. His body suffered the effects of years of tasting and sniffing chemicals. He was often bedridden, but with Michael Faraday's help, he continued to make discoveries. He designed the arc lamp, a device that used a discharge of electricity between carbon rods to generate a dazzling source of light.

When Davy was asked what was his greatest discovery, he promptly replied "Michael Faraday." As his life drew to a close, Davy wrote about his early interest in fly-fishing and a series of articles about his travels. He traveled despite the effects of a stroke and died in Geneva, Switzerland, at the age of 50.

FRANCIS SCOTT KEY

1779–1843
UNITED STATES LAWYER
MAJOR ACCOMPLISHMENT: WROTE THE UNITED STATES NATIONAL ANTHEM

FRANCIS SCOTT KEY WAS A Maryland lawyer who practiced in both Baltimore and Washington, D.C. In the late summer of 1814, Washington, D.C., had fallen to the British, who then advanced up the Chesapeake Bay to attack Baltimore.

Francis Scott Key received an urgent request to help free an American citizen, Dr. William Beames. The doctor had been taken prisoner by the British when they overran Bladensburg, Maryland. Key agreed to the dangerous mission. He gathered a packet of letters from friends of the doctor and from President Madison himself, stating that the doctor was a civilian and had not participated in the fighting. Key also gathered written statements from wounded British soldiers who confirmed that the doctor had treated them with the same care that he had given American soldiers.

Francis Scott Key and Colonel John Skinner, an American in charge of exchanging prisoners, sailed under a flag of truce past old Fort McHenry to meet the British ships. They came alongside the flagship *Tonnant* of Admiral Alexander Cochrane. The admiral received them, read the packet of letters, and agreed to release the doctor.

From the busy activity, Key could see that the British planned to begin their attack the next morning. Admiral Cochrane decided not to release Key and the others until after the battle. The British believed their firepower would make short work of the old, poorly repaired Fort McHenry.

The shells from the British ships pounded the fort all through the day and then throughout the night. The battle raged for 25 hours. In addition to 1,500 cannon bombshells, the British released Congreve fire rockets that were intended to ignite the wooden buildings inside the fort.

On the morning of September 14, to nearly everyone's amazement, Fort McHenry had not fallen. The sight of the American flag still flying at daybreak over the fort inspired Francis Scott Key to scratch out a poem on the back of an envelope. He titled the composition, "The Defence of Fort M'Henry."

The British sea forces stalled, and the land attack was repelled. The British withdrew. Admiral Cochrane lost the battle, but kept his word. He released Francis Scott Key, Colonel Skinner, and Dr. Beames. When Key arrived back in Baltimore, he went to his room at the Indian Queen Hotel and completed the poem. His brother-in-law had copies printed and distributed, and it was published the next week in the Baltimore *Patriot*.

The next month the song was published as sheet music with the title "The Star Spangled Banner." Although immediately popular and used as the anthem by the American armed forces, more than 110 years passed before it became the official national anthem in 1931.

The last three lines of the song were:

And this be our motto, "In God is our Trust"
And the star-spangled banner in triumph shall wave
O'er the land of the free and the home of the brave.

During the Civil War, Secretary of the Treasury Salmon P. Chase sent an order to the Director of the Mint in Philadelphia. Chase wrote, "No nation can be strong except in the strength of God, or safe except in His defense. The trust of our people in God should be declared on our national coins."

The director remembered the phrase "In God is our Trust" from Key's song. He shortened it to "In God We Trust" and put it on a one-cent piece. Eventually all coins carried the motto, but it was not required on paper money. In 1956, it became the official U.S. motto to be placed on currency as well as coins.

After the War of 1812, Francis Scott Key continued to practice law and write poetry. His book *The Power of Literature and Its Connection with Religion* was published in 1834. Because of the circulation of American currency in foreign countries, his words have been read by more people in more countries than those of any other American writer.

PETER MARK ROGET
1779–1869
ENGLISH PHYSICIAN

MAJOR ACCOMPLISHMENT: AUTHOR OF *ROGET'S THESAURUS*

PETER MARK ROGET LED several lives. As a physician he investigated the medical properties of newly discovered gases, established medical schools, and practiced medicine for 50 years. As a scientist, he made a better slide rule, investigated the persistence of vision, became an editor of the *Encyclopedia Britannica*, and contributed 300,000 words on science subjects. As a Christian, he volunteered free service at a charity hospital and wrote one of the Bridgewater treatises to promote the evidence of design in creation. In his spare time he engaged in a passion for chess and developed a pocket chess set. Yet, his greatest achievement came after he retired.

Although born in London, Roget was educated at the University of Edinburgh, the "place to be" during the late 1700s and early 1800s. After earning a medical degree, he spent a year in Bristol at the pneumatic clinic of Dr. Thomas Beddoes. In the late 1700s, a variety of new gases had been discovered, and doctors believed that some of the gases might have medical possibilities. The teenage chemist Humphry Davy was on the staff of Beddoes's clinic. Davy had discovered laughing gas (nitrous oxide) and used it as a painkiller. Roget was one of the people Davy persuaded to test the gas by inhaling it.

After a stint at the air clinic, Roget moved to Manchester where he helped found a medical school. In 1808, he moved to London, and there he stayed until his retirement, 32 years later.

Medicine alone could not utilize all of his talents. In 1814, he developed an improved version of the slide rule. Before the invention of small electronic calculators, engineers and scientists relied on the slide rule for quick and easy math calculations. The rule and moving part, the slide, were marked so numbers could be multiplied or divided by the simple act of moving the slide and a hairline cursor. Rather than the numbers themselves, their logarithms were added or subtracted.

Slide rules were either circular or linear, but neither design was capable of raising numbers to powers or taking roots. Roget overcame this limitation by developing a slide rule with a log-log scale. Roget's slide rule permitted calculating the power or root of any number. The fixed part of the slide rule was marked in logarithms of the logarithms of numbers, while the slide scale had the logarithm. He perfected his design in 1815, and it remained in common use until the 1960s. For this work, he was elected to the Royal Society.

In 1820, Roget began working on vision with the great English scientist Michael Faraday. Roget's interest had been aroused when he watched the wheels of a passing carriage through the slats of a venetian blind. The spokes of the wheel appeared curved, although they were perfectly straight. He built a portable device to study the effect. He concluded that an image of the spokes remained on the retina of the eye as the next spoke came into view.

He published his results in the transaction of the Royal Society. The descriptive title was "Explanation of an Optical Deception in the Appearance of the Spokes of a Wheel Seen Through Vertical Apertures." In the paper, he stated that an image "will remain for a time after the cause has ceased." In later years, his finding became known as the persistence of vision. By showing a series of still pictures quickly enough, the illusion of motion can be achieved. Roget's work is often cited as the start of theoretical study of motion pictures.

In 1827, Roget became the secretary of the Royal Society. The position involved numerous duties, including writing summaries of the latest in scientific advances. He was noted for being able to communicate his exact meaning. In this, he had a secret weapon. Starting in 1805, he had become interested in the meanings of words. Scientists grouped similar objects into classes in the natural world. In the same way, he put words in categories based upon similar meanings and thoughts. He added to his system of verbal classification over the years.

Roget was 61 years old when he retired from medical practice in 1840. He had a rough handwritten collection of words that he had grouped, not in alphabetical order, but according to ideas. Roget spent

12 years extending and improving his manuscript. It was published as *Roget's Thesaurus of English Words and Phrases* in 1852. *Roget's Thesaurus* was instantly successful.

Peter Mark Roget was one of the eight scientists selected to write a Bridgewater treatise. Roget, the son of a French Protestant pastor, was well-known for his Christian service including his free treatment of needy cases at a charity clinic that he helped found. Roget's Bridgewater treatise was "Animal and Vegetable Physiology Considered with Reference to Natural Theology."

Roget continued to add words to his thesaurus. His son and grandson continued the effort after his death. The book has never gone out of print and became the third best-selling book of all time after the King James Bible and Webster's Dictionary. Roget's name became synonymous with synonyms.

WILLIAM BUCKLAND
1784–1856
BRITISH MINISTER AND GEOLOGIST

MAJOR ACCOMPLISHMENT: IDENTIFIED THE FIRST
DINOSAUR

WILLIAM BUCKLAND GRADUATED from the University of Oxford and was ordained in the Church of England. Because of his training in geology and mineralogy, he became a professor of geology at Oxford University. He was the first true paleontologist, and the first researcher to name a dinosaur.

As a hobby, Buckland collected fossils. Among the bones that he uncovered in southern England were those of an ancient mammal. He had also come across a lower jawbone that had dagger-like teeth and fragments of a limb bone from the animal. It was not a mammal, and his analysis of the fragments identified it as a large, extinct lizard-like creature. In a paper published in 1824, Buckland named it *Megalosaurus*, a name meaning "large lizard."

Although dinosaur bones had been discovered several times, their study had not become a separate discipline. When the name dinosaur ("terrifying lizard") for these reptiles came into use in 1841, it became clear that Buckland's discovery belonged to the newly named group. He had been the first person to give a scientific name to a species of dinosaurs.

Buckland's discoveries were influential among scientists and captured the imagination of the public. He recreated the scene of his fossil finds. In a book published in 1822, he described a feeding frenzy of ancient hyenas as they tore their prey apart. He became a popularizer of science, an important role as scientific disciplines became more complex and filled with jargon.

He agreed with Georges Cuvier that the surface of the earth had been shaped by a series of worldwide disasters, with the last one being the Flood. He accepted Louis Agassiz's statement that glaciers had made their mark on vast regions of Europe and North America. He was the first scientist to find evidence of scratch marks left by glacial flow on rocks in England.

Buckland's scientific work was done from the viewpoint of his religious beliefs. The scientific community acknowledged his abilities as a scientist by electing him to the Royal Society. The Church of England recognized his abilities as a clergyman by making him dean of Westminster Cathedral.

In 1837, Buckland was invited to provide an entry in the Bridgewater treatises. Francis Henry Egerton, the Earl of Bridgewater, gave 8,000 pounds to the Royal Society for the purpose of publishing books that showed the power, wisdom, and goodness of God as manifested in the creation. Buckland was a natural choice for the project. He was a member of the Royal Society, a founder of paleontology and a clergyman. His entry was titled *Geology and Mineralogy Considered with Reference to Natural Theology*. Rather than a simple pamphlet, the completed manuscript was printed in two volumes.

William Buckland wrote a number of books on science and Scripture, including *Relics of the Deluge*. One of his goals was to reconcile the latest geological discoveries with the Bible. He believed religion should embrace science, using the natural theology argument that both came from the same source.

WILLIAM PROUT

1785–1850

ENGLISH PHYSICIAN AND CHEMIST

MAJOR ACHIEVEMENT: MADE THE FIRST TABLE OF
ATOMIC WEIGHTS FOR THE CHEMICAL ELEMENTS

PROUT WAS THE SON OF A tenant farmer, but managed to attend the University of Edinburgh and graduate with a medical degree. He chose digestive ailments as his specialty. This led him to a study of metabolism, a poorly understood aspect of how food energy is used by the body.

During his digestive studies, Prout discovered hydrochloric acid in the stomachs of animals, and presumably, it would be in human stomachs. This was an astonishing discovery because hydrochloric acid was a powerful acid. It could eat its way through metal, burn a hole in cloth, and dissolve flesh. Although present in diluted form in the stomach, scientists were nevertheless stunned that the lining of the stomach was able to withstand its action.

In studying digestion, Prout followed the trend of the time of putting objects into categories. He classified foods as fats, carbohydrates, and proteins. Other chemists and nutritionists quickly accepted these categories.

Prout noticed that when the atomic weights of elements were compared with the weight of hydrogen, they were close to whole numbers. Carbon was 12 times the weight of hydrogen, oxygen 16 times, and so on. He proposed that all elements might be built of hydrogen atoms. Prout's suggestion touched off a flurry of study in chemistry to prove or disprove his hypothesis. Chemists found that chlorine had an atomic weight of 35.5, which showed the idea in error. However, in proving him wrong, chemists had collected information that helped Mendeleev in the 1860s develop the periodic table of the elements.

Although Prout's hypothesis appeared to have failed, it was revived in the early 1900s. Modern chemistry established that the mass of a hydrogen atom is in the proton. Atoms of elements do have atomic weights that are multiples of the mass of a proton.

Prout was another of the scientists selected to write one of the Bridgewater treatises. In his treatise he took to task those philosophers who smiled at ignorant savages who imagined a god in every cloud and heard a spirit voice in every wind. Philosophers and atheist scientists had made the laws of nature their god, an idea no more absurd than that of the untaught savage. "Both are alike ignorant," William Prout concluded.

MICHAEL FARADAY
1791–1867
ENGLISH CHEMIST AND PHYSICIST
MAJOR ACCOMPLISHMENT: DISCOVERED
ELECTROMAGNETIC INDUCTION

MICHAEL FARADAY IS universally placed near the top of any list of the greatest scientists of all time. He made both theoretical and practical discoveries in chemistry, electromagnetism, and optics. His mind ranged from applications of science in daily life to abstract concepts that became central to theoretical physics.

Faraday's father was a blacksmith and his mother a farmer's daughter. The family moved to London in search of a better life. Faraday, who had nine brothers and sisters, grew up in poverty. His formal education was limited to learning to read, write, and do simple arithmetic. His parents did teach him the Christian faith and instilled in him the concept of providence — God would provide. Throughout his life, he had no particular concern about the future, but concentrated on the work for that day.

At age 13, he began work in a book bindery. Faraday read the books that passed through the shop. In his spare time, he repeated some of the scientific experiments that he encountered. An artist who rented a room from the bookshop owner taught Faraday the rudiments of drawing.

A customer gave Faraday tickets to a series of lectures by Humphry Davy, the best-known scientist in London. Faraday attended the lectures and made a notebook of the speeches. He drew pictures that illustrated the demonstrations and bound the book in leather. He presented the notebook to Humphry Davy as a way of introduction and asked for a position as Davy's assistant.

Davy, who worked at the Royal Institution, had no opening for an assistant. However, Davy never exercised caution around chemicals. He was always tasting and sniffing them and sometimes his experiments resulted in explosions. An explosion left Davy temporarily blinded and while his sight recovered, he hired Faraday to read to him.

After three months, Davy could see again. Faraday was dismissed, but rehired almost immediately because of an unexpected opening. Davy had married earlier in the year, and decided to combine a honeymoon with a two-year-long European vacation. Michael Faraday accompanied him with a portable laboratory. Faraday, who had never been out of London, suddenly found himself traveling throughout Europe and meeting the most important scientists of his day.

Michael Faraday

Faraday investigated the action of the powerful batteries that Davy used to free elements from their oxides. When electricity flowed in a solution containing dissolved salt such as sodium chlorine, the metal would plate out on one of the electrodes. The chemical action of electricity was not well understood. After a series of experiments, Faraday discovered the two principles of electrolysis. First, chemical action was proportional to the amount of electricity that flows. Second, the weights of substances removed from the solution were proportional to the equivalent weights of the substances. (Equivalent weight was a measure of an element's chemical combining power; or in modern chemical terms, atomic weight divided by valence.)

Faraday showed that an electric current could produce mechanical action. He built a device in which a wire rotated around a magnet while current flowed in the wire. It was the first electric motor.

In 1821, the year he invented the electric motor, Michael Faraday married Sarah Barnard. He preferred to stay close to his laboratory, so they lived in an attic apartment above the Royal Institution.

Electricity could only be made at that time by chemical methods. Faraday took on the challenge to generate electricity by mechanical action — the opposite action of an electric motor. Faraday worked on this problem more than ten years. The breakthrough came in 1831 when he thrust a bar magnet into a coil of wire and a small electric current flowed. He improved upon this by spinning a copper disk between the poles of powerful magnets. He touched the disk at the center and at the edge with copper brushes attached to a wire. The wires drew away a continuous supply of electricity. Faraday had made the first electric generator.

As part of his research, he also found he could transfer electricity from one coil of wire to another. When he sent electricity through the first coil, it produced a flow of electricity in the second coil. Although close together, the two coils were independent of one another. In addition, if the number of turns of wire in each coil were different, then the voltage from the secondary coil would be different from the voltage of the electricity flowing in the primary coil. Faraday had invented the first electric transformer to step-up or step-down voltage.

Faraday never patented his inventions but lived on a small salary from the Royal Institution.

In his theoretical work, Faraday used a compass to map the magnetic field around a wire in which electricity flowed. Because of his lack of mathematical training, he often used visual pictures to represent the abstract concepts of physics. He invented the idea of lines of force to show a magnetic field.

The idea of lines of force drew ridicule from the physicists of his day. However, James Clerk Maxwell put the concept of lines of force on a firm mathematical footing. From Faraday's work, Maxwell developed the four electromagnetic equations that became essential in understanding electromagnetism.

Faraday showed a relationship between electricity, magnetism, and light. His earlier work showed that an electric current could produce a magnetic field and a moving magnetic field could generate electricity. This discovery was known as electromagnetic induction. Faraday tested the optical properties of glass by subjecting them to an intense magnetic field. The magnetism twisted the plane of polarized light. This was the first indication that light had an electromagnetic nature. It began the search, still going on today, to relate the fundamental forces of nature in a single unified theory.

Faraday strove to live a humble life that depended on God. When his income exceeded his needs, he gave away the excess. He turned down a knighthood. He declined an offer to become president of the Royal Society. This determination to stay focused on his research allowed Faraday to make scientific achievements matched by few individuals.

His Christian duty was central to his life. His Bible was well-used for his study. He seldom missed a church service. As elder of the congregation, he also prepared and gave some of the sermons. He did not engage in arguments about whether discoveries in science and Scripture agreed. He believed that there could be no difference between the two because they both had the same Maker.

He remembered his own childhood of poverty and gave free Christmas lectures about science to children. One of his best-known talks was about a candle.

In 1862, Faraday gave his last lecture because of failing memory. He said, "The old candle is about to go out." He resigned from the Royal Institution, and he and his wife moved into a nearby cottage provided by Queen Victoria. When he died in 1867, he could have been buried in Westminster Abby, but he expressly asked for a simple funeral and an ordinary gravestone.

SAMUEL FINLEY BREESE MORSE

1791–1872

AMERICAN ARTIST AND INVENTOR

MAJOR ACCOMPLISHMENT: INVENTED ELECTRIC

TELEGRAPH

SAMUEL MORSE WAS BORN into a scholarly family — his father Jedidiah Morse was a clergyman and the author of a textbook on geography. Samuel attended Phillips Academy in Andover and Yale College. He proved to be a merely adequate student. He enjoyed sketching likenesses of the students, and earned some money by drawing portraits for students to send home to their parents.

In 1812, Morse sailed to England to study at the Royal Academy. Once in London, Morse wrote to his parents. "I only wish," he wrote, "you had this letter now. But 3,000 miles are not passed over in an instant." The fastest mail ship took a month to cross the Atlantic.

After two years in England, Samuel Morse returned to the United States. He married and settled in New Haven, Connecticut. His portrait business took him all along the eastern seaboard. At the height of his fame a tragedy struck. He was in Washington D. C. painting the portraits of famous Americans. Back home, his wife unexpectedly became sick and died. The letter telling of the terrible news was eight days in the mail.

This personal tragedy caused Samuel to become more aware of his good fortune in other areas. Each night he would ask himself, *Have I received a particular blessing today and not been thankful for it?*

He had become concerned that because of the separation of church and state, children in the United States were not receiving a full education. He said, "Education without religion is in danger of substituting wild theories for the simple common sense rules of Christianity."

To remedy the problem, he promoted the idea of Sunday schools. In his hometown, New Haven, Connecticut, he began a Sunday school, one of the first in the United States. He said, "The soul of freedom is true religion exerting its moral power on an educated population."

He moved to New York City, and he and his brother launched the New York *Journal of Commerce*. They made the unusual decision not to carry advertisements for subjects they did not approve, such as those of theaters with immoral plays.

At age 40, Morse took a vacation to Europe. He had become America's best-known, most successful portrait painter. He spent weeks in the Louvre and painted *Gallery of the Louvre*. More than a hundred years later, in 1985, this painting sold for three million dollars, the highest price ever paid up to that time for a painting by an American artist.

Also visiting Paris were James Fenimore Cooper and the great German naturalist Alexander van Humboldt. They often came to the Louvre to watch Morse work and talk about the events of the day. The topic of conversation was the fall of Warsaw, Poland, to the Russian army. The news came by the French semaphore system, which was a method of signaling messages by means of towers with jointed arms that moved up and down. The system had been tried in the United States, but proved too slow for the vast country.

In 1832, Morse boarded the *Sully* for the return trip to America. The shipboard conversation turned to electricity. One passenger said that the length of a wire did not slow the flow of electricity. Morse had heard of a new invention, an electromagnet, which could be turned on and off. Suddenly, Morse realized that messages could be sent great distances through a wire. Samuel sketched his basic design. In his invention, electricity flowed through a circuit of wire. The current caused an electromagnet to raise and lower a metal lever. A pencil attached to the lever marked dots and dashes on a moving strip of paper. He called his invention a telegraph. He devised the Morse code, the dots and dashes that stood for letters of the alphabet. Within a few months after landing in New York, Samuel showed a crude form of the telegraph to several businessmen. They were unimpressed. One said, "It is useful only for the lady of the house to send for the maid in the cellar!"

Samuel struggled to interest people in the telegraph. He pointed out that because of the lack of speedy communication, England and the United States blundered into the War of 1812. They fought a bloody battle in New Orleans 11 days *after* signing a peace treaty.

American businessmen showed no interest. Morse traveled to Europe to try to sell it to the French government, but he failed in this, too. However, he met the artist-inventor Louis Daguerre, who announced his invention of the photograph process as Morse left for America.

When Morse returned to the United States, he built his own camera and developing equipment. He took the first photographic portrait in America. To raise money for the telegraph, he taught the process to students. One of his students was Mathew Brady who would become famous as a photographer of the Civil War.

He still could not interest anyone in the telegraph. However, his faith in God did not waver. "I am perfectly satisfied that, mysterious as it may seem to me, it has all been ordered in view of my Heavenly Father's guiding hand."

Finally, after 12 years of trying, Samuel convinced the United States government to pay for a test line between Baltimore and Washington, D.C. Samuel demonstrated the telegraph on Friday, May 24, 1844. The message — "What hath God wrought" from Numbers 23:23 — had been chosen by the daughter of the commissioner of patents.

The telegraph began to earn a profit. Samuel gave the first money from his invention to a church in Washington so the congregation could begin a Sunday school.

The telegraph became one of the top ten inventions of all time. Honors showered upon him. Yale conferred upon him an honorary LL.D. degree. The letters stood for Latin words meaning "doctor of letters." Playfully, Samuel always insisted that LL.D. stood for "Lightning Line Doctor."

Once its importance became known, people who claimed to have invented the telegraph filed more than 600 lawsuits. Yet, not a single one prevailed, and Morse was universally recognized as the inventor of the practical telegraph. Morse, however, gave God the credit. "I agree with that sentence of Annie Ellsworth, 'What hath God wrought!' It is *His* work."

In 1900, Morse was inducted into the Hall of Fame for Great Americans. Oddly, as other inventions such as the telephone and e-mail have become the modern standard, Morse is today being re-found as an artist. He had both a technical competence and an ability to render a positive aspect of the subject's character. His powerful portraits include those of Lafayette and William Cullen Bryant. His non-portrait paintings helped establish a style known as "democratic art." He produced a giant canvas showing the legislature in action late at night in the Capitol building. Morse is recognized as one of America's great artists.

CHARLES BABBAGE
1792–1871
ENGLISH MATHEMATICIAN AND INVENTOR
MAJOR ACCOMPLISHMENT: DESIGNED THE FIRST
PROGRAMMABLE COMPUTER

CHARLES BABBAGE WAS THE son of a wealthy English banker. Science, especially mathematics, fascinated him. He studied at Cambridge in 1810, but found that science had gone into suspended animation following the great gains of Newton a century earlier. Babbage took his education into his own hands by studying science books from France that were more up-to-date.

Babbage read about a remarkable invention by Joseph Marie Jacquard. The Frenchman invented a way to mechanically control a cloth-weaving loom with punched cards. Holes punched in a series of cards controlled the pattern in the woven fabric. When a loom operator finished a particular bolt of fabric, he could replace the cards with a different set to weave a different intricate pattern to the next bolt of cloth.

Babbage was aghast that France and not England had developed the new technology. He blamed it on the stagnant nature of science in England. While still a student at Cambridge, Babbage teamed with John Herschel (son of William Herschel who discovered Uranus) and other students to found the Analytical Society. The goal was to introduce modern mathematics into English science. As Christians, they also pledged to leave the world a better place than they had found it.

Babbage knew that many of the hand-calculated mathematical tables contained errors. He built a mechanical calculator that could generate tables of logarithms to eight decimals. He called it a "difference engine." The name came from the way the final answer was calculated by a series of numbers based on differences of the previous result.

In 1823, he gained government funding to build a full-size version with a 20-decimal accuracy. His intense work on the machine damaged his health. This was compounded by the deaths of his father, wife, and two daughters in 1827. He went to Europe for his health, but came back even more exasperated at the pace of scientific discovery in England when compared to France.

He wrote a controversial book that was published in 1830. He had been elected to the Royal Society, but in his book, *Reflections on the Decline of Science in England*, he denounced the organization as obsolete. He wrote, "The Council of the Royal Society is a collection of men who elect each other to office and then dine together at the expense of this society to praise each other over wine and give each other medals." He found many others who agreed with him, and they began a rival organization, the British Association for the Advancement of Science.

During the periodic gaps when he ran out of money for his computing machine, Babbage became an expert at time and motion studies. He wrote the influential book *On the Economy of Machinery and Manufactures*.

The British Postal Commission contracted with him to investigate the pricing of mail delivery. Babbage concluded that the cost of collecting and stamping a letter in accordance with weight and distance would cost more than it was worth. The best choice, he said, would be to charge the same flat rate, one penny, for a 1/2-ounce letter. The British government adopted his recommendation and it proved entirely successful. Postal authorities from other countries came to England to learn how it worked. This time Britain led the world.

By 1834, Babbage should have completed the difference engine. The government had spent 17,000 pounds and he had sunk 6,000 pounds of his own money into the machine. (At that time a working man made about 100 pounds a year.) However, he suspended work on it for something even grander. He developed plans for a vastly superior machine that he called an analytical engine.

He envisioned the five essential components that made it a mechanical version of a modern computer. Punched cards brought variables (input) into the mill (central processing unit) to be acted upon. The store (memory) mechanically saved variables and intermediate results. The control (computer program) on punched cards instructed the mill's action. A printer or punched cards gave the final answer (output.) The machine even had bells and whistles that showed it was working and announced intermediate results.

It was an audacious undertaking. The machine could be called an engine because it was as large as a steam engine but densely packed with gears and wheels as small as those found in a watch. Despite 50 years of work, despite spending an immense sum of money, and despite his single-minded determination, Charles Babbage never finished the analytical engine.

Charles Babbage

Charles Babbage, however, did not begrudge his time working on the engine. He said, "If it is the will of that Being who gave me the endowments which led to the discovery of the analytical engine that I should not live to complete my work, I bow to that decision with intense gratitude for those gifts."

Babbage read with interest the eight Bridgewater treatises that were published in the 1830s. The Earl of Bridgewater had left 8,000 pounds to the Royal Society for the production of essays on the power, wisdom, and goodness of God. Because of his opposition to the Royal Society, Babbage would hardly have been invited to participate in preparing one of the essays.

Babbage wrote one anyway without the Royal Society's invitation or blessing. He titled it the *Ninth Bridgewater Treatise* and published it himself in 1837. Babbage had noticed that people were often surprised as his original difference engine turned out the results. The series of numbers apparently had no pattern until suddenly the answer emerged. He proposed that the miracles of the Bible were not exceptions to the laws of science, but had been latent in the design that God had "programmed" into nature.

Sixty years after his death, Howard H. Aiken, a student at Harvard University, came across Babbage's description of the computer. Atken, working with IBM, constructed Mark I, the first general-purpose calculating machine. An electronic computer replaced it a few years later. Charles Babbage had been a hundred years ahead of his time.

JOSEPH HENRY
1797–1878
A MERICAN SCIENTIST

M AJOR ACCOMPLISHMENT: FIRST DIRECTOR OF
S MITHSONIAN I NSTITUTION

JOSEPH HENRY IS CONSIDERED America's greatest electrical experimenter between the time of Benjamin Franklin and Thomas Edison. He was born in Albany, New York, and was raised by his mother who earned income by running a boarding house. Henry became interested in electrical experimentation when he read a book on science given to him by one of the boarders.

He decided to become a scientist and enrolled at Albany Academy, a local college. He had not attended high school, but with the help of the dean of the college, he compressed the four years of high school study into seven months. He earned college tuition by teaching at a country school. After graduation, he worked for a time as a surveyor and then starting in 1826 he taught science at the college.

He experimented with electromagnets that had been invented by William Sturgeon, an English scientist, in 1825. Sturgeon wrapped bare copper wire around an insulated bar of iron. When electricity flowed, the bar became magnetic and when the current was turned off, the bar lost its magnetism. Sturgeon's strongest electromagnet could lift nine pounds.

Henry built magnets that were more powerful than those built by Sturgeon. He found that the magnet could be made stronger by increasing the current or by increasing the number of turns of wire. Rather than insulating the bar, he insulated the wire to wind it in layers. Insulated wire was not available, so he talked his wife into sacrificing her silk petticoats to science. He spent hours wrapping the wire in strips of silk. With 800 turns of wire, the electromagnet lifted 27 pounds.

He abandoned the tedious task of winding wire with fabric. Instead, he painted the wire with shellac. By 1832, he could demonstrate an electromagnet that lifted more than 2,000 pounds. When he showed it at the College of New Jersey, he was offered a teaching position at the college. (The College of New Jersey was renamed Princeton University in 1896.)

His students at Princeton helped him string a wire from his laboratory to his home, a distance of just over a mile. By pressing a button at the laboratory, the electromagnet rang a bell at home, announcing to his wife that he was starting home. It was essentially a very long doorbell, but also very close to being the first telegraph.

Henry built electric motors, generators, and transformers. The press of teaching duties interrupted his summer experiments. Sometimes nine months would elapse between the time he made a discovery to the time he published the finding. Because of this delay, someone else — notably Michael Faraday — published first and received credit for the discovery.

In one experiment, Henry wrapped a needle in a coil of wire and measured whether it became magnetic during a lightning strike. It did, even when the lightning strike was eight miles away. He found evidence that wireless communication was possible years before Rudolph Hertz's experiments with radio waves in 1885.

In 1836, Joseph Henry visited England where Faraday, Sturgeon, and other scientists gave him a warm welcome. He and Faraday became instant friends. They had much in common, including growing up in poverty, a humble nature, and strong Christian faith. Neither Faraday nor Henry patented their inventions. Both helped others to perfect inventions.

For instance, Samuel F.B. Morse came to Henry for help with the telegraph. Morse had come to a dead end because his buried telegraph line failed to work. Also, over long distances, the signal became too weak. Henry agreed to keep confidential his aid during the week-long discussion. After the meeting, Morse strung the wires on tall poles with glass insulators to hold them. He strengthened the signal with an electrical relay that Henry had designed a year earlier.

In 1846, Henry accepted the assignment to run the newly created Smithsonian Institution. He is credited with funding the scientific exploration of the West, and with the use of the telegraph to collect weather data that led to the establishment of the United States Weather Service. He became science advisor to Abraham Lincoln during the Civil War.

After the Civil War, Henry continued as director of the Smithsonian. In 1875, Alexander Graham Bell visited his office with the telephone design that at that point had proven unsuccessful. As he had done 40 years earlier for Morse, Henry examined Bell's design, suggested improvements, and encouraged him to continue. In 1876, Henry was one of the judges at the Philadelphia Centennial. Bell had entered the telephone in the contest too late to be eligible for an award, or even to have a choice location for its demonstration. Henry, however, brought the judges around to see the telephone and arranged for it to receive a special certificate of merit.

Henry was a founder of the American Association for the Advancement of Science. He discovered the property known as self-induction in electrical circuits, and the measure of its strength, the henry, is named in his honor. In 1915, he was inducted into the Hall of Fame for Great Americans.

SOJOURNER TRUTH
1797–1883
AMERICAN ABOLITIONIST
MAJOR ACCOMPLISHMENT: SUCCESSFULLY USED
    AMERICAN JUDICIAL SYSTEM TO PURSUE RIGHTS
    FOR FORMER SLAVES

SOJOURNER TRUTH WAS BORN in Hurley, New York, at a time when slavery was legal not only in the South but also in New York state. She was one of 13 children. Her mother succeeded in instilling in her the concept of Jesus as a loving Savior who would protect her despite her burden of slavery. Known only by a first name, Isabella (and called Belle), she was forced to marry an older slave and had five children. All but one was sold into slavery and removed from her.

At the end of the American Revolutionary War, slavery had been legal in the northern states, but was being gradually phased out, usually by freeing slaves when they reached a certain age. In 1824, New York announced that slaves born before July 4, 1799, would be freed on July 4, 1827. Isabella's master, John Dumont, promised to release her a year early provided she worked extra hard. She agreed, and when he reneged on his promise, she ran away, taking infant daughter Sophia with her.

The nearby Van Wagener Quaker family hid Isabella until they could purchase her freedom. She lived with the Van Wageners until the deadline passed for all slaves in New York to be freed. She was 30 years old.

One of her sons, Peter, had been sold into slavery and taken to Alabama, an action that was against New York statutes. With the help of the Van Wageners and other Quakers who opposed slavery, she sued to secure his release. She became the first former slave to successfully use the court system in this way.

She moved to New York City and worked as a maid and house cleaner. In early life, she had been taught only the Dutch language and received no education. She learned to speak English as a teenager, but with a Dutch accent. She never learned to read or write.

She became associated with Elijah Pierson, head of the "Kingdom of Matthais" cult. She worked with the zealous religious missionary for almost ten years. However, she left following a series of public scandals against the leader, including adultery and murder charges.

In 1843, as part of her break with the cult, she took the name Sojourner Truth. Her last name came from John 8:32 "And ye shall know the truth, and the truth shall make you free." She began preaching along the eastern seaboard. With her imposing six-foot height and electrifying presence, she drew large crowds. She exhorted listeners to show their love for God by their active concern for others. She had a ready wit. When a heckler told her that her speeches had no more effect than that of a flea, she said, "Perhaps not, but Lord willing, I'll keep you scratching."

In the early 1850s, she met Amy Post, Lucretia Mott, and other advocates for women's suffrage. Sojourner realized that women were kept isolated and uneducated to prevent them from exercising the few rights they did possess. Like slaves, women were denied education, jobs, and public roles in society. Sojourner added women's rights to her cause. She began attending women's suffrage meetings.

At a meeting in Akron, Ohio, she listened quietly while speakers endured hecklers who claimed women were too weak physically for the jobs they sought. Suddenly Sojourner strode to the lecture platform and gave what became her best-known speech. "I have plowed, I have planted, and I have gathered into barns. And ain't I a woman? I have borne children and seen most of them sold into slavery, and when I cried out with a mother's grief, none but Jesus heard me. And ain't I a woman?"

She also became an advocate of temperance. Like many other women, she believed alcohol caused sexual violence, prostitution, and the destruction of working families.

She settled near Battle Creek, Michigan, and purchased a home. She raised money by selling a business card with her portrait and a book, *The Narrative of Sojourner Truth*. She had dictated it to her neighbor Olive Gilbert.

During the Civil War, she raised money and supplies for African-American volunteers. In 1864, she moved to Washington, D.C. to work toward the idea of granting the freed slaves farmland in Kansas and other prairie states. She found that the city's trolley system would not stop for African-Americans. When injured while trying to board a trolley, she brought a civil suit and won. She made history again when President Abraham Lincoln officially received her in the White House, the first former slave so honored.

After the Civil War, Sojourner's grandson, Sammy Banks, traveled with her. He could read and write. However, he died in 1875 at the age of 24. Sojourner returned to her home near Battle Creek to live with her two daughters. By then, she had earned her place as one of the best-known women in America.

MATTHEW FONTAINE MAURY

1806–1873
AMERICAN OCEANOGRAPHER
MAJOR ACCOMPLISHMENT: FOUNDER OF
OCEANOGRAPHY

MATTHEW FONTAINE MAURY MADE an exhaustive study of the oceans. He mapped trade winds, charted ocean currents, and built elevation profiles of the ocean floor. He charted the floor of the Atlantic Ocean between the United States and Europe and planned the route of the trans-Atlantic telegraphic cable.

Maury joined the navy as a midshipman at the age of 18. He made an around-the-world voyage, and during the next 14 years he was promoted to lieutenant. However, his sea-going career ended because of a permanent leg injury during a stagecoach accident. The Navy retired him from active duty by assigning him as the superintendent of Depot of Charts and Instruments. He was not expected to work, or if he did, to do only light duty.

Maury, however, took the position seriously. He dedicated his life to a scientific examination of the ocean — not only its surface, but throughout its depths. He collected charts and navigation instruments. In poring over old ships' logs, he compiled ocean-wind and ocean-current charts that aided speedier travel of sailing ships. He published his results as *Wind and Current Charts for the North Atlantic* in 1847.

He also became aware of the Gulf Stream, which other scientists believed was ill-defined and diffused. Its exact nature could not be determined because of the lack of reliable information. He designed new logbooks to collect better information and distributed them to American sailing vessels. However, because of the vast expanse of the oceans, international cooperation was needed. He became the guiding hand behind an international oceanography conference in Brussels, Belgium, in 1853. The conference developed uniform methods of recording ocean data and reporting sea conditions.

His decision to more carefully map the Gulf Stream came from his reading of the Bible in Psalm 8:8 that there are "paths in the seas." Rather than a diffuse and unpredictable current, Maury mapped a current with a definite width, depth, speed, and direction. His description of the Gulf Stream became a classic of scientific exposition.

Matthew Fontaine Maury

"There is a river in the sea," Maury said. "In the severest droughts it never fails, and in the mightiest floods it never overflows. Its banks and its bottom are of cold water, while its current is of warm. The Gulf of Mexico is its fountain, and its mouth is in the Arctic Seas."

He published *Physical Geography of the Sea* in 1855. It earned him the title of "Founder of Oceanography" and established the new science. The textbook was extremely successful and even more remarkable because of his insistence on accepting the literal words of the Bible in guiding his study of the ocean.

Businessmen began making plans to lay a submerged telegraph cable from the United States to Europe. Cyrus Field, the president of the Atlantic Cable Company, asked Maury to chart the ocean floor for the best route for the cable. During this research, Maury discovered the Mid-Atlantic ridge. The plateau became the route for the cable from Newfoundland to Ireland.

By the start of the Civil War, Maury had risen to the rank of commander. However, he followed his state of Viriginia into the Confederacy and became head of the harbor defenses. The end of the war found him on a mission to England for the Confederacy. He assumed he would be unwelcome in the United States, but after two years all was forgiven. He returned in 1868 and taught meteorology at the Virginia Military Institute.

Matthew Fontaine Maury earned the title "Pathfinder of the Seas." The "charts" of his Depot of Charts and Instruments became the Hydrographic Center of the Department of Defense, and the "instruments" part was merged with the United States Naval Observatory. The Naval Academy at Annapolis named Maury Hall in his honor, and Virginia celebrates his birthday as a state holiday.

He was elected to the Hall of Fame for Great Americans in 1930. On his tombstone at the United States Naval Academy is inscribed Psalm 8:8 with the "paths in the seas" phrase.

LOUIS AGASSIZ

1807–1873

SWISS-AMERICAN SCIENTIST

MAJOR ACCOMPLISHMENT: ESTABLISHED THE

EXISTENCE OF THE ICE AGE

LOUIS AGASSIZ, A Swiss-American naturalist, was one of the great figures of scientific discovery. He revolutionized scientific understanding of glacial activity. He was also a science teacher without peer.

Louis Agassiz was the son of a Swiss protestant preacher who was descended from the French Huguenots that had fled France following the persecution by Louis XIV. Agassiz became fascinated with the glaciers in the high Alps that were visible from his home. His father insisted that he study medicine. He attended Zürich, Heidelberg, and Munich, where he earned a medical degree. However, he never practiced medicine. He spent a year in Paris attending lectures and working at Georges Cuvier's museum.

He returned to Switzerland to become the professor of natural history at Neuchâtel. It was a small town, but near the glaciers that he wished to explore. He spent the summers of the next four years studying the glaciers. The local people claimed that the glaciers were slow moving rivers of ice. He proved their contention to be true. He found a cabin that had been built 12 years earlier on the ice. He located its wreckage a mile down the glacier from its original location. He drove stakes across the ice. When he came back the next summer, those in the center had moved more rapidly than those stakes at the edges.

Agassiz examined enormous boulders, called foundling ("orphan") stones, on the valley floors around Neuchâtel. The erratics looked out of place because the type of stone was found only in the mountains. Agassiz believed the boulders had been carried to the valleys by the moving glaciers and dropped when a warmer climate melted the ice.

The evidence he amassed proved conclusively that glaciers had once been more extensive. He concluded that a great Ice Age had covered much of the earth's surface years ago.

At a gathering of scientists, he gave a word picture of the dramatic events. "Many years ago a long winter settled over a land previously covered with rich vegetation, where great beasts like those found in India and Africa freely roamed. Death entered with its terrors. With one blow of its violent hand it destroyed a mighty creation and wrapped all nature in a shroud of ice.

"Europe was buried under a vast mantle of ice. Everything was still; plants, animals, lakes — even oceans. All over, creation fell silent. Rivers ceased to flow in the icy blast of perpetual winter, the sun's warmth was powerless over this deep invasion by the north."

In 1846, Louis Agassiz visited the United States on a lecture tour. He had a unique ability to make details of scientific investigations fascinating to the public as well as to students. He called his lectures "Plan of Creation." The lectures were exceptionally successful and the Boston newspapers reprinted them.

Agassiz had married the sister of a college roommate. When she died, he decided to return to the United States and made it his permanent home. In North America, he found signs of an ancient Ice Age. Agassiz believed that when the Ice Age glaciers melted, they created most of the earth's fresh water lakes. Glaciers had carved out the five Great Lakes of North America.

During an expedition to the Midwest, he mapped out a sixth lake that had once covered an area in Minnesota, North Dakota, and part of Canada. He found the remains of deltas from rivers that once flowed into the sixth Great Lake. The ghost lake was called Lake Agassiz in his honor.

Agassiz settled in Massachusetts as professor of zoology at Harvard. In addition to being a groundbreaking scientist and spellbinding teacher, he was also an able fundraiser. He built the Museum of Comparative Zoology to house his extensive collections of fossils and animal specimens. Louis Agassiz looked upon his classification efforts as tracing out the order put in the universe by the Creator. He said, "God wrote the books of nature; I am only His librarian."

He married Elizabeth Cabot Cary in 1850. Together they began a series of science lectures for women. She accompanied him on his travels to South America and combined the information he developed with her own personal observations in the successful book *A*

Journey to Brazil. She later became the president of Radcliffe College.

In 1860, Agassiz was asked to comment on Darwin's theory of evolution. He said, "I can say only that evolution is a desolate theory, using the laws of matter to explain away all the wonders of creation. It is a system that rejects God, substituting for our Creator only the impersonal, chance actions of physical forces."

When Louis Agassiz died, almost every naturalist in the United States had either studied under him or studied under someone he had trained. His classes were popular because he enlisted his students as co-workers in his discoveries. He encouraged them to make close and accurate observations before venturing into speculation.

Louis Agassiz was named to the Hall of Fame for Great Americans in 1930.

Louis Agassiz

WILLIAM GLADSTONE
1809–1898
BRITISH POLITICIAN

MAJOR ACCOMPLISHMENT: FOUR TIMES PRIME

MINISTER OF BRITAIN

WILLIAM GLADSTONE WAS prime minister for a total of 16 years on four separate occasions and was a member of the House of Commons for the entire span of his political career — 63 years. He worked to ensure that common people had a say in the government (a stand that was considered liberal), but he embraced conservative religious views. A classical scholar, he accumulated a library of 32,000 books in six languages and read nearly all of them. With his great learning, he wrote on subjects ranging from critical studies of ancient Greek scholars to essays about Christian hymns.

Although born in Liverpool, Gladstone was of Scottish descent. His father was a prosperous corn merchant, dealer in West Indies sugar, and member of Parliament. His parents were evangelical Christians. The strong religious convictions that Gladstone learned from them sustained him through turbulent political conflicts.

He attended the University of Oxford where he finished first in the classics and mathematics. He intended to become a clergyman, but his father convinced him that he would better serve the nation as a statesman. With the help of his father's friends, Gladstone entered the House of Commons in 1832.

Gladstone began his political career as a member of the Conservative Party that supported the aims of the monarchy and control of everyday life by the powerful Church of England. However, the party fell out of favor in 1846, and Gladstone was in political quarantine until 1859.

He had married Catherine Glynne in 1839. She was everything a politician needed — witty, charming, and supportive. She encouraged him during the time of his isolation, and became a steadying influence during his public life. They raised eight children.

During this time his views changed dramatically. He came to realize that working class families, not the aristocracy, were the strength of the nation. However, lower classes were excluded from the political process. Those without land could not vote, yet the heavy taxes they paid supported a civil service closed to them and a military dominated by wealthy individuals who had purchased their commission. Taxes paid by the poor went to the Church of England, whose schools would not educate their children.

In 1860, Gladstone became the chancellor of the exchequer in the Whig government. He instituted a series of reforms to reduce taxes, and in 1868 became prime minister for the first time. Gladstone became leader of the new liberal party. A liberal in Britain at that time was one who supported changes to encourage participation in government by working families and the poor.

The reforms Gladstone introduced improved the democratic process by implementing secret ballots and allowing people without land to vote. He strengthened the civil service by competitive promotions based on merit, and ended the military practice of purchased commissions. He eliminated the practice of flogging in the navy (at least during peace time), improved the condition of dock workers, and created an education program for all children between the ages of 5 and 13. He also started the post office savings bank for small accounts so working families could put aside some money.

His championing of democratic principles made him a hero of the lower classes but an enemy of the rich. He was thoroughly reviled by the 10,000 most powerful and wealthy individuals in Britain and thoroughly loved by the rest.

However, reforms caused disruptions in daily lives. Even those who benefited from them grew weary, and his party was voted out of office in 1874. Gladstone waited for the controversy to die down. He came into power again in 1880 and continued where he had left off.

One of his goals was to avoid excessive taxes and reduce the size of government. He took the unusual step of serving as both prime minister and chancellor of the exchequer. He also resisted the added expense of becoming involved in needless wars. Gladstone is often not ranked among the top prime ministers because he never led the country during a major military conflict. Overlooked is the fact that his skill as a leader prevented war from being necessary. Queen Victoria came to detest Gladsone because of his resistance to the growth of her empire at the expense of human lives.

Gladstone tried to diffuse the simmering discontent in Ireland. During his last two ministries, he addressed what he described as, "Ireland, Ireland! That cloud in the west, that coming storm."

He was for home rule in Ireland, a measure he called "an act of justice and wisdom." Although his bill granting home rule passed the House of Commons, it died in the House of Lords. He used other measures to bring about reform. Irish Catholics had to pay taxes that supported the Anglican Church. He removed this irritant. Englishmen owned vast stretches of Irish land and sometimes evicted tenants whose families had worked the land for centuries. Gladstone's measures required landowners to compensate victims of removal.

Gladstone's critics could not touch his intellectual and moral power, so they pointed to minor idiosyncrasies. He chopped down trees as a way of exercise. Lord Randolph Churchill (father of Winston Churchill) said, "The forest laments, in order that Mr. Gladstone may perspire." Others labeled as bizarre his walks through London at night to counsel prostitutes. What his amused critics do not mention was that Gladstone and his wife opened a home so the women could learn a different trade and start a new life.

He became prime minister for the last time in 1892, at the age of 83. He resigned two years later when it became clear that his last remaining goal, home rule for Ireland, would fail.

During his retirement, he built a public library (called the Iron Library because of its construction of metal), and stocked it with his 32,000 books. He transported the books himself with a wheelbarrow from his study to the library a quarter mile away.

Gladstone's religious views guided his political life. He spoke against immorality without a hint of hypocrisy. His profound devotion to Christianity, his daily Bible study, and regular church attendance resonated with the common people who made him one of the most popular and influential statesmen in English history. He was buried in Westminster Abbey.

HENRY RAWLINSON
1810–1895
English Assyriologist and diplomat
Major accomplishment: deciphered Persian
cuneiform inscriptions

HENRY RAWLINSON IS credited with bringing the history of ancient Bablyon and Assyria alive through his interpretation of cuneiform writing. He began as a British cadet in the army of the East India Company. In 1833, he was assigned to Persia (Iran) to train the shah's army.

While in Persia he became interested in strangely shaped inscriptions on clay tablets. Looking more like bird tracks than a written alphabet, the markings appeared to have been made in soft clay by a wedge-shaped knife. They were called cuneiform, from the Latin word *cunei* meaning "wedges." Some scientists thought they were decorations or brief inscriptions but not a complete written language.

Although thousands of the clay tablets were later discovered, at that time most examples of cuneiform were only fragments on monuments and other objects. Rawlinson learned of a longer inscription high on a cliff along the road from Persia to Babylon (Iraq). He decided to investigate and found why the inscriptions had lasted through the ages. They were nearly inaccessible at 1,700 feet on the sheer side of Mount Bisitun. He made the heart-pounding climb many times over the next two years and transcribed the writing while hanging from a rope.

The writing was of three styles, and he chose the simplest one to attack. After two years, he succeeded in translating the first two paragraphs. The writing had been commissioned by Darius I, king of Persia. Darius used the mountainside billboard to describe how he came to the throne and to warn those who might threaten the Persian Empire. The statement itself had been seen before in other languages. An Aramaic language version had been found on papyrus in Egypt.

Before Rawlinson finished the work, he had to leave Persia because of the changing political climate. He became a British counsel at Kandahar, Afghanistan, and later at Baghad, Iraq. He continued to collect cuneiform writing and other valuable antiquities. He shipped these to the British museum in London.

He managed to return to Persia and obtain additional examples of the cuneiform script. This time he was able to make a complete translation of the Behistun writing, and developed the grammar so other samples could be translated.

The second language on the cliffside was Assyrian. He and other scholars managed to translate it as well. The third language on the cliff of Bisitun was Elamite, an extinct language of Mesopotamia. The country of Elam and Elamites are mentioned in Genesis.

Rawlinson was knighted in 1855. He served three years in Parliament and then returned to the Middle East as counsel at Tehran, Iran. The translations by Rawlinson and his books on the history of Assyria allowed scholars to understand the history of Persia, Babylon, and Mesopotamia as it related to the Bible. Darius I was the ruler who authorized the Jews to rebuild the temple at Jerusalem (see Ezra 6:12).

JAMES SIMPSON

1811–1870

BRITISH PHYSICIAN

MAJOR ACCOMPLISHMENT: PIONEERED THE USE OF
CHLOROFORM AS AN ANESTHETIC

JAMES SIMPSON WAS THE seventh son of a baker in Bathgate, Scotland. His family was poor and could only afford to send one child to school. Because he showed the greatest promise, he was the one chosen. He entered the University of Edinburgh at age 14, earned his medical degree by the time he was 21, and then stayed on at the university as an assistant professor. With his success, he could send money home. He became a full professor in 1830.

He believed the future of medicine required the implementation of the latest discoveries. He trained students to examine diseased tissues with a microscope, a step that few other physicians followed. He read widely, studied the history of medicine, and tested new ideas.

In 1846, Simpson learned of American experiments with ether (diethyl ether) as a painkiller during surgery. He experimented with the substance but encountered problems. Ether was difficult to procure in the pure form, and the powerful, suffocating odor caused patients to struggle against its administration. The less pure form gave inconsistent results. Ether was highly volatile and would explode if exposed to a spark. Gaslights or oil lanterns illuminated operating rooms and the open flame was a constant danger with ether in use.

After a year of experiments with other gases, Simpson discovered the anesthetic properties of chloroform. It had a pleasant smell and gave consistent results.

Some doctors refused to use ether or chloroform. They objected, saying that pain served a medical purpose. However, Simpson answered the medical objections with a paper that he presented in 1847: *Account of a New Anaesthetic Agent.*

He also had to answer religious objections to the use of chloroform during surgery. Simpson had become interested in painkillers

James Simpson

after reading that God had put Adam into a deep sleep to create Eve. It was the first surgical operation, and God chose to do it without pain to Adam. Although this had taken place before the fall from the garden, Simpson believed the principle that God did not rejoice in needless pain still applied.

Queen Victoria learned of Simpson's use of anesthesia. In 1853, the queen had her doctor, John Snow, administer chloroform during the birth of her eighth child, Prince Leopold. The criticism of anesthetics for surgery and in obstetrics all but ended.

Chloroform had a very narrow safety range, and it acted as a poison in long operations. Balanced anesthesia of several gases replaced it in modern operating rooms. However, chloroform is still used in primitive conditions. It is inexpensive and easy to transport and store. Hot temperatures do not affect it, and an open flame will not cause it to explode.

James Simpson was a Christian and Bible scholar. He wrote a religious tract in which he identified Jesus as his Savior as his greatest discovery. "I must tell others about Him," Simpson wrote. " 'With His stripes we are healed.' "

DAVID LIVINGSTONE
1813–1873
SCOTTISH MISSIONARY, PHYSICIAN, AND EXPLORER
MAJOR ACCOMPLISHMENT: OPENED A PATH INTO THE
INTERIOR OF AFRICA

AT AGE TEN, DAVID LIVINGSTONE began work at the Blantyre Cotton Mill. His workday began at 6 a.m. and ended at 8 p.m. Two hours of school lasted until 10 p.m. To find time to study, he propped a book up on the machines at the mill. As he passed by, he read a line and thought about it as he worked.

David Livingstone grew up with a sense of a Christian purpose. In addition to his Christian faith, he developed an intense desire to travel and an interest in science. He believed a missionary who knew some other profession, such as medicine, would be welcome in foreign countries. He studied both theology and medicine, and received a medical degree from the University of Glasgow in 1838.

He traveled to London for additional medical studies and to train to be a missionary. Although officials of the Missionary Society approved of his zeal, they hesitated to sponsor him. His sermons did not have polish. The Society assigned his practice sermons to small country churches where his lack of elegance would go unnoticed.

While in London, he attended a lecture by Robert Moffat, a Scottish missionary to Africa. Moffat's missionary station was at Kuruman north of Cape Town. During the talk, Moffat said, "In the vast plain to the north, I have sometimes seen, in the morning sun, the smoke of a thousand villages, where no missionary has ever been."

"The smoke of a thousand villages" caught Livingstone's attention. Here was a place he was needed. He convinced the Missionary Society to let him go to Africa. He worked for a few months at Kuruman, which was the last outpost before the Kalahari Desert. Then Livingstone set out on his own.

Livingstone's goal was to "preach the gospel beyond every other man's line of things." He also believed that commerce with the Africans for their native products would be beneficial to both Europeans and the natives. He believed that commerce and Christianity would work hand in hand.

He married Mary, the daughter of Robert Moffat. She was the most experienced female traveler in Africa. Despite the hardships, Mary and their four children accompanied him on a trip across the Kalahari Desert. Her mastery of the Bushman language was invaluable. Livingstone reached the Makololo people who lived on the shores of Lake Ngami.

Livingstone became determined to find a better route into the interior of Africa. In 1852, he sent Mary to England with their four children so they could receive an education.

In Cape Town he took additional training in navigation and gathered supplies. He traveled exceptionally light — he put his supplies, clothing, notebooks, navigation equipment and a projector and glass slides for telling the story of Jesus in five tin containers no bigger than hatboxes.

His journey took him north from Cape Town, across the Kalahari to the Makololo people. He turned west and struck out across Africa for the Atlantic Ocean. A small band of the Makololo accompanied him. They gathered some of their products, including ivory, to learn the going price at the coast. In the villages where he was welcomed, he set up his magic lantern projector and told the story of Jesus in pictures.

All along the way, he calculated his latitude and longitude with a sextant and chronometer. He measured elevation by the temperature at which water boiled. He noted the plants and animals, and charted the position of rivers and other features. His journals became a model for other explorers.

He made contact with the outside world at Luanda, a Portuguese port in what is now Angola on the Atlantic Ocean. He sent a detailed report back to England of his two-year journey.

Rather than returning to England, he left Luanda and retraced his steps. He followed the Zambezi east toward the "smoke that sounds," a huge waterfall. He measured the falls and gave it the name Victoria Falls, after Queen Victoria of England. He continued east and eventually arrived at the Indian Ocean. He became the first European and probably the first human being to travel the entire width of Africa.

In England, his first group of reports from Luanda had created a sensation. His disappearance for another two years caused an even greater interest in his exploits. He returned to England in 1856 as a national hero.

Before his African adventure, the missionary society had nearly dismissed him because he lacked a polished speaking style. Now he spent six months speaking in England and Scotland to capacity crowds. Four different groups welcomed him: the London Missionary Society, the Royal Society, the Royal Geographical Society and the College of Physicians in Glasgow.

He wrote the book *Missionary Travels and Researches in South Africa*. It set a publishing record by selling 70,000 copies as quickly as they could be printed.

When he returned to Africa, he became disheartened by what he saw. His exploration had not opened Africa to commerce but to the slave trade. He became a powerful voice calling for the complete abolition of slavery. Except for one short visit home, Livingstone spent the rest of his life in Africa. His letters had to be carried by caravans run by slave traders. Because of his opposition to slavery, they intercepted and destroyed his canvas pouches of mail. Some guides who had deserted him reported that he had died.

Four separate expeditions, including one by the Royal Geographical Society, failed to find him. No one knew if Livingstone was alive or dead. Then in 1871, American newspaper reporter, Henry Morton Stanley, equipped one of the largest and most expensive expeditions ever mounted. He found Livingstone in the town of Ujiji on the eastern shore of Lake Tanganyika.

Nervous in the presence of the great man, Stanley could not think of anything to say except, "Dr. Livingstone, I presume."

Stanley discovered that Livingstone did not need to be rescued and did not intend to return to England. Stanley and Livingstone explored Lake Tanganyika together. Then Stanley returned to civilization to file his newspaper report.

A year after the meeting with Stanley, Livingstone's two assistants, Chuma and Susi, found his still body beside his cot. He was kneeling as if in prayer. His native guides buried his heart at the foot of a nearby tree. They then dried and wrapped Livingstone's body and carried it, along with Livingstone's papers, to the Indian Ocean for the trip home.

Livingstone's accomplishments were many. He proved that the interior of Africa was not a desert as many geographers believed. He inspired countless Christian missionaries to work among the Africans.

He worked tirelessly to end the slave trade. His most famous quote is from a letter he sent back with Stanley. His plea to end the slave trade is engraved on the black marble covering his burial site in Westminster Abbey: "All I can say in my solitude is, may Heaven's rich blessing come down on everyone — American, English, Turk — who will help heal this open sore of the world."

JAMES DWIGHT DANA
1813–1895
AMERICAN MINERALOGIST
MAJOR ACCOMPLISHMENT: AUTHOR OF *SYSTEM OF MINERALOGY* AND FOUNDER OF MODERN MINERALOGY

JAMES DWIGHT DANA WAS BORN in Utica, New York and educated at Yale. His mentor was Benjamin Silliman, founder and editor of the influential *American Journal of Science*. Silliman encouraged Dana's interest in minerals, which remained a hodge-podge of scientific information. Some researchers focused on their physical properties, others on internal structures, and still others on the properties of the crystals. No single classification system had been developed to bring together the unrelated facts.

Although Dana realized that many properties should be taken into account for the classification of minerals, he concluded that chemistry was the chief way to identify them scientifically. At age 24, Dana published a massive 580-page book, *A System of Mineralogy*. It became the standard for the study of minerals and crystals.

After his graduation from Yale, he accepted the position of instructor of mathematics to midshipmen in the United States Navy. The assignment took him with the crewmen on a cruise to the Mediterranean. The floating classroom gave him contacts that led to his selection as the chief scientist on an expedition to the South Seas and Antarctic regions. During the four-year voyage, he amassed a vast collection of information about minerals, corals, volcanoes, and the structure of ocean basins. During the next ten years, he published 7,000 printed pages about the expedition that included many illustrations that he made himself.

Upon his return, he became co-editor of the *American Journal of Science* with Benjamin Silliman. Two years later he married Henrietta Silliman, the professor's daughter. The couple made New Haven, Connecticut, their permanent home. Dana accepted the post as professor of natural history at Yale in 1849. Later, when it appeared that he might be lured away by rival Harvard, the position of professor of geology and mineralogy was created for his benefit.

In 1848, he published *Manual of Mineralogy*, a textbook organized around the chemistry of minerals and crystals. Dana revised and updated the book throughout his life. By the time of its third edition in the 1850s, it became the standard for mineral classification and the model format for textbooks. Dana's son, Edward, continued to keep the *Manual of Mineralogy* up-to-date after his father's death, and the 22nd edition of the book is in print today.

Like his mentor Silliman, Dana was a Christian. He accepted the Bible as sacred and believed in the special creation of the species. Although he accepted the variations seen in fossils as a type of evolution, he believed they were a manifestation of a divine design for the continual improvement of life.

JAMES PRESCOTT JOULE

1818–1889

BRITISH SCIENTIST

MAJOR ACCOMPLISHMENT: PROVIDED EXPERIMENTAL

PROOF OF THE LAW OF CONSERVATION OF ENERGY

JAMES PRESCOTT JOULE WAS an amateur scientist who grew up near Manchester, England. He received some instruction from John Dalton who taught at a Protestant school in Manchester. Mostly, however, Joule was self-taught and did experiments in a home laboratory.

Joule's first interest was measuring temperature changes. He designed thermometers that could detect changes to 1/200 of a degree Fahrenheit. With these thermometers, he gauged the change in temperature in a variety of settings. During his honeymoon, he stopped the carriage to measure the temperature of the water both above and below a waterfall. He attributed the gain of heat at the bottom to the mechanical motion of water changing into heat energy when it plunged into the lower pool.

His accurate thermometers made it possible to measure minute changes in temperature. For instance, he measured the temperature of a container of water, stirred the water, and then measured the temperature rise caused by the stirring. Scientists measured heat energy by British thermal units (the calorie is the metric unit) and mechanical energy in foot-pounds (erg is the metric unit). Scientists did not have a conversion between the two. Joule let falling weights turn a paddle that caused a rise in the temperature of water. He measured the distance the weight fell and compared it to the rise in water temperature. He calculated the conversion between British thermal units and foot-pounds (1.00 Btu equaled 778 ft. lbs.).

Scientists still debated whether heat was a substance or a form of energy. Joule's experiments showed that it was a form of energy. As long as the paddle turned, it produced a never-ending supply of heat. He explained heat as the energy of motion of the atomic particles that made a substance.

However, Joule was an amateur scientist and was unknown in the scientific community. After having the report of his work rejected by scientific journals, he brought the discovery to the scientific world in an unusual way. He gave a free lecture and arranged for his talk to be reprinted in the Manchester paper. The newspaper came to the attention of William Thomson (later known as Lord Kelvin.) Although William Thomson was only in his early twenties, he had already become a well-respected scientist, and he publicized Joule's work.

Joule and Thomson worked together. Joule was always conducting unusual experiments, such as forcing water through a small opening to measure whether it gained or lost temperature (it gained), or letting a gas escape from a container to see how it changed temperature (it grew cooler.) Joule and Thomson found that the temperature of a gas fell as it was allowed to expand freely. Known as the Joule-Thomson effect, it became the basis for the refrigeration industry.

A wire became warm when a current flowed through it. However, scientists had no simple formula to predict the heating effect. Joule measured the heat emitted by an electric circuit and developed Joule's law: the amount of heat produced is proportional to the resistance of the wire and the square of the current. Long distance power transmission lines avoided excessive heat loss with Joule's law. A lower current at extremely high voltage generated less heat but carried the same power as a higher current at ordinary voltage.

Joule found that energy transfers from one form to another were not 100 percent efficient. He showed that the loss of energy was balanced by a release of heat energy. This observation became known as the law of conservation of energy, also called the first law of thermodynamics.

Joule earned the respect of England's greatest scientists — William Thomson, G.G. Stokes, and Michael Faraday. In 1849, he was invited to speak before the Royal Society, and he became a member the next year. The unit of energy in the metric system, the joule, is named after James Prescott Joule.

He never held a position at a college or university. He financed his scientific work out of his own pocket. Toward the end of his life he fell into hard financial times. Queen Victoria granted him a pension because his work had proven to have an economic benefit to the empire.

Joule was a modest, unassuming man and a sincere Christian believer. Like Thomson, Stokes, and Faraday, he saw laws such as the law of conservation of energy as a design in nature. He said, "It is evident that an acquaintance with natural laws means no less than an acquaintance with the mind of God therein expressed."

GEORGE GABRIEL STOKES

1819–1903

BRITISH PHYSICIST

MAJOR ACCOMPLISHMENT: DEVELOPED LAW OF VISCOSITY
DESCRIBING MOTION OF A SOLID THROUGH A FLUID

GEORGE GABRIEL STOKES, KNOWN affectionately as G.G., was the son of a clergyman and born in Ireland. He attended the University of Cambridge and finished at the head of his class in mathematics, a position known as "first wrangler." He became Lucasian professor of mathematics at Cambridge, the chair once held by Isaac Newton.

Like Newton, Stokes applied mathematics to physics, and developed the law of viscosity, which described the frictional resistance of solids moving through a liquid or gas. It had a practical application in measuring the resistance of water to the motion of a ship. Decades later, the formula became the centerpiece of Robert Millikan's oil drop experiment that measured the electrical charge on a single electron.

Stokes studied light and the property of fluorescence, a term he coined. Certain crystals glowed when struck by invisible ultraviolet rays. He found that ordinary glass was opaque to ultraviolet light, but quartz was a clear window. Ultraviolet imaging telescopes use quartz optics.

Stokes next explained the cause of Fraunhofer lines. Astronomers found puzzling, dark bands that crossed the sun's spectrum. During his lectures, Stokes developed the explanation that atoms of each element emitted a distinctive group of colored bands when heated white hot and viewed through a spectroscope. For instance, the metal sodium glowed with two bright yellow bands. Elements in the upper atmosphere of the sun were relatively cooler and absorbed the same colors that they would have emitted if hotter. From the light alone, astronomers could identify elements in the sun, stars, and dark clouds of gas.

Stokes did not publish his ideas. When German physicist Gustav R. Kirchhoff published the proposal, Stokes's friends claimed that he had priority. Stokes, who had a warm and generous character, insisted that Kirchhoff had a more detailed form of the idea and refused to pursue the matter. Repeatedly, Stokes formulated theories and allowed others to develop them more fully.

Since the time of Isaac Newton and Christiaan Huygens, scientists had argued about the nature of light. Newton had developed his optical theory with light as particles, and Huygens had developed his theory with light as waves. Both theories could explain refraction and reflection. The wave theory more easily explained interference and diffraction. However, its one failing was that physicists believed waves needed to be carried by a medium. Physicists hypothesized a luminiferous ether that filled space and carried the waves.

Stokes developed the properties of the luminiferous ether. According to his calculations, ether would have the rigidity of steel for the speedy light waves, but be nearly frictionless for the slower moving planets. His development of ether's contradictory properties gave several opportunities for scientific testing. The Americans Albert Michelson and Edward Morley proved that the speed of light was a constant in a vacuum, which could only be true if the earth had no motion in relation to the ether. The ether could only exist if the earth were the center of the universe and everything revolved around it. This effectively killed the idea of interstellar ether.

One of the scientists that Stokes helped, James Clerk Maxwell, showed that light waves were electromagnetic in nature and did not require a medium to carry them.

Stokes lived to see the exciting second scientific revolution that began in 1895 with the discovery of x-rays. Stokes proposed that they were like ultraviolet light, but far more energetic.

Stokes is often compared to Isaac Newton, not only for his breakthrough discoveries, but also for the way his life paralleled Newton's. They both held the same chair at Cambridge, both developed laws of motion, both investigated light and optics, both served in Parliament, and both were elected president of the Royal Society. Both were knighted for their scientific accomplishments. In 1872, Cambridge inherited the papers that Newton left in the care of his niece Catherine Conduitt. Stokes was one of the faculty members who reviewed the papers and catalogued them.

Like Newton, Stokes was a staunch Christian. Stokes wrote the book *Natural Theology*, published in 1891. For years, he had supported the Victoria Institute. It was founded in London in 1865 as a Christian evidence society. George Gabriel Stokes was one of those who served as president of the organization.

FRANCIS (FANNY) JANE CROSBY

1820–1915

AMERICAN HYMNWRITER

MAJOR ACCOMPLISHMENT: WROTE MORE THAN 6,000 HYMNS

FANNY CROSBY WAS BORN in the country cottage of John and Marcy Crosby in Putnam County, a rural area north of New York City on the Connecticut border. She was the youngest of three daughters and one son. At age six weeks, her eyes became infected. The family doctor was away, and his replacement proved incompetent. Fanny Cosby lost her vision, either from the infection or the doctor's negligence. Her father died when she was one year old and her mother, who was 21 years old, earned a living as a maid.

Grandmother Eunice Crosby took care of Fanny. One of Fanny's earliest memories is being held in her grandmother's rocking chair and listening to her read from the Bible. Her grandmother guided her development and helped build her Christian character. The grandmother not only read the Bible, but also explained how it applied personally to Fanny, and taught her the importance of prayer.

The Crosby family encouraged Fanny to live a normal life. She climbed trees, cared for pets, rode horses, journeyed into the mountains by wagon, and sailed on the Hudson River. At age five she visited New York City. During the New York City trip, doctors examined her damaged eyes. They decided she could not be treated and would be blind for life.

During this time, Fanny developed her memory, which she claimed was no better than that of other people. However, she memorized great stretches of the Bible including the Gospels, Proverbs, and Song of Solomon.

When Fanny was nine, the family moved to Ridgefield, Connecticut, where Fanny's mother was employed as a maid in the Hawley home. Mrs. Hawley took an interest in the young girl. Members of the Hawley family were politically connected and Mrs. Hawley introduced Fanny to the visitors. Later, Fanny had an easy presence around people in high places, including presidents, because of Mrs. Hawley's influence.

Fanny entered the New York Institution for the Blind in 1835. Teaching was by lectures and reading aloud. The Braille system of embossed dots had not made its way to America from France. When it did come into common use shortly after her graduation, Fanny chose not to use it.

The subject that gave her the most trouble was mathematics. Her feeling toward the course was summarized by one of her rhymes:

Fanny Crosby

> I loathe, abhor, it makes me sick,
> To hear the word, Arithmetic!

She was called to the office and warned about her playful rhymes. The school labeled the activity as a distraction from her class assignments. However, the secretary of the institution, Grover Cleveland, encouraged her to continue composing poems. He offered to copy them for her. Later, when Grover Cleveland became president, he invited Fanny to the White House.

The school, always in need of funds, discovered that she was undaunted by visiting dignitaries. She became the tour guide and ushered around visiting businessmen, generals, and congressmen. Visitors included statesman Henry Clay, poet William Cullen Bryant, publisher Horace Greeley, and singer Jenny Lind.

Fanny was sent to the state assembly in Albany and the national Congress in Washington, D.C., to interest lawmakers in the work of the school. She met John Quincy Adams after he left office and eventually met all of the presidents of the 1800s who held office after Adams.

After graduation at age 27, she stayed on as an instructor. Her book *The Blind Girl and Other Poems* was published when she was still a student, and two more came out when she was a teacher. She also wrote patriotic songs such as "The Pilgrim Fathers" and others of a secular nature such as "There's Music in the Air." She was not yet writing religious hymns.

While still a student, she met Alexander Van Alstine. He was a blind music student. He became a teacher at the school, too. Fifteen years after they met, Fanny and Alexander were married in 1858. He insisted that she keep her name because it had already become well-known. She resigned from the school, probably to avoid being asked to leave because married female instructors were frowned upon. Alexander resigned, too. He could earn more as a private teacher of music and church organist in New York City.

In 1860, Fanny began supplying hymns to Bigelow and Main Company, a publisher of songs for Sunday schools. Her first hymn to become well-known was "Pass Me Not, O Gentle Savior" written in 1864. She was 44 years old and had another 51 years to go in her songwriting career. She became the most prolific hymnwriter in history, with 6,000 published songs to her credit, and perhaps another 3,000 other works that were not printed. Most hymnals today contain several of her songs: "More Like Jesus," "Safe in the Arms of Jesus," "Near the Cross," "Rescue the Perishing," and "I Am Thine, O Lord."

She could compose a song quickly. William Doane was going to a Sunday school convention in Cincinnati. He needed lyrics to fit the melody that he had already composed. He sat down at her piano and played the tune. During the next 20 minutes, she completed "Safe in the Arms of Jesus." The song, written in 1868, was played at President Grant's funeral.

She prayed that God would let her write lyrics that harmonized with the music. She looked for words that fulfilled the technical requirements of number of syllables and accent but also agreed in subject matter. She wanted the words to encourage salvation and conversion.

One of her most popular songs was "Blessed Assurance," written in 1873. Some of her better songs were overlooked until after her death. For instance, "To God Be the Glory" became a favorite only after George Beverly Shea sang it at a Billy Graham Crusade in 1954.

Fanny Crosby died just short of 95 years of age. On the night of her death, she dictated a letter to a friend and included a poem. She was buried in Bridgeport, Connecticut, where she had lived after the death of her husband. Her tombstone has the words:

> Blessed assurance, Jesus is mine. Oh, what a foretaste of glory divine.

JOHN WILLIAM DAWSON

1820–1899

CANADIAN GEOLOGIST

MAJOR ACCOMPLISHMENT: ENHANCED THE STATUS OF
McGILL UNIVERSITY, MONTREAL, CANADA, INTO
A WORLD-CLASS INSTITUTION

SIR JOHN WILLIAM DAWSON WAS born in Nova Scotia, Canada, and studied geology at the University of Edinburgh. He studied under Charles Lyell, the Scottish geologist, who taught that natural processes currently at work had caused the geological changes in the earth. This uniformitarianism contrasted with Georges Cuvier's catastrophism theory of rapid and sudden changes. Most people believed that catastrophism was more consistent with the Bible's account of the earth's creation.

Upon his return to Canada, Dawson became superintendent of education for Nova Scotia. His specialty was plant fossils and coal strata.

In 1855, Dawson became professor of geology at McGill University. James McGill, a Scottish fur trader, had opened the school in 1829. When Dawson came on board he was put in charge of its reorganization, and during the next 38 years, he advanced it into a school with a worldwide reputation.

While he served as president of the institution, he continued to teach and publish scientific papers, averaging about ten each year. He wrote several books, including *The Dawn of Life* and *Air Breathers of the Coal Period*.

Dawson was an evangelistic Christian and anti-evolutionist. During his life, he was a careful and reverent student of Holy Scripture. He believed in Bible reading for spiritual guidance. He said, "Those that aim to be Christian teachers should be fully armed to contend for the truth."

In 1874, Dawson was invited to deliver a series of lectures in New York on the "Relations of the Bible to the Sciences." Samuel F.B. Morse had established the lectures at the Union Theological Seminary. The title of Dawson's talk was "Nature and the Bible."

Dawson pointed out that God "reveals science by raising up gifted minds to interrogate nature. He reveals spiritual truths directly through human minds." He also made the observation that "We cannot rest in the general statement that the Bible is not intended to teach science, any more than we can excuse inaccuracy to historical facts by the notion that the Bible was not intended to teach history."

FLORENCE NIGHTINGALE
1820–1910
BRITISH NURSE AND MEDICAL ADMINISTRATOR
MAJOR ACCOMPLISHMENT: ESTABLISHED NURSING AS A
MEDICAL PROFESSION

FLORENCE NIGHTINGALE WAS named for Florence, Italy, the city where she had been born while her wealthy father and mother were on an extended vacation. She grew up in England. Her family maintained two comfortable estates, a country home in Derbyshire and another in London.

Her father and mother saw to her education and it was thorough. She learned French, German, and Italian, as well as Greek and Latin. Mastering those languages allowed her to read books on history, philosophy, and mathematics and continue her education on her own.

Nightingale's mother and father expected her to grow into a highborn lady who limited her activities to social occasions. However, at age 17, Nightingale became convinced that God had planned something different for her. She believed she had a mission — if only she could determine what it was. Eventually, she became convinced that her special work was nursing.

Her mother was aghast. In England, nursing was menial labor. Nurses were not considered a part of the medical profession. A woman with the ability to be a nurse could live a better life as a maid, so the only women who took a job as a nurse were those who could find no other employment. Often they were women of low morals or alcoholics.

However, Florence began rising well before dawn to study nursing in secret. Since there were few books about nursing, she also read about medicine and hospital administration, not only in English, but also in other languages. She became an expert on public health and hospitals.

She had no source of income, and had to depend on her family to provide her the money for any training that she received. Her research revealed that nurses enjoyed better reputations in other countries. In 1849, she managed to take a few months of training at a nursing school in Alexandria, Egypt, and at Kaisenwerth, Germany. In May 1850, she wrote in her diary, "God, I place myself in Thy Hands."

When she returned to London, she was appointed superinten- dent of the Institution for the Care of Sick Gentlewomen in London. It was an administrative position, not a nursing one. By then, she had come to see her role as a medical reformer.

When the Crimean War broke out in 1854, Nightingale volun- teered to go to a large British hospital in Turkey. She set out with 38 nurses and on the way learned she had been put in charge of all nursing operations of the war. She collected additional nurses along the way. She accepted Catholic and Protestant nurses and had her hands full trying to keep the two groups, who had received different training, working together.

The conditions at the hospital were appalling. Rats overran the place, and one wing of the building stood above a cesspool. She had to overcome overcrowding, lack of sanitation, contaminated water, and shortages of food and medical supplies. She had brought some supplies but those quickly ran out. The army supply line had broken down and her request for materials went unanswered.

The Crimean War was one of the first to be covered in a mod- ern way. Reporters were on the scene, and newspapers carried tele- graph dispatches and illustrated the fighting with lithographs pre- pared from photographs taken at the scene.

In the evening when her administrative duties were finished, Nightingale lit a lantern and made the final check of the wards. The newspapers portrayed Nightingale as the "lady with the lamp" and made her a hero.

The *London Times* reported on the disgraceful condition of the hospital and her struggle with the lack of supplies. The *Times* ap- pealed for funds, and the public gave an outpouring of 30,000 pounds. Nightingale was able to purchase supplies directly. Almost immedi- ately, the death rate fell by two-thirds. When the soldiers tried to give honor to her, she would instead say, "Give praise to God."

In 1858 she returned to England as a hero. Additional money had been raised and she used it to found the Nightingale School and Home for Nurses in London. She wrote three textbooks for use in the school: *Notes on Hospitals* (1859), *Notes on Nursing* (1860), and *Notes on Nursing for the Laboring Classes* (1861). The school and the textbooks marked the start of nursing as a medical profession.

Her primary interest was improving the welfare of soldiers in the British army. Public adoration would weaken her ability to deal effectively with military authorities. She refused public receptions and controlled her visitors. She sank so far from public sight that some people thought she had died. However, she continued to be engaged behind the scenes.

She was appointed to the Royal Commission on the Health of the Army. Her experience during the Crimean War had taught her how to work with military leaders. She exercised considerable patience and discretion. She kept her recommendations confidential until they were implemented.

Nightingale, whose education included mathematics and statistics, collected and analyzed data to summarize information about public health. However, her listeners' eyes glazed over when she presented columns of figures. To make it easier to understand she invented that mainstay of power presentations — the pie chart.

She retired from public view. She became an invalid and seldom ventured from her home in London. However, she carried on brisk correspondence, questioned guests, and read extensively. She became the foremost authority on India and the problems facing the British army in the subcontinent. Viceroys who were assigned by the British crown to govern India always consulted her before taking office.

About 1900, Florence Nightingale became blind. In 1907, King Edward VII conferred the Order of Merit to Nightingale for her services to the armed forces. She was the first woman so honored. She died in 1910 at the age of 90.

RUDOLF VIRCHOW
1821–1902
GERMAN PATHOLOGIST
MAJOR ACCOMPLISHMENT: FOUNDER OF THE STUDY OF
CELLS AS THE HOST OF DISEASES

VIRCHOW WAS BORN IN what is now Poland and educated at the University of Berlin. He received his medical degree in 1843. During his internship at Charité Hospital, he described the first case of leukemia. While at the hospital he began editing a journal that became known as *Virchow's Archive*. He continued to publish it for the next 50 years.

The Prussian government called upon him to investigate an outbreak of typhus fever in one of the provinces. He reported that neglect of the basic human services by the government contributed to epidemics. His scathing report did not endear him to the ultra-conservative Prussian government. He also upset the leading doctors by pressing that all doctors and surgeons be treated equally. When disorder against the government broke out in Berlin, Virchow took the wrong side. He was dismissed from Charité Hospital.

He accepted a position at the University of Würzberg in the newly created post of pathological anatomy. The next year, 1850, he married Rose Mayer and they had three sons and three daughters.

While at Würzberg, Virchow began to investigate the cause of diseases. Biologists had accepted cells as the building blocks of living organisms. However, doctors believed that cells could come into existence in the body from undifferentiated tissue, and that these cells were the ones that became diseased. Virchow showed that all cells were derived from cell division. More importantly, he showed that diseased cells arose from normal ones. His statement "all cells arise from cells" became the easily grasped principle of cellular pathology.

In 1856, Virchow returned to Berlin. He immediately became involved in politics and won an election to the Berlin City Council. He improved public health through hygiene instruction in schools. He opened a school for nurses and designed hospitals. He developed the plan to provide pure water in the city and disposal of sewage.

In the 1860s, Louis Pasteur and Joseph Lister proposed the germ theory of disease. According to Pasteur, diseases arose from germs attacking the body from outside. Virchow suggested that the germs might release toxins that caused cells to become diseased. However, he did not fully accept the germ theory of disease. He turned his attention to other areas of interest.

Virchow's hobby had been amateur archaeologist. He investigated an unusual find in a small cave in the Neader Valley near Dusseldorf, Germany. A local high school teacher came into possession of old bones that the teacher believed were from a gorilla.

Virchow had developed the modern methods of autopsy in which the whole body is systematically examined. He applied this skill to the ancient skeleton. He stated that the bones were from a human. The larger brow ridge had been caused by arthritis and the curved thighbone was a condition common to rickets.

In the 1860s, Darwin's theory of evolution took the scientific world by storm. Scientists re-evaluated the bones and declared them to be the skeleton of a member of an ancient apelike race. The skeleton was put together with legs bowed, back bent and shoulders drooped. The result made the Neanderthal Man, as the skeleton was called, look short and awkward.

Virchow maintained throughout his life that insufficient scientific evidence existed to justify the theory of evolution. In the 1880s, when he was elected to the German Reichstag, he voted for a law that banned the teaching of Darwin's theory in schools. Later, archaeologists agreed that his first ideas about Neanderthal Man were closer to the truth than the picture based on the theory of evolution.

In 1874, Virchow met Heinrich Schliemann, who had uncovered the site of Troy, the legendary city of Homer's epic *Iliad*. Virchow accompanied Schliemann to Troy. He helped with the excavations there and at archaeological sites in Egypt.

He served in the German Reichstag from 1880 to 1893. During Germany's wars, Virchow designed hospital trains and portable field hospitals. He served in the hospitals on the front lines. The government offered to make him a nobleman, but because of his years of support for ordinary citizens, he declined.

LOUIS PASTEUR
1822–1895
FRENCH CHEMIST AND BIOLOGIST

MAJOR ACCOMPLISHMENT: ESTABLISHED THE GERM
THEORY OF DISEASE

LOUIS PASTEUR IS KNOWN today as a medical researcher. However, he began his career as a chemist and never earned a medical
degree. Pasteur grew up in the small French town of Arbois where he
helped his father who was a tanner. Louis Pasteur was a slow, plod-
ding student. He earned ordinary grades because he worked so slowly
that he often turned in his assignments late.

When Louis grew older, his father sent him to a teacher training school in Paris, which was far from home. Young Pasteur grew so
homesick he could not continue his studies. He left Paris to study at
a school closer to home. Two years later he returned to Paris and
successfully began studying to be a chemist.

While still a student, he used a microscope to make several
important discoveries about crystals produced in living things. The
microscopic study encouraged an interest in biology.

Through the microscope, Pasteur saw a bewildering number of
tiny living things. Some naturalists believed new ones continually
appeared. Louis rejected the idea of spontaneous generation. Through
a series of decisive experiments, Pasteur firmly established the biological principle that all living things arise from living things. He
made the discovery at the same time that Darwin announced his
theory of evolution. Pasteur opposed the idea of evolution throughout his life.

He became the director of the science program at the University of Lille. Pasteur followed the stages of fermentation with a microscope and proved that yeasts were living organisms. Certain microscopic organisms that he extracted from buttermilk would cause
fresh milk to sour. But the milk would be unchanged if heated to kill
the microorganisms. This process of purification became known as
pasteurization, named after Pasteur. His friends assured him that his
patents on the process would make him wealthy. Pasteur, however,

gave the discovery to the public. He believed he had a duty to help others.

After his success with pasteurization, Pasteur investigated the disease of silkworms that was devastating the French silk industry. Pasteur proved that germs caused disease in silkworms. His solution was to destroy all of the silkworms and mulberry bushes they ate, and then re-establish the silkworms by selecting disease-free eggs.

In the 1860s, the combined discoveries of Louis Pasteur and Joseph Lister, the Scottish surgeon, helped establish

Louis Pasteur

the germ theory of disease — although 20 years elapsed before it was fully accepted by the physicians of their day. The germ theory of disease was the single greatest medical discovery of all time.

Like Lister, Pasteur was a humble person who lived by New Testament principles. Pasteur began each day with Bible study and prayer. Louis often spoke to his family about the importance of Christian faith. In letters to his sisters, he told how he read the New Testament to let its simple truths guide his life. He encouraged them to pray for one another.

Much of Louis Pasteur's scientific triumphs can be traced to his decision to base his work upon experimental facts, which sometimes took months to establish. As Louis said, "In everything, I believe, the secret of success is prolonged efforts."

Sometimes he overcame the objections of scientists by enlisting public support. One of his best-known demonstrations was his public test of his anthrax vaccination.

On February 28, 1881, Louis Pasteur described his new anthrax vaccine to the French Academy of Science. His idea that tiny bacteria could kill vastly larger organisms seemed ridiculous to many people, including veterinarians. They refused to believe that a chemist could have solved the problem that had baffled them for centuries.

Hippolyte Rossignol, editor of *Veterinary Press*, demanded a field test. Pasteur accepted the challenge. On May 5, 1882, at a farm near Melun, France, the public test began. A large crowd gathered to watch and take sides. Twenty-five sheep would be given the vaccine. Another 25 would be left untouched. A few weeks later, all 50 would be given a virulent strain of deadly anthrax.

A reporter asked, "How many will survive?"

Pasteur explained, "All of the control sheep will die. All of the vaccinated ones will live. The ones I treated must live or you can tell your readers the experiment failed!"

After giving the vaccine to the 25 animals, Pasteur returned to his laboratory in Paris. Two weeks later, his assistants gave the vaccinated animals a booster shot. Newspapers carried a day by day account of the health of the animals. On the last day of May, Pasteur and his assistants came back to the farm. They injected all animals with a very powerful and deadly strain of anthrax.

"The results will be clear within 48 hours," Pasteur told the judges. He rode the train back to Paris to wait out the results. Pasteur acted more confident in public than he felt in private. Too many things could go wrong. The vaccine could have been prepared wrong, stored or shipped improperly. His vaccinated sheep could get sick and die from an entirely different disease.

That evening Pasteur could not eat. The next day newspapers reported that some of the vaccinated sheep appeared sick. After another sleepless night, he awoke to the doorbell ringing.

A telegraph arrived. Pasteur's hands shook so badly he couldn't open the envelope. His wife tore open the envelope and read the telegraph to him. "Sick sheep among vaccinated lot all completely recovered. Unvaccinated sheep all dead or dying. Stunning success." Hippolyte Rossignol himself had sent the telegraph.

Louis Pasteur could claim complete victory. Never again did anyone seriously challenge the germ theory of disease.

Pasteur was a methodical worker who chose his battles wisely. The climax of his career was the development of a vaccine for rabies, a dreaded disease for the very good reason that it killed every victim. After four years, Pasteur developed a serum and had cautiously tested it on dogs, but never on a person.

A mother brought her little boy, Joseph Meister, to see Louis. A mad dog had savagely attacked the nine-year-old boy. "My remedy is untried and possibly dangerous," Louis Pasteur told the woman. "I'm not ready to try it on a human being."

"My son is doomed anyway," she cried.

Reluctantly, Pasteur agreed to do what he could. On July 7, 1885, Pasteur began the treatment. One of Louis Pasteur's assistants simply could not bear the tension of another case with so much at stake and asked to be excused. A doctor on Pasteur's staff gave the actual vaccination because Pasteur himself had not been licensed to practice medicine.

During the ten days of the treatment, Pasteur could not work. He sat by the little boy's bed. Pasteur ate little and slept hardly at all. Finally, on July 16, they gave the final injection. Even if the mad dog hadn't given Joseph rabies, the last injection would give it to him anyway. Joseph would die the horrible, suffocating death of rabies.

As the days passed, Joseph Meister showed no ill effects. The boy never developed rabies. Joseph Meister became the first human being to escape the certain death of rabies.

Throughout his life, Pasteur grew in his Christian faith. He said, "The more I study nature, the more I stand amazed at the work of the Creator."

Louis Pasteur became one of the most respected medical researchers of his, or any other, time. The Pasteur Institute was built by public donations after his discovery of the vaccine for rabies. It became one of the great research institutions in the world. Joseph Meister, the boy Pasteur saved, grew up to work at the institute. Louis was 70 years old at its opening and worked there until his death three years later. After his death, the English surgeon Stephen Paget wrote a biography about Pasteur. Paget said, "Here was a man whose spiritual life was no less admirable than his scientific life."

JEAN HENRI FABRE

1823–1915

FRENCH BIOLOGIST

MAJOR ACCOMPLISHMENT: FOREMOST OBSERVER AND
WRITER ON THE BEHAVIOR OF INSECTS

JEAN HENRI FABRE WAS BORN in St. Léons, France. Until he started school, he spent his time in a nearby village with his grandparents. Fabre enjoyed being outdoors. As a small child he became fascinated with butterflies and grasshoppers. His family was not wealthy. He moved several times as a child, and dropped out of school to work selling lemons. However, he passed a test to enter teacher training school. After three years of study, he gained his teaching certificate.

He began teaching at age 19. He was fortunate to be assigned to a school at Ajaccio on the Mediterranean island of Corsica. Known as "the scented isle" because of its luxuriant vegetation, it was a naturalist's paradise. During his four years on the island, he developed his style for studying nature. He combined patient observation with detailed but interesting description of the insects' behaviors.

The usual practice by biologists was to capture insects, kill and dissect them. A dead insect held no charms for Fabre. He felt an insect was better described by its fascinating behavior than by its body parts. He said, "You rip up the animal and I study it alive; you turn it into an object of horror and pity, whereas I cause it to be loved. . . . I make my observations under the blue sky to the song of the cicadas."

When he moved back to the continent, he investigated the production of dyes from plants. He discovered the dye alizarin that became useful as a biological stain to make visible features of microscopic subjects. He also improved the production of a natural red dye for coloring fabrics. He earned three patents for this work, which gave him some financial independence.

French government officials realized that the education of adult workers was not keeping pace with the rapidly changing technology. School officials hired Fabre to create an evening course for adults.

His course material did not follow the rigid teaching methods then employed. Critics objected that his books were too entertaining and easy to read.

He scoffed at this idea of making his textbooks more difficult to read. He said, "Were I to take their word for it, we are profound only on condition of being obscure."

Fabre resigned rather than change his course material. He began writing nature guides. He wrote with the eyes and mind of a scientist and the heart of a poet. He had an exceptional ability to paint word pictures of his subjects. People could distinguish flowers from his precise descriptions of aromas and fragrances.

He became friends with Louis Pasteur. Like Pasteur, he criticized the idea of spontaneous generation. He also concluded that the theory of evolution was false. He lived to see most of the main ideas of evolution proposed, but he never accepted the theory.

During the period of 1879 to 1907 he wrote ten volumes in his scientific series *Souvenirs Entomologiques* ("Recollections of Insects"). He filled the books with direct, patient observations of insect behavior. The books established him as the foremost authority on insects. Following the scientific books, he wrote popular books such as *The Life of the Spider* and *The Life of the Caterpillar*. His influence was bolstered by a long writing career that lasted until 1915, the year he died at age 92.

His writing impressed not only scientists such as Louis Pasteur, but also literary giants such as Victor Hugo who said, "Fabre is the Homer of the insects."

Fabre wrote books for children, and some of his material made its way into textbooks for French school children. His critics opposed his frequent religious references in the books. Fabre responded, "Without Him I understand nothing; without Him all is darkness. . . . Every period has it mantras. I regard atheism as a mantra. It is the malady of the age. You could take my skin from me more easily than my faith in God."

WILLIAM THOMSON (LORD KELVIN)

1824–1907

SCOTTISH PHYSICIST

MAJOR ACCOMPLISHMENT: DEVELOPED THE LAWS OF
THERMODYNAMICS

ALTHOUGH WILLIAM THOMSON WAS born in Belfast in what is now Northern Ireland, his mother was Scottish, and his family moved to Scotland when he was six years old. William Thomson became a college professor by the time he was 22. He taught science at the University of Glasgow, Scotland, and held the position for 53 years. He was an effective teacher who introduced laboratory exercises in science education. He influenced how science was taught throughout the last half of the 1800s.

In 1847, Thomson began work with James Joule, an amateur scientist who had a fascination for measuring changes in temperature. Because of his study of heat with Joule, Thomson discovered that heat was the energy caused by the motion of atoms and molecules of a substance. When a substance cools, its atoms move more slowly.

Thomson defined absolute zero as the temperature at which all motion ceased. He proved that this temperature was the same for all substances. At -273° C (-459° F) atoms and molecules lost all of their heat energy. It is the coldest temperature possible.

In later life, William Thomson received the title Lord Kelvin. He became well-known under that name. Scientists named the absolute temperature scale in his honor. The Kelvin scale is measured in Kelvin degrees and starts at absolute zero, 0° K.

While studying heat, Thomson developed the second law of thermodynamics; also known as the law of entropy. When energy changed from one form to another, some energy became the random motion of atoms and molecules. The second law of thermodynamics stated that the universe became more disorganized as concentrated forms of energy changed into the random motion of heat energy.

Along with heat, electricity interested Thomson. He had developed formulas for the flow of heat in a conductor. To his surprise, the same equations described the flow of electricity in an electrical conductor. This discovery gave him some hope that the various theories about electricity, magnetism, and thermodynamics could be combined into a single theory. Although he pursued that goal, he realistically did not expect to see it accomplished in his lifetime. However, when his work was combined with that of his friends, Michael Faraday and James Clerk Maxwell, it was definitely established that magnetism, electricity, electromagnetism, and light were related.

William Thomson

In the 1850s, Cyrus Field attempted several times to lay a transAtlantic telegraph cable. The first four cables broke. The fifth was completed in 1858, but the signal was unreliable. Thomson calculated that the current used to transmit the signal was too strong. Thomson was only one of many technical advisors, and his proposal to use a weaker signal was ignored. After a month of unreliable service, the telegraph cable quit working entirely. With the start of the Civil War, the project was abandoned.

In 1859, Darwin announced his theory of evolution, and Thomson jumped into the controversy. He opposed Darwin and brought much mathematical and physical evidence to bear in opposition to the theory. The concept of evolution violated the second law of thermodynamics. He convinced the scientific world that biological theory had to conform to the well-established laws of physics.

Thomson calculated the age of the earth in 1862 based on its temperature and the rate at which heat is lost. Evolution required a vast extent of time, yet Thomson calculated that the age of the earth was far short of the time needed for evolution. He said, "With regard to the origin of life, science . . . positively affirms creative power."

He lived to see the discovery of radioactivity, which he had not known about when he first calculated the age of the earth. He redid the calculations by taking into account the heat generated by natural radioactivity in the rocks of earth. Once again, he found that the earth was still too young to support the vast ages that evolution required.

After the Civil War ended, Cyrus Field put together another attempt to lay a cable. This time he used the largest steam ship of the day, the *Great Eastern*. It was five times the size of any other ship and made laying out the cable easier.

Cyrus Field put William Thomson in charge of technical matters. Rather than a powerful electric current, Thomson chose to use a small current and designed a mirror galvanometer, an extremely sensitive device, to respond to the reduced signal. Thomson's sensitive instruments succeeded in detecting the faint electrical signals, and the telegraph was a success. Queen Victoria knighted William Thomson for his efforts regarding the trans-Atlantic telegraph.

Thomson was a devout Christian. The Bible was the most important book in his life. He encouraged religious instruction for the school children of England.

BERNHARD RIEMANN
1826–1866
GERMAN MATHEMATICIAN

MAJOR ACCOMPLISHMENT: DEVELOPED A SYSTEM OF
GEOMETRY THAT BECAME THE MAIN TOOL OF
MODERN PHYSICS

BERNHARD RIEMANN WAS THE son of a Lutheran pastor. Despite growing up in poverty, Riemann received a good education. He graduated from high school with grades quite good in German, Latin, Greek, French, and English, good or better in religion and Hebrew, and excellent in mathematics. Overall, he was judged a first-class student.

Riemann wanted to be a minister like his father. However, he was excessively shy. He could only speak in public by preparing thoroughly, writing out fully what he wanted to say, and sticking to the script. The painful shyness did not forecast success for a future as a preacher.

He excelled in mathematics, which was generally seen as a solitary profession. His father agreed that Riemann should pursue a career as a mathematician. He received a Ph.D. in mathematics in 1851.

He was interested in the geometry of complex mathematical functions. He developed a geometry based on the assumption that on some surfaces, any two lines would eventually meet. For instance, on the globe of the earth, if two travelers traced out any two great circles, their paths eventually crossed. The meridians are great circles, and they all meet at the poles.

In 1854, he prepared a lecture for admission to the faculty at Göttingen. It became one of the most celebrated lectures in the history of mathematics. He described a new geometry as logically consistent as Euclid's geometry that had been in use for 2,000 years. Karl Gauss, the greatest mathematician of the age, was in the audience. Gauss reported that he became dizzy at the vista Riemann's lecture opened to him.

Riemann became a teacher, but it was without a salary. Students who attended his classes paid him directly. He was overjoyed when his first course drew eight students. He was afraid he would have only three. In 1857, Riemann became a paid professor of mathematics at the University of Göttingen, a position he held until his death.

He revolutionized every branch of mathematics that he touched. At least 13 principles, theorems, surfaces, matrices, and mathematical constructions carry his name. Riemann showed how to recast complex algebraic formulas into geometric ideas. With the rise of modern physics, Riemann's surfaces became the foundation of modern physics. Einstein used Riemann's methods in developing the theory of relativity.

In 1862, Bernhard Riemann married Elise Koch, a friend of his sisters. He had grown up in poverty and he often suffered from illness. But for one golden year, he enjoyed good health, a well-paying job, and a warm family life.

It did not last. The next year he fell ill with a lung infection. He experienced fits of coughing, painful breathing, and suffered alternate chills and fevers. During the summer recess, he traveled to Italy for rest. He and his wife saw the sights of Naples, Florence, and the other great Italian cities.

The rest did him good, but by the next year his health had ebbed lower than the summer before. Although friends said they could find a job for him at Pisa University, it was too late. He died in the summer of 1866.

Although he made mathematical research his profession, Riemann continued to study the Bible. Riemann persevered in his faith and remained a sincere Christian all his life. Richard Dedekind, a great thinker on the cutting edge of mathematics, said of Riemann: "He reverently avoided disturbing the faith of others; for him the main thing in religion was daily self-examination."

He died at the age of 39. His wife was at his side holding his hand. He felt the end coming and began reciting the Lord's Prayer. He died while saying the words "Forgive us our trespasses." The inscription on his tombstone is a quotation in German from Romans 8:28. In English, the inscription states: "All things work together for good to them that love God."

LEWIS WALLACE

1827–1905

AMERICAN LAWYER, MILITARY LEADER, AND WRITER

MAJOR ACCOMPLISHMENT: WRITER OF *BEN-HUR*

LEWIS WALLACE, KNOWN AS LEW, was an inventor, youngest general in the Union Army during the Civil War, a judge in the trial of the assassination conspirators of President Abraham Lincoln, and a territorial governor of New Mexico. Yet, Lew Wallace is remembered today as the writer of *Ben-Hur: a Tale of the Christ*, the best-selling book of the 1800s.

Lew Wallace's father was a lawyer and governor of Indiana. Wallace left school at 16 to work in the county clerk's office and to study to be a lawyer. At that time one could pass the bar by reading about law under the oversight of a lawyer. Wallace interrupted his studies to become a volunteer in the Mexican War (1846–1848). Foreign cultures fascinated him, so his participation was an excuse to travel to Mexico.

After war's end, another year of study qualified him for the bar, and he began practicing in Indianapolis. When the Civil War began, he organized six regiments of volunteers from Indiana. He became a brigadier-general, and the youngest Union general in the war. During the Battle of Shiloh, he received conflicting orders and his men did not join the battle until the second day.

Although Grant finally prevailed, his army suffered huge casualties during the first day. Grant and his generals looked for someone to deflect the criticism of the Shiloh disaster, and Wallace took the blame. He was sent home to await further orders. He finally redeemed himself by successfully defending Cincinnati against General Kirby Smith. Using mostly a civilian force, he improved the city's fortifications so that Kirby Smith chose not to attack.

Wallace was given a command near the end of the war. He went up against Confederate General Jubal A. Early who was marching on Washington. Wallace lost the battle, but this time he became a hero. Wallace delayed the Confederate general long enough for Washington to be reinforced, and Early never reached his objective.

Because of his training as a lawyer and his military experience,

Wallace was chosen to preside over several military courts of inquiry after the Civil War. He was assigned to the military court that tried the conspirators in the Lincoln assassination. He led the court at the trial of Henry Wirtz, Confederate commandant of the notorious prisoner of war camp at Andersonville.

He became a civilian again in 1865 and returned to law practice. However, in 1878, President Rutherford B. Hayes appointed him governor of the territory of New Mexico. His chief assignment was to quell a cattleman's conflict so bloody it was known as the "Lincoln County Wars."

Wallace held a secret meeting with William Bonney (Billy the Kid.) The young desperado agreed to testify for a reduced sentence, but escaped from jail while awaiting his own sentencing. He was arrested again and convicted of murder, but escaped again. Wallace issued his death warrant and Sheriff Pat Garrett tracked down Billy the Kid and killed him at Fort Sumner, New Mexico.

Wallace soon became thoroughly disgusted with the bickering, bribes, and dishonesty in New Mexico. As he sat in the Palace of Governors in Santa Fe, he bleakly surveyed the problems he faced: bad schools, a high crime rate, no state prison, Indian unrest, corrupt state politicians, and warring cattlemen. He said, "All calculations based on experiences elsewhere fail in New Mexico."

To divert himself, he began writing a story set in the Roman Empire during the life of Christ. It began with the wise men coming to find the baby Jesus and ended with the crucifixion. The main character was the young Judah Ben-Hur, who lost his family and freedom because of a corrupt Roman officer.

Although Ben-Hur was a fictional character, the historic details made the events come alive. The book had the subtitle, "A Tale of the Christ" and presented Jesus as the Savior of the world. The story unabashedly used a miracle of Jesus to advance the story line.

The book, published in November 1880, immediately became a best seller. It had a deep spiritual impact on its readers. President Garfield read the book, and when he learned that the author was his man in New Mexico, he asked if Wallace desired some other appointment.

Any other appointment would do as far as Wallace was concerned. He happily took the position as minister to the Ottoman Empire in Turkey. He became friends with the Sultan and was given privileges denied most other westerners. He took the opportunity to tour the Holy Land, which was under the control of the sultan.

When he returned to the United States, Wallace became an inventor. He designed railroad switches, an apparatus for molding fence posts, and an improved fishing rod. In all, he was awarded seven patents.

Lew Wallace continued to write. But his reputation rested upon *Ben-Hur.* The book was the best seller of the 1800s. The Broadway play of 1899 included a chariot race with live horses galloping at top speed on a treadmill. The silent-era movie version appeared in 1925, and the blockbuster motion picture (11 academy awards) appeared in 1959. *Ben-Hur* was translated into many languages and has never been out of print.

Wallace began *Ben-Hur* as a short story for magazine publication. The story languished on his desk because he was dissatisfied with it. His own religious convictions were weak. One day he took a train from his hometown of Crawfordsville to attend a political convention in Indianapolis.

As he moved down the train greeting people, he was invited into the private stateroom of Robert G. Ingersoll, a lawyer and orator. Ingersoll was known as the "Great Agnostic" because of his antireligious views. He said, "Come in, I feel like talking." Wallace agreed, provided Ingersoll addressed a series of questions: Is there a God? Is there a devil? Is there a heaven? Is there a hell? Is there a hereafter?

To each of these questions, Ingersoll answered, "I don't know." During the next two hours, Ingersoll gave a spellbinding speech that wove together all of his arguments for unbelief in God, Christ, and heaven.

Until then, Wallace's interest in religion had been one of indifference. He'd read great sermons and heard others, but mostly he focused on the skill of their oratory rather than the content of the message. His discussion with Ingersoll aroused for the first time in his life the importance of religion. He wanted to more fully explore what the Bible taught.

His little story had left Jesus as a child in Bethlehem. He decided to study and to write what he learned in an expanded story. The study resulted in *Ben-Hur.* More importantly, Wallace developed — in his words — "a conviction amounting to absolute belief in God and the divinity of Christ."

JOSEPH LISTER
1827–1912
SCOTTISH SURGEON
MAJOR ACCOMPLISHMENT: FOUNDER OF ANTISEPTIC MEDICINE

JOSEPH LISTER'S PARENTS WERE Quakers, and he grew up with strong religious training. He attended Quaker schools that gave a greater emphasis on science than the established schools. With this preparation, he earned a medical degree with honors. Later, he married the daughter of one of his professors. He and his wife were faithful members of the Episcopal Church.

In 1861, he was appointed surgeon of the Glasgow Royal Infirmary. A new research group had been formed to reduce infections following surgery. At the time, scientists believed gangrene and other infections were caused by bad air. As evidence, they pointed to the fact that a simple fracture usually healed without difficulty. But a compound fracture (one in which the bone protruded through the flesh into the air) often became so badly infected the patient died.

Joseph Lister

A gangrene infection was noted for its disagreeable odor. Lister knew that some cities treated the sewers with carbolic acid to reduce the stench. He began experiments with carbolic acid. He painted the wounds with acid. It was weak enough not to damage human flesh too severely.

The results were promising. In 1865, he learned of Pasteur's theory that germs caused diseases and that germs were carried in the air. Lister now had a scientific explanation for why his use of carbolic acid proved effective. Carbolic acid killed germs. He began a more systematic approach to keep germs from the operating table. He sprayed the air of the operating room with a fine mist of carbolic acid.

Most doctors washed their blood-soaked hands after a surgical operation. Lister washed his hands *before* going into the operating room. Most doctors wore blood-encrusted operating coats. Lister wore a clean linen apron. He became the first white-robed doctor. After he finished the surgery, he washed the incision and bandages with an acid solution.

Lister toured Europe and the United States to demonstrate his discovery. It was adopted in France because of the work of Louis Pasteur, and in Germany where infection had become so bad that officials threatened to burn the hospitals. In Munich, antiseptic surgery changed the dismal record of four deaths out of every five surgery patients to less than one death in two hundred patients.

Physicians in other countries found alternate methods to exclude the germs, such as steam heating the bandages and operating instruments. In the United States, Dr. Joseph Lawrence developed a disinfectant that could be used during operations that was gentler to human tissues than carbolic acid. Later, it was named after Joseph Lister and sold under the name Listerine.

Lister's lectures and publications spread the word so thoroughly that missionary and doctor David Livingstone in Africa began using antiseptic methods. Livingstone was 1,000 miles from any hospital. Yet, doctors in London continued to resist the germ theory.

Lister, a Christian, had a gentle nature and an even temper. Although firm in his convictions, he refused to engage in heated discussions. Instead, he let his results speak for themselves.

London was the chief medical city of the world, and without the endorsement of doctors there, the germ theory would take years to gain acceptance.

At age 50, Lister moved to King's College Hospital in London. His goal was to overcome resistance to the germ theory by the example of his successful surgeries. He did operations that no one else would attempt. For instance, wiring the bones together could more easily set some simple fractures. However, the procedure changed a simple fracture into a compound fracture that exposed the bone to the air. The success of his antiseptic surgeries forced London doctors to accept his methods.

Starting in about 1880, the fact that germs caused infections was universally accepted. Lister became the president of the Royal Society upon the retirement of Lord Kelvin (William Thomson). Lister became the first physician to belong to the House of Lords, and he became physician to Queen Victoria. Joseph Lister died in 1912 at the age of 84.

Joseph Lister became the greatest surgeon of all time. He believed God directed his work. Lister said, "I am a believer in the fundamental doctrines of Christianity."

WILLIAM S. PITTS

1830–1918

AMERICAN PHYSICIAN AND SONGWRITER

MAJOR ACCOMPLISHMENT: WROTE "THE LITTLE
BROWN CHURCH IN THE VALE"

WILLIAM PITTS WAS BORN IN Orleans County, New York. As a
young man, he taught school in rural Rock County, Wisconsin.

In 1857, Pitts boarded the stagecoach to visit his future bride
who lived in Fredericksburg, Iowa. The stagecoach stopped in
Bradford, Iowa, to change horses. The trip had left Pitts stiff and
dusty. He exercised by walking to a grove of trees a short distance
from the small village. The surroundings could not have been
more pleasant: cool shade trees, lush grass, a soft breeze, and singing birds.

To Pitts's eyes, the location seemed perfect for a little country
church.

After a visit with the woman he loved, Pitts returned to his
home in Wisconsin. The vision of a church in the pleasant grove
refused to fade from his mind. Finally, Pitts described the persistent
scene in song:

> There's a church in the valley by the wildwood,
> No lovelier spot in the dale;
> No place is so dear to my childhood,
> As the little brown church in the vale.

With the vision captured in words, Pitts put aside the song and
forgot about it.

About this time, John K. Nutting arrived in Bradford. He was a
young and energetic minister who took over leadership of a strug-
gling congregation. The good people of Bradford had no church building. They worshiped in an abandoned store with doors and windows
missing. The new minister encouraged his congregation of pioneers
to begin a building. They did the labor with their own hands and
used donated materials. They quarried the stone for the foundation.
They cut oak trees and dressed the lumber for the framing. They

painted the church building with the color of paint donated to them by a local merchant — brown.

Unknown to the church builders, Pitts, the songwriter, moved to Bradford to teach at the academy. When he revisited the wooded vale, what he saw could not have surprised him more. A little brown church now stood on the very spot that had inspired his song.

In 1864, the congregation completely finished the building. At the dedication ceremony, Pitts's vocal class from the academy sang "The Little Brown Church in the Vale" in public for the first time. Later, Mr. Pitts sold the song to a Chicago publisher for $25.00. The money helped pay for medical studies. Pitts became a doctor and practiced in Fredericksburg, Iowa, for over 40 years.

In 1916 church members collected money to reunite William Pitts and John Nutting. Both men were well into their eighties. The writer of the song and the builder of the church came together again after almost 60 years. Over time, the song became well-known around the world.

JAMES CLERK MAXWELL
1831–1879
SCOTTISH PHYSICIST

MAJOR ACCOMPLISHMENT: DEVELOPED FOUR CONCISE
EQUATIONS THAT SUMMARIZED ALL THAT WAS
KNOWN ABOUT MAGNETISM, ELECTRICITY, AND LIGHT

JAMES CLERK MAXWELL'S FATHER WAS A well-to-do lawyer who owned a townhouse in Edinburgh and an estate in the country. Maxwell's early education was by his father who taught him science and his mother who taught him the other subjects, including Bible. When he was eight years old, he successfully memorized Psalm 119, the longest chapter in the Bible.

In 1841 he began formal studies at Edinburgh Academy. As a farm boy dressed in rustic clothes and with a bit of a stammer, he suffered at the hands of bullies. However, he learned how to overcome his stammer and slowly moved to the head of his class. He attended Cambridge University where he developed the ability to use mathematics to solve real world problems.

He took a teaching position at a small college in Aberdeen so he could be near his father who was in poor health. (His mother had died when he was eight.) At Aberdeen, he tackled the question of the rings of Saturn. Scientists debated whether the rings were solid, liquid, or gas. Maxwell's calculations showed that gaseous or liquid rings would disperse into space. Solid rings would be broken up by Saturn's gravity. The rings had to be composed of a myriad of small solid particles. (A century later when space probes took close-up photographs of the rings, astronomers were not surprised to find that he had been entirely correct.)

In 1796 the French astronomer Simon Laplace proposed the "nebular hypothesis" for the formation of the planets. He ascribed their origin to the contraction of a gaseous nebula. Maxwell's studies showed that the random motion of the molecules of a gas would not have allowed objects of planetary size to form.

While in Aberdeen, James met the college president and his daughter, Katherine Dewar. She and James married, just as the college merged with another school and his position became redundant.

He was offered a position as science teacher at King's College, London. While there, he combined the kinetic theory of heat — that heat is due to the motion of atoms and molecules — with the atomic theory of matter to produce the kinetic theory of gases. From a few simple assumptions, he applied probability and statistics to develop all of the gas laws.

The test of a theory was its predictive power. Maxwell stated that pressure and density would not affect the viscosity (internal friction) of a gas. Laboratory tests proved this counter-intuitive prediction correct, and established Maxwell's reputation as a physicist.

James and his wife had taken a home near Hyde Park. His neighbors learned of his devotion to the teachings of Jesus. When they were sick, he was at their door to offer his help. James would bring them water, change the bed linens, and feed those too weak to feed themselves. Should they be agreeable, he would stay and read aloud from the Bible and say a prayer.

The Maxwell country estate had been neglected, and several tenement farmers depended upon it for their livelihood. Maxwell retired from King's College and returned to the farm. He and his wife also enjoyed riding their horses in the countryside. At the end of the day, he called family, visitors, and servants for devotions. In one of his prayers he said, "Almighty God, who has created man in Thine own image, and made him a living soul that he might seek after Thee . . . that we may believe on Him whom Thou has sent to give us the knowledge of salvation and remission of our sins."

He had time to experiment and correspond about science. Scientists had come to a confusing dead end in their understanding of magnetism and electricity. The great English scientist Michael Faraday had made many imposing discoveries, but Faraday had received no mathematical education as a child. Most of his ideas about electricity and magnetism were based on physical pictures rather than mathematical models. Faraday's visual ideas included lines of force and magnetic and electric fields.

Maxwell took on the daunting task to give a mathematical foundation to Faraday's work. He developed four equations, known as Maxwell's field equations, that summarized everything known about magnetism and electricity. He showed that the back and forth motion of an electric charge produced an electromagnetic field. The field radiated outward from its source at the speed of light. This was powerful evidence that light was itself an electromagnetic radiation. All of the laws of optics could also be derived from the field equations.

Maxwell's equations predicted that a circuit in which electricity rapidly switched back and forth would generate electromagnetic waves. A similar circuit would detect the waves. In the late 1880s, German scientist Rudolf Hertz made the first radio receiver and transmitter.

The importance of Maxwell's field equations can hardly be overemphasized. Albert Einstein called Maxwell's achievement "the most profound and most fruitful that physics has experienced since the time of Newton."

Maxwell moved back to Cambridge to be the first director of the Cavendish Laboratory. He also became the science editor for the *Encyclopaedia Britannica*. In one article, he stated the physical evidence showing that the universe has a Creator. "The exact equality of each molecule to all others of the same kind gives it, as Sir John Herschel has well said, the essential character of a manufactured article."

Maxwell's brilliant career was ended at age 48, when he died of cancer of the stomach. He was buried at the country church that he had helped build near his country estate.

DWIGHT L. MOODY
1837–1899
AMERICAN EVANGELIST

MAJOR ACCOMPLISHMENT: ORIGINATED THE MODEL
FOR EVANGELIC CAMPAIGNS IN LARGE CITIES

DWIGHT MOODY WAS BORN on a small farm near East Northfield, Massachusetts. Dwight's father was a bricklayer, but also an alcoholic, and did not provide particularly well for the family. The father died when Dwight was four years old, leaving his mother to raise nine children in near poverty.

When Dwight was 17 years old, he moved to Boston to work as a shoe salesman in a store owned by his uncle. His mother had taken him to a Unitarian church when he was a boy, but in Boston, he began attending a Congregational church. While there, he dedicated his life to Jesus. He said, "I was in a new world. The birds sang sweeter, the sun shone brighter. I'd never known such peace."

After two years in Boston, he moved to Chicago. Another uncle helped him find work in a boot store. In his spare time, he visited hotels and boarding houses to distribute religious tracts. His greatest efforts were for the children of poor families. At that time, churches raised money by a pew fee — members paid an annual sum for the space they occupied in the pews. Moody rented four pews and brought in enough children to fill them.

Over the next four years, he proved his ability as a salesman and saved $7,000. He gave up his assured income to work full time as an evangelist. He had no formal religious training and had not been ordained. With most pulpits closed to him, he concentrated on opening a Sunday school for slum children.

In the summer of 1858, he taught children in the open air along the shores of Lake Michigan. In the fall, he moved his class into an abandoned freight car. It soon proved too small. Businessmen saw the good work he was doing and arranged the use of a vacant building that had once been a saloon. He offered pony rides, picnics and games with prizes. The Sunday school grew to 500 children.

Dwight L. Moody

He moved into larger quarters, a hall over the city's North Market. Although rent-free, it was used during the rest of the week for other activities. He spent his Sunday morning sweeping and cleaning. He held classes in the afternoon so teachers would be available after they had attended morning services at other churches.

In 1860, attendance grew to 1,500. It was the largest Sunday school in Chicago. President-elect Abraham Lincoln visited the school while on his way to Washington, D.C. for his inauguration. Moody was 23 years old.

He became involved with the Young Men's Christian Association. Moody agreed with the aims of YMCA. During the industrial revolution, a great number of young men came to large cities from rural areas. The homesick young men became easy targets for saloons and other disreputable activities. The YMCA gave them a positive outlet for their energies. However, the Civil War nearly paralyzed the development of the YMCA in Chicago. Moody revitalized the program and served as the president of the Chicago chapter. He also served as a volunteer chaplain with Union troops at Shiloh, Chattanooga, and Richmond.

He married Emma Charlotte Revell in 1862. He was 25 years old and she was 19. She became an important part of his ministry. She did almost all of his correspondence. She had been born in England, so after the Civil War, he took her back to England for a visit. He wanted to meet some of the great English preachers, including Charles Spurgeon.

While in England, he heard a statement that is usually attributed to John Knox: "The world has yet to see what God will do with a man fully consecrated to Him." An English minister, Henry

Moorhouse, told him, "Teach what the Bible says, not your own words, and show people how much God loves them."

Moody developed a simple, conservative preaching style. He emphasized a personal relationship with God and avoided denominational differences.

The change in his ministry came after the Great Chicago Fire. The blaze that burned for three days in early October 1871 destroyed one-third of the city and left 90,000 people homeless. Moody lost his home, the YMCA building, and the place he preached. A meeting place was quickly built — the Northside Tabernacle — and he used it as a relief shelter for the homeless.

Following the Chicago fire, Moody embarked on a decade-long series of urban revival meetings. During his work in Sunday schools, Moody had learned the importance of lively songs to keep the children's attention. Moody realized he needed a dynamic song leader. He heard Ira A. Sankey sing at a YMCA convention in Indianapolis. Moody convinced him to give up his job and accompany him to England.

In 1873, Moody, Sankey, and their families toured England. The effect of Sankey's gospel music and Moody's preaching was stunning. At one location, a crowd of 15,000 people surrounded the meeting hall. Moody preached from a carriage and Sankey led the singing from the roof of a nearby shed. In Ireland, special trains brought in people from the surrounding areas. In London, he held a meeting in the 4,000-seat Crystal Palace. The crusade in London lasted for four months.

Moody and Sankey held similar revivals in the United States. By 1884, however, he changed his focus to smaller cities.

Moody established several schools, including a seminary for young men and a similar one for women in Massachusetts. In Chicago he began the Moody Bible Institute to train Christian workers. Moody published several books compiled from his spoken words at gospel meetings.

Early in his life, Moody set the goal of telling at least one person about Christ every day. Moody never kept records of attendance or conversions, but in all he spoke to several million people. In a comment about his own death, he said, "Some day you will read in the papers that D.L. Moody is dead. Don't you believe a word of it! At that moment I shall be more alive than I am now; I shall have gone up higher."

PHILIP P. BLISS
1838–1876
AMERICAN HYMNWRITER
MAJOR ACCOMPLISHMENT: WROTE "ALMOST
PERSUADED" AND OTHER HYMNS FOR EVANGELISTIC
GOSPEL MEETINGS

PHILIP P. BLISS WAS BORN IN Rome, Pennsylvania. His parents were dedicated Christians. He received his spiritual education from his father's songs and prayers, and from his mother who read the Bible to him and told him Bible stories. The family was poor, and he received practically no education except what he learned at home.

Bliss was a large, ungainly boy who walked into town barefoot to sell vegetables door to door. He was 10 years old before he heard a piano being played at a customer's home. At age 11, he left home to work in sawmills and lumber camps. Because of his muscular body and large size, he was able to do a man's work.

Somehow he managed to pick up an education, and he passed an examination to be a teacher. While still a teenager, he became the schoolmaster in Hartsville, New York. During the summer, he continued to find work as a laborer.

The next year he taught at an academy in his hometown of Rome, Pennsylvania. He met Lucy Young and they were married when he turned 21. She was a poet and musician. Philip, like his wife, loved to sing, but he had no formal training. She taught him all she knew, and helped him learn how to combine words with music. She believed he could earn a living as a music teacher.

Philip, however, had learned enough about music to know his own shortcomings. He needed more schooling. Lucy's grandmother made it possible by giving them $30. At that time, a farm worker earned about that much in two or three months. The newlyweds moved to New York where Philip attended the Normal Academy of Music. He made the most of the six-week course.

During the next four years, he alternated between taking music classes and conducting music workshops. As the Civil War ended, he and Lucy moved to Chicago. He became the leader of the choir at his church and served as superintendent of the Sunday school. The Root and Cady Music Publishers offered him a position at $150 per month, a fabulous sum to Bliss. He was paid to do what he enjoyed doing. He arranged conventions for musicians, represented the company at singing schools, and sponsored sacred concerts.

Bliss began writing songs. Two of his first efforts were "Hold the Fort" and "Jesus Loves Even Me." Because his employment gave him everything he and his wife needed, Philip released the songs — and all the others that he wrote — without copyright. He earned not one cent from them.

While in Chicago, Bliss attended one of Dwight L. Moody's revival meetings. Moody was looking for someone to be his song leader. He offered Bliss the position. Bliss had a well-paying job and one that met his every expectation for Christian service. He declined. Ira Sankey became Moody's song leader.

In 1873, Bliss received a letter from Moody who was in Scotland. Again, Moody encouraged Bliss to become a touring singer with an evangelist. After a long time of prayer, Bliss became convinced it was God's will for him to join forces with evangelist Major Daniel Whittle. They began their tour in 1874.

Bliss had three factors that made his songwriting efforts effective. He could write the words, then set them to music, and he could sing the songs. He also benefited from hearing preachers make their point with pithy stories. On several occasions, Bliss converted the point of the stories into songs with a message.

For instance, during one of Dwight L. Moody's sermons, he heard the story of a passenger boat attempting to make Cleveland harbor on Lake Erie at night during a storm. The pilot missed the channel because the two lower guide lights for the main beacon had gone out. The ship crashed against the rocks and was destroyed. Bliss wrote the song, "Let the Lower Lights Be Burning."

Because he conducted the song service, Bliss saw the effect of a song upon the audience. The first song at the end of the gospel sermon, known as the invitation song or altar call song, came at an important moment during the crusade. The most popular invitation song was "Just As I Am" that had been in use for 25 years.

In 1874, Bliss completed an invitation song but put it aside thinking it of slight merit. He did not sing it in public until two years later at a gospel meeting in New Haven, Connecticut. He saw firsthand the effect that it had on the audience. The song was "Almost Persuaded."

> Almost persuaded now to believe;
> Almost persuaded Christ to receive;
> Seems now some soul to say,
> "Go, Spirit, go Thy way,
> Some more convenient day
> On Thee I'll call."

When Moody came back from England, Sankey and Bliss combined the songs they had written with others to produce a successful songbook, *Gospel Hymns and Sacred Songs*. Bliss would not accept royalty for his songs, and distributed the $60,000 he earned to charities.

In November 1876, Bliss sang at a meeting that Moody held in Chicago. It was for church leaders, and 1,000 ministers attended. After the meeting, he and his wife took the train back to spend Christmas with his mother at Towanda, Pennsylvania.

His mother could be pleased with the progress of her barefoot boy. Bliss was 38 years old, and after 12 years of writing songs, he had risen to the top of his craft. Already people were speaking of Bliss as the American Charles Wesley.

On December 29, 1876, Philip and Lucy boarded the Pacific Express train back to Chicago. The two engines pulled 11 passenger cars and luggage coaches through a blinding snowstorm. Outside of Ashtabula, Ohio, the engines passed over a trestle weakened by floodwaters. The first engine reached the other side, but the second engine and all of the passenger cars plummeted 75 feet into the ravine. The wooden coaches shattered. Philip survived the crash and crawled to safety. Five minutes after the crash, the engine set the wooden coaches afire.

Philip realized Lucy had not made it out of the wreckage. He crawled back inside and found her pinned by one of the metal seats. He would not give up as the flames forced other rescuers out. He and Lucy died together.

The tragedy shocked the entire nation. More than 12,000 people attended the service in his memory in Chicago. Music publishers set aside the royalties from his songs as a trust fund for his two daughters.

Bliss's luggage reached Chicago. Inside were some of his un-published songs. One was "I Will Sing of My Redeemer." The next year, 1877, James McGranahan set it to music. That same year Thomas Edison invented the phonograph and recorded "I Will Sing of My Redeemer" to demonstrate his invention.

Some songs were unfinished. One is believed to have been the last words he had written. It began, "I know not what awaits me. God kindly veils my eyes. . . ."

JOHN WILLIAM STRUTT (LORD RAYLEIGH)

1842–1919

BRITISH PHYSICIST

MAJOR ACCOMPLISHMENT: RECEIVED NOBEL PRIZE
FOR HIS DISCOVERY WITH JOHN RAMSAY OF THE
INERT GAS ARGON

JOHN WILLIAM STRUTT IS BETTER KNOWN by his title Lord Rayleigh. He did not enjoy good health as a child. After being tutored at home, he entered Eton at age ten, but spent most of the time in the school dispensary. His early education came under a private tutor and ordained minister, George Townsend Warner. His parents and his tutor gave him a firm grounding in the Christian faith.

When Rayleigh entered Trinity College at Cambridge, England, he was behind the other students. However, by the time he graduated, he earned first place in the mathematics competition. Upon graduation, he received a teaching fellowship at Trinity and held the position until 1871.

He excelled as a teacher because of his ability to explain difficult subjects so that average people could understand. The electromagnetic theory of James Clerk Maxwell was taken more seriously because Rayleigh explained it clearly and simply. Later, he contributed science articles to the *Encyclopaedia Britannica*.

Lord Rayleigh lived a quiet and unassuming Christian life. Those who met the serious young man were not aware he was from an aristocratic family.

In 1871, he resigned from Trinity College to marry Evelyn Balfour. She was intelligent, wealthy, and from a powerful family. Her brother was a force in English politics. He would later be British prime minister.

Rayleigh was stricken with rheumatic fever shortly after his marriage to Evelyn. He turned the distressing time into an enjoyable holiday. The couple traveled to Egypt and took a houseboat journey on the Nile. While on the extended vacation, he began a study of sound vibrations that resulted in his breakthrough book, *The Theory of Sound*.

He returned to England when his father died. In addition to the title of Lord Rayleigh, he inherited an estate of 7,000 acres. Dozens of tenant families depended upon the farm for their livelihoods. Although Rayleigh wanted a career in science, he felt an obligation to the tenants. He dedicated himself to improving the estate. By applying the latest knowledge of agriculture, it became a model farm. After three years, he left management in the hands of his younger brother.

In his study of sound, Rayleigh investigated the property of resonance. If sound waves of the correct wavelength strike a tuning fork, the tuning fork begins vibrating. This understanding of how waves work provided him the clue to explain why the sky was blue.

No scientist had found a suitable explanation of why the sky was blue. Rayleigh showed that if light waves struck a particle of a suitable size in the atmosphere, the particle first absorbed the energy and then emitted it in all directions at the same wavelength. Although referred to as scattering, the process was much more complex than merely reflection of the light from an uneven surface.

Rayleigh developed the formula to predict the amount of scattering. It depended on the wavelength and size of the particles. Atoms and molecules of the atmosphere scattered the shorter wavelength of blue light ten times as much as red. Blue light came from all directions in the sky, while red passed through unaffected. Sunsets were red but the sky was blue.

In 1891, Rayleigh measured the density of various gases. He prepared nitrogen gas in two different ways — by releasing nitrogen from nitrogen compounds and by extracting it from the atmosphere. According to Rayleigh's sensitive measurements, identical volumes of nitrogen gas from the air weighed more than the nitrogen gas liberated from nitrogen compounds. The two samples should have been identical.

One by one, Rayleigh eliminated every possible explanation for the discrepancy. Finally, he concluded that the sample from the air contained a heavier gas mixed in with the nitrogen. However, despite his considerable skill, he could not separate the mystery gas from the sample.

He wrote a letter to the scientific magazine *Nature* and frankly asked for help. A year later William Ramsay, a young Scottish chemist, asked to tackle the problem. Ramsay and Rayleigh worked together although they were miles apart in different laboratories. The new technology of the telephone made it possible. For the first time, two scientists collaborated by long distance.

Ramsay passed the nitrogen gas over red-hot magnesium. The nitrogen reacted with the metal and was removed from the sample. He was left with a small bubble of gas. Nitrogen was itself the least active gas known at that time. Yet, the mystery gas was far less reactive than nitrogen.

In 1894, Rayleigh and Ramsay announced that they had found a new element that made up about one percent of the atmosphere. Chemists were astonished that the gas had been so long unobserved. Gases in the atmosphere in far less concentrations had been detected — ozone, carbon dioxide, sulfur dioxide, and water vapor. It was as if chemists had found a flea on a dog but missed seeing the dog entirely.

Rayleigh and Ramsay named the gas argon, from a Greek word for "inert." In 1904, Rayleigh was awarded the Nobel Prize for physics for his work in studying the density of gases and for the discovery of argon. Ramsay received the award in chemistry in the same year.

Rayleigh donated the cash reward that accompanied the prize to the University of Cambridge. Later, he became chancellor of the university. Lord Rayleigh displayed a personal charm and a generous nature. His home became a gathering place for scientists from all over the world. He was recognized as the leader of science in the British Empire and was elected president of the Royal Society in 1905.

In the introduction to his collection of scientific papers, he quoted from the Bible: "The works of the Lord are great, sought out of all them that have pleasure therein" (Ps. 111:2).

WILLIAM MCKINLEY
1843–1901
TWENTY-FIFTH PRESIDENT OF THE UNITED STATES
MAJOR ACCOMPLISHMENT: RESTORED UNITED STATES
PROSPERITY AND HELPED MAKE THE UNITED
STATES A WORLD POWER

WILLIAM MCKINLEY WAS BORN IN Niles, Ohio, where his father worked in a pig-iron foundry. His parents were Puritans. His mother was from Scotland and deeply religious. She taught McKinley the importance of living a righteous life. His mother moved to Poland, Ohio (near Youngstown), so he could attend a private academy. She hoped he would be a minister when he grew up. He worked in a post office and taught school to pay for his education.

He was 18 when the Civil War started. McKinley saw action in the fierce battle at Antietam, where 120,000 men fought. McKinley escaped without a scratch, although several horses were shot out from under him. Following a particularly heroic effort to get supplies to exhausted troops, Col. Rutherford B. Hayes made him an assistant on his staff. Later, Hayes became president and encouraged McKinley's political career. He described McKinley as "one of the bravest and finest officers in the army."

McKinley cast his first vote for president on a Shenandoah Valley battlefield where a military ambulance had been converted into a voting booth.

After the Civil War, McKinley became a lawyer in Canton, Ohio. The young lawyer was still a simple country boy. At one reception, he was served a dessert of what he thought was custard. He mentioned to another guest that it had unfortunately become frozen. The guest explained that it was ice cream. He had never tasted ice cream.

McKinley attended a large church in Canton, and became the Sunday school superintendent. He loved children and spoke to them about the love of God. He taught the children his favorite songs, "Nearer, My God to Thee" and "Jesus, Lover of My Soul."

William McKinley married Ida Saxton, the daughter of a banker. Both William and Ida loved children, and they were filled with joy at the birth of a daughter. The daughter died after four months. Later, a second daughter lived for four years, but succumbed to typhoid fever. Ida was devastated by the loss and never fully recovered.

In 1876, McKinley was elected to the U.S. House of Representatives. While a representative, McKinley pushed high tariffs to protect domestic manufacturers, an idea that Lincoln had supported.

During 1893 the country was plunged into a depression. In 1894, McKinley averaged more than a speech a day in support of Republican candidates. Because of his work for the party, the Republicans nominated him as their candidate for president.

The Democrat candidate was 36-year-old William Jennings Bryan, one of the best orators the country had ever heard. He was noted for his "cross of gold" speech against keeping the gold standard.

McKinley was an effective speaker, too. He had a powerful baritone voice and delivered his speeches with a musical cadence. McKinley's wife Ida had a relapse and was bedridden. McKinley believed in the importance of family and caring for one another. He made the decision to sit out the campaign to stay in Canton with his wife.

He did speak, but only from the front porch of his home. Railroads ran trains at reduced fares to bring visitors to hear him. He won the presidency with an electoral vote of 271 to 176. The Chicago *Times-Herald* called for an interview, but he was not available because he was in prayer with his wife and mother.

William McKinley used as his guide for public service the quotation from Micah 6:8, ". . . what doth the LORD require of thee, but to do justly, and to love mercy, and to walk humbly with thy God?" In Washington, he attended church and joined quietly in the services. He prayed over major decisions and sought the prayers of others.

He said, "My belief embraces the divinity of Christ and a recognition of Christianity as the mightiest factor in the world's civilization."

By 1897 his positive outlook had restored the nation's confidence and the hard times caused by the Panic of '93 were replaced by prosperity. He slowly began ending the isolation of the United States. He negotiated trade agreements with other countries to lower tariffs when the countries competed equally.

McKinley's greatest challenge was what to do about Cuba, which was seeking to eliminate Spanish rule. Spanish troops put down a rebellion and sent thousands to confinement camps. The American public sided with the Cubans. A frenzy of newspaper reporting inflamed public sentiment for American intervention.

On February 15, 1898, the American battleship *Maine* exploded under mysterious circumstances in Havana harbor. Congress declared war on Spain. The war ended in less than four months with a stunning United States victory over Spain, a country that had been a world power for more than 500 years.

McKinley had the difficult task of deciding what to do with Cuba, Puerto Rico, Guam, and the Philippines. He had entered office saying, "We want no wars of conquest. We must avoid the temptation of territorial aggression." In the end, he decided that the islands would not survive without United States protection. They became American territories.

In the election of 1900, McKinley ran against Bryan again and easily won re-election. In four years he had made the United States a recognized world military power. Now he wanted to make it an economic power. McKinley understood the importance of foreign trade. In 1901 the Pan-American Exposition was held in Buffalo, New York. Its purpose was to encourage unity and commerce among the countries of North and South America. McKinley spoke at the exposition to show his support for the purpose of the fair.

After the speech, McKinley greeted visitors. A man in the receiving line thrust out what appeared to be a bandaged hand. The man carried a concealed gun and fired twice. The first bullet struck McKinley in the ribs. The second bullet hit his stomach. Leon Czolgosz, the shooter, was an anarchist who hated authority.

As the crowd began to beat Czolgosz, McKinley ordered his bodyguards, "Don't let them hurt him." He then was helped to a chair where he warned a friend to be careful how he broke the news to his wife, Ida. Then he whispered to the exposition director his regrets that the shooting had marred the trade show.

The wounds did not kill him, and he would have lived had it not been for infection. Once gangrene set in, his doctors and McKinley himself knew that hope was gone. "It is useless, gentlemen," he said. "I think we should have prayer." He survived for eight days. He whispered, "Goodbye, all, goodbye. It is God's will. His will, not ours, be done."

The whole nation mourned. Churches opened their doors to pray and to sing his favorite song, "Nearer, My God to Thee."

ARCHIBALD H. SAYCE

1845–1933

BRITISH LANGUAGE SCHOLAR

MAJOR ACCOMPLISHMENT: WROTE THE FIRST ASSYRIAN

GRAMMAR

DURING HIS LIFE, SAYCE LEARNED about 20 ancient and modern languages. He could translate directly from one to another without going through English as an intermediate step. He became the foremost expert on the Assyrian language. The Assyrian influence was vast in the ancient world. When Sayce found a reference in an untranslated language, he would search the Assyrian records for the same event. Although not reported in identical ways, knowing that two different scripts referred to the same event helped in the translation.

One of the languages he tackled was the Hittite language. The Hittites were mentioned extensively in the Bible. Abraham had dealings with them, Esau married a Hittite woman, and Bathsheba was the wife of a Hittite. The Hittites were among the first to smelt iron. They had a military advantage because their iron weapons were harder than the bronze weapons of their neighbors. However, their culture collapsed about 1200 B.C. Historically, very little was known about them outside the Bible.

The Hittites spoke the Anatolian language. Sayce found inscriptions in the language on monuments, short sayings on helmets and shields, and cuneiform tablets relating business transactions. He also found an Assyrian and Anatolian inscription that appeared to tell about the same event. Because of his knowledge of Assyrian, Sayce was the first scholar to make progress in deciphering the Hittite language.

For 28 years, starting in 1891, he was professor of Assyrian studies at Oxford University in England. However, he suffered from tuberculosis and recurring bouts with pneumonia. At every opportunity, he escaped the cold, damp climate of England for the dry, desert climate of Egypt. He outfitted a barge on the Nile as his home, and stocked it with an extensive library.

Sayce had been ordained at age 25. His Bible studies had been based on what was known as higher criticism. According to higher criticism, historical and archaeological evidence showed that biblical accounts could not be literally true. Yet, higher criticism was first proposed in the early 1800s when historical information was severely lacking.

As Sayce uncovered the historical context, the archaeological evidence showed that individuals and kingdoms mentioned in the Bible had existed. Sayce grew in his Christian beliefs and wrote extensively about history and the Bible. One of his books in this area was *The Early History of the Hebrews*. By the start of the 1900s, he had helped discredit the books of higher criticism written decades earlier. He wrote *The Higher Criticism and the Verdict of the Monuments*.

He influenced three generations of archaeologists. Archibald Sayce was noted for his warm character. He corresponded extensively and gave the same good-natured reply to his harshest critics as to beginning archaeology students.

JOHN AMBROSE FLEMING
1849–1945
BRITISH ELECTRICAL ENGINEER

MAJOR ACCOMPLISHMENT: INVENTED THE FIRST
VACUUM TUBE THAT USHERED IN THE ELECTRONICS
AGE

JOHN AMBROSE FLEMING, THE SON of a minister, attended Cambridge University. While at Cambridge, he worked for James Clerk Maxwell in the Cavendish Laboratories. Maxwell had predicted the existence of radio waves. In 1885, Rudolf Hertz produced and detected them. That same year, Fleming accepted the newly created position of professor of electrical engineering at University College in London.

Hertz's radio equipment could only send an on or off signal across the room. Ambrose Fleming worked with Gugielmo Marconi to develop a practical wireless telegraph that communicated over long distances with the Morse code. To test his invention, Gugielmo Marconi set up a receiver in St. Johns, Newfoundland. Fleming operated the transmitter in Cornwall, England. In 1901, Fleming sent the first wireless signal across the Atlantic. He keyed in the dot-dot-dot of the letter s that Marconi detected in Newfoundland.

The electrical devices in common use at that time were the telegraph, telephone, and electric light. Fleming served as a consultant for Edison's Electric Light Company. In one of Thomas Edison's experiments, he put a cool wire near a white-hot filament. The wire, which was not connected to a battery, received a slight electric current from the filament. Electrons boiled away from the filament and jumped across the gap to the cool wire. Edison saw no particular application for this, but did report it in a technical journal. It became known as the Edison effect.

Fleming replaced the wire with a small metal disc. He gave the metal plate a positive charge to increase the attraction of electrons from the hot filament. It was a one-way trip — electrons traveled from the hot wire to the plate but not the other way. The device filtered out the backward flow of an alternating current, such as a

radio signal. It detected radio waves and converted them to weak direct current that could be played through a radio headset.

In 1905, Fleming patented his invention. It became known in the British Isles as a Fleming valve and in the United States as a diode. Fleming's diode was the first electronic vacuum tube. The American inventor Lee De Forest made a simple modification that changed it into an amplifier of radio waves. Human speech and music could be carried by radio waves. On Christmas Eve 1906, an experimental radio station in Boston transmitted the song "O Holy Night" followed by a Bible reading.

Fleming wrote more than a hundred scientific publications including *The Principles of Electric Wave Telegraphy*. He continued to develop useful applications of electricity. He designed electrical systems for lighting ships and for heating. Knighted in 1926, he is generally considered the founder of modern electronics.

John Ambrose Fleming died in 1945 at the age of 95. He lived to see vacuum tubes become the key invention of the electronic age. He was an active Christian who opposed evolution and wrote a book defending the biblical account of creation.

CHARLES M. SHELDON
1857–1946
AMERICAN MINISTER AND INSPIRATIONAL WRITER
MAJOR ACCOMPLISHMENT: AUTHOR OF *IN HIS STEPS*

CHARLES SHELDON WAS BORN in New York, but grew up in the Dakota Territory where his father had been sent to establish churches. Sheldon was educated at Andover Theological Seminary in Maine. After graduation, he worked as an editor on a Christian publication and served as a minister at Waterbury, Vermont.

As a young pastor, Sheldon often found himself being chastised by the leaders of the congregation. They objected to his campaign against the practice of renting pew seats to members. They found fault with him because during one bitterly cold day, he kept his hat on during a graveside funeral service. They didn't like it when he exercised by playing tennis with a group of lawyers. In addition, he took Mary Abby Merriam, a single woman of marrying age, on a buggy ride.

Everet Merriam, the young woman's father, approved of Charles Sheldon as a possible husband for his daughter. However, nothing developed because the Merriam family moved to Topeka, Kansas. The Central Congregational Church in Topeka, Kansas needed a preacher. Everet suggested Charles Sheldon to the congregation. Sheldon came for a visit, delivered a sermon, and was invited to fill the post.

Everet Merriam suggested that Sheldon stay in their large house, a move that put Charles Sheldon and Mary (called May) Merriam in daily contact with one another. The arrangement ended when Sheldon's parents relocated to Topeka. He moved in with them.

Topeka in 1889 was experiencing change and an economic slump. Sheldon felt he needed to understand better the problems that people faced in Topeka. He made a list of the different segments of the community. Each week he concentrated on a different group of people. The first week he rode the streetcar and talked to workers. He spent a week on the campus of the local college and attended sports events. He worked at the *Topeka Daily Capital* as an unpaid reporter. He visited the hospital and accompanied doctors on their rounds. He researched court cases as an assistant to a lawyer. He visited the segregated African American section in Topeka.

In one experiment, he dressed in shabby clothes and tried to find work. He walked the streets for three days, stopping at shoe stores, restaurants, and hotels. No work was to be had. He became immersed in his role as an unemployed man. He became so desperate he volunteered to shovel coal at the Santa Fe rail yard for no pay. The next day he was hired for half a day and earned 50 cents.

In another experiment, he and a friend who was African American ate at cafes and restaurants in town. Sometimes they would enter together, and other times the black man would go in first. In all cases, they received service without question. However, when they tried to enter the YMCA, the black man was denied access because of his color.

Sheldon's sermons encouraged people to take their Sunday Christianity and put it into action every day of the week. He believed Christians had a responsibility to serve the poor and disadvantaged. Although his sermons grew out of the social gospel movement, he presented his case so convincingly that the sermons found a ready acceptance.

After two years of sporadic courtship, May Merriam and Charles Sheldon were married on May 20, 1891. Sheldon never thought about money. May learned to empty his pockets so that he left home with only enough cash for the day's activities. Otherwise, he would give a needy person all that he had.

The Sunday evening worship services were poorly attended. Sheldon's father, also a preacher, suggested he drop the evening worship entirely. Instead, Sheldon decided that people were bored with the preaching. He resolved not to preach, but instead read an interesting story that he wrote himself.

Each week he read a chapter, and within three weeks, the Sunday evening service attendance matched that on Sunday morning. For 28 years, starting in 1891, he read on Sunday evening from a story that he wrote. In all, he wrote 30 novels.

In 1896, he began reading *In His Steps*, a fictional story about a pastor named Henry Maxwell. The book was based on Sheldon's weeks of working at various places in Topeka. Henry Maxwell was a thinly disguised version of Charles Sheldon himself.

In the story, the pastor of the fashionable First Church of Raymond challenged his congregation not to do anything without first asking, "What would Jesus do?" The book then followed the effect that question had upon different individuals. Characters included a newspaper editor and a young woman who was a talented singer.

A few weeks into the reading of *In His Steps*, Sheldon received a letter from The *Advance*, a weekly Chicago publication. The publication offered $25.00 to serialize the story for its 21,000 readers. The *Advance* had published two of his other books, and he had donated the stories without payment. *In His Steps* had been rejected by two book publishers. He was happy for the magazine to publish the manuscript.

In His Steps became Sheldon's best-known book and a worldwide best seller. However, The *Advance* failed to meet the conditions to secure a proper copyright, and the book fell into public domain. About 65 unauthorized editions were published. A single publisher in London sold three million copies.

Wealth was not one of Sheldon's goals, and he did not regret the loss of the copyright. It did make him the best-known clergyman in the world. People assumed that such a successful author must be fabulously wealthy as well. They wrote heartbreaking stories asking for aid that he could not provide.

The connection between the character (Maxwell) and the creator (Sheldon) became even more blurred in March 1900. The publisher of the *Topeka Daily Capital* offered Sheldon the opportunity for one week to publish the newspaper as he believed Jesus would. The newspaper had a circulation of 10,000. However, because of the publicity of the project, it was reprinted in New York, Chicago, and London. The circulation jumped to 360,000.

Sheldon was a prohibitionist, so he purged the paper of alcohol advertisements. In the sports section he refused to cover prize fights, and reduced the society page's coverage to those events that helped ordinary citizens.

Periodically Sheldon's phrase "What would Jesus do" was revived and became popular. In the 1990s, it made its appearance as a bracelet and other products with the abbreviation WWJD. Often, people were unaware of its origin. Although Sheldon did not make any money from the pirated copies of *In His Steps*, he wrote hundreds of other items including several successful books. Charles Sheldon died at age 89 in 1946.

WILLIAM (BILLY) SUNDAY
1862–1935
AMERICAN EVANGELIST
MAJOR ACCOMPLISHMENT: PREACHED TO ABOUT
100,000,000 PEOPLE

BILLY SUNDAY WAS BORN in 1862. He never saw his father, who disappeared into the smoke of the Civil War. His mother tried to raise her three sons in a log cabin in Ames, Iowa. When he was 12, he was sent to an orphanage for two years. He toiled at a variety of jobs as a teenager, including working as a janitor in a hotel and as an assistant undertaker. His formal education ended with his high school graduation.

At age 21, he became a professional baseball player for the Chicago White Sox. He played in the major leagues for seven years. In 1886, Billy Sunday responded to a street preacher from Chicago's Pacific Garden Mission. Shortly after becoming a Christian, Billy Sunday met Helen Thompson. She was 18. Two years later they were married. Although he had the respect of the players and fans, he found it difficult to continue as a ballplayer, especially since he refused to play on Sunday. A year after his marriage, he resigned from baseball. He began his full-time Christian work with the YMCA. After helping other traveling evangelists, he began his own revival ministry in 1896.

Billy and Helen had four children. Helen took the lead in raising their children while Billy Sunday was on the road. After their children were grown, Helen traveled with him and did much of the planning for his evangelistic campaigns. The ten years from the time she joined him in 1907 until 1917 were the most effective of his 40-year career.

Billy Sunday built temporary wooden structures for his campaigns. Sawdust covered the floor. One of his phrases was "hitting the sawdust trail" to encourage believers to respond to the gospel and dedicate their lives to Christ.

A mainstay of his campaign was an attack on liquor. Brewers, distillers, and saloon owners felt the aftermath of his campaigns —

citizens often voted to make their county "dry." Billy Sunday himself had struggled with alcohol before he became a Christian. He spoke ardently to ban liquor sales. He said, "Whiskey is all right in its place — but its place is hell."

His New York campaign in 1917 was the peak of his career. It was the catalyst for the final push for prohibition. Two years later, the 18th amendment outlawing the sale and distribution of alcohol was added to the Constitution. Most people obeyed the ban and alcohol consumption was cut by more than one-half until prohibition was repealed in 1933.

Billy Sunday confined his preaching entirely within the United States. He preached to about one hundred million people. A substantial percentage of the population of the country heard him in person. Billy Sunday's career declined after 1917, in part because of the distraction of World War I and in part by the changing nature of the country from rural to urban.

He continued to preach until his death. One of his best-known statements is often quoted (sometimes without credit.) He said, "I'm against sin. I'll kick it as long as I've got a foot, and I'll fight it as long as I've got a fist. I'll butt it as long as I've got a head. I'll bite it as long as I've got a tooth. And when I'm old and fistless and footless and toothless, I'll gum it till I go home to Glory and it goes home to perdition!"

GEORGE WASHINGTON CARVER

1864–1943

AMERICAN AGRICULTURAL CHEMIST

MAJOR ACCOMPLISHMENT: DEVELOPED COMMERCIAL
PRODUCTS FROM PEANUTS AND SWEET POTATOES

GEORGE WASHINGTON CARVER WAS the son of a slave woman. He was born during the dark days of the Civil War. Shortly after his birth, bandits kidnapped him and his mother. A Union scout rescued George, but his mother, Mary, vanished, never to be seen again. George himself was near death. His future could not have appeared more dismal — born into slavery, a black orphan being raised by a poor family, seriously ill, and his life unsettled by the fighting of the Civil War.

Moses and Susan Carver raised George as their own and gave him their last name. Young Carver developed a strong desire to learn more about God's creation. Later in life he explained, "I love to think of nature as an unlimited broadcasting system through which God speaks to us every hour, if we will only tune in."

He chose a life's work that would help others. "It is service to others that measures success," he said. Poor farmers needed his help the most. Many lived on small 40-acre plots of worn-out land. Those who planted the same crop year after year robbed the soil of its minerals.

He spoke to the farmers in his polite but compelling way. "Rotate your crops," he explained. "Grow cotton one year, then peanuts or sweet potatoes the next year. They restore nitrogen to the soil." Farmers at the mercy of exhausted land put his suggestions into practice. They succeeded almost too well. Prices for peanuts and sweet potatoes fell because they were so plentiful.

Carver found new uses for the produce. From peanuts, he developed 300 products including everything from dyes and soap to milk and cheese substitutes. From sweet potatoes, he developed more than a hundred new products, such as molasses and rubber.

He gave God the credit. "Most of the things I do are just cooking," he said. "These are not my products. God put them here and I found them." In his unassuming way, he described himself as merely a "cookstove chemist."

When George Washington Carver died in 1943, his passing was noted by the president of the United States and by the great Albert Einstein. Both spoke about his dedication and service to common people.

A few years later the United States opened the Carver farm, near Diamond, Missouri, as a National Monument. Many of George Washington Carver's prized possessions are on display, including a Bible, well worn from years of reading and study.

Throughout his life, Carver had a profound religious faith, one to which he attributed his successes. He often quoted from a poem by Edgar A. Guest: "God has equipped you for life, but He lets you decide what you want to be."

ROBERT A. MILLIKAN
1868–1953
AMERICAN PHYSICIST

MAJOR ACCOMPLISHMENT: RECEIVED NOBEL PRIZE
FOR MEASURING ELECTRICAL CHARGE OF AN
ELECTRON

ROBERT A. MILLIKAN ATTENDED elementary school in the tiny village of Maquoketa, Iowa. His father was a minister of the gospel at the local church. Robert had to work hard to succeed at his schoolwork. He was a slow learner. He despaired of earning good grades. His *McGuffey's Reader* taught, "If you find your task hard, then try, try again. Time will bring you your reward."

Robert Millikan took the advice to heart. Every lesson received his best efforts. After high school graduation, he attended Oberlin College. He took his first science course, one on physics. The textbook was a head-scratching puzzlement. His instructor had not been trained in science. Despite Robert's persistent efforts, the course was a complete loss.

When he graduated, the college asked him to continue as the science teacher. Although Robert had his doubts, he agreed to the assignment. He spent the entire summer preparing to teach. Unknown to Robert, school officials had written letters recommending him to Columbia University in New York City. Looking at his high scores, officials at Columbia thought he must be a special genius.

Columbia University offered him a scholarship, which he accepted. Robert was the only physics student at Columbia. After his first year, school officials saw that he was not a brilliant genius, but merely an ordinary student who tried hard. They took away his scholarship to divert the money to bright students who majored in more important subjects than science.

Disappointed, Millikan returned to the Midwest. He took summer science courses at the University of Chicago. In 1895 he went to Europe to study science. He attended lectures by Max Planck in Berlin, but the mathematics was far too difficult for him to comprehend.

On Christmas Eve,1895, the Berlin physics professors and students met Wilhelm Röntgen from Würzburg. Röntgen displayed the first x-ray photographs. They showed keys and coins photographed through a leather wallet. A few months later, French scientist Becquerel discovered the strange rays coming from uranium. The discoveries by Röntgen and Becquerel created a sensation in physics.

Robert Millikan had the unexpected good fortune to be in Europe at the start of the second scientific revolution. (The first scientific revolution dated from the early 1600s with the discoveries of Galileo and Kepler.) While in Europe, Robert received a telegraph offering him a position at the University of Chicago. Robert eagerly accepted, although his teaching load was too great for research.

After ten years, Robert made time in his busy schedule for research. He selected as his goal to measure the charge of the electron. J.J. Thomson, in England, had discovered the electrically charged subatomic particle in 1897. Thomson named it an electron because of its role in producing electricity. Like the speed of light, the charge of the electron figured in many equations of science.

J.J. Thomson had tried to measure the charge of a single electron but never succeeded.

Millikan built his own apparatus to time the fall of an oil drop that had been given an electric charge. He then turned on an electrical field and measured the change in velocity. The apparatus he designed was extremely sensitive. Once, as he watched, the drop suddenly changed speed. It had gained an electron.

Millikan applied the law of viscosity (developed decades earlier by George Gabriel Stokes) for measuring the resistance of air to the falling drop of oil. Millikan did not arrive at an answer he trusted for three years. Then, he spent another three years to double-check his conclusion.

In 1912, after six years of experiments, Millikan announced his discovery. The scientific world was stunned. Here was a 44-year-old scientist with no other achievements in physics. Yet, his oil drop experiment proved him a scientist of the first order. Robert Millikan's oil drop experiment became a classic. Most physics laboratory classes used it as an example of a well-designed experiment. It was simple to understand and easily repeated.

Robert returned to Chicago and took up other problems. He experimentally confirmed Einstein's equation for the photoelectric effect, the observation that the speed of an electron released from a metal depends on the color of the light but not its brightness. Millikan also measured another fundamental quantity of physics, known as Planck's constant, named for Max Planck. The constant related the energy of a discrete bundle of light, called a photon, to its frequency (color).

Max Planck won the Nobel Prize in physics in 1918, and Albert Einstein won in 1922. Millikan had given their work a scientific footing.

In 1921, Millikan moved to the California Institute of Technology where he tackled the problem of a mysterious background radiation detected all over the earth, but whose source could not be identified. He proved that the rays came from outer space. He coined the term for them — cosmic rays.

Millikan received the 1923 Nobel Prize in physics.

Like so many other scientists, he could not look at nature without seeing intelligent design. He said, "The atheist is irrational and unscientific because he asserts that there is nothing behind or inherent in all the phenomena of nature except blind force."

Some newspapers were surprised at his outspoken religious views. He explained that science and religion should work together to make the world a better place. He said, "Why is it that all the world is still willing to say of Jesus, 'Never man spake like this man?' Is it not because He literally spake two thousand years ago the words of everlasting life — the words of rich, full abundant, satisfying, unselfish living for all times and all places."

He spoke to numerous groups on the role of science and religion in the modern world and wrote books on the subject. At a lecture at Yale University in 1928, he said, "The prophet Micah said 2,500 years ago, 'What doth the Lord require of thee but to do justice, to love mercy, and to walk humbly with thy God?' Modern science, of the real sort, is slowly learning to walk humbly with its God, and in learning that lesson it is contributing something to religion."

OSWALD CHAMBERS
1874–1917
SCOTTISH MINISTER
MAJOR ACCOMPLISHMENT: WRITER OF THE
DEVOTIONAL BOOK *MY UTMOST FOR HIS HIGHEST*

OSWALD CHAMBERS GREW UP in Scotland and attended the University of Edinburgh. Although he had become a Christian while a teenager, he studied art and archaeology at the university. After graduation, however, he felt a call from God to the Christian ministry.

He began as a teacher at a small theological college in Dunoon. It was located in western Scotland, on the northwestern shore of the Firth of Clyde. However, Chambers wanted to be a full-time preacher. He became a traveling preacher in the British Isles. In 1908, he began a tour to the United States and then to Japan.

While aboard the ship to America, he became acquainted with a young woman named Gertrude Hobbs. He learned that she had left school early because of sickness and to help her mother at home. She studied Pitman shorthand and became a stenographer.

They parted company when the ship docked but wrote to each other. Two years after the shipboard meeting, Oswald and Gertrude married. They felt their special calling was to run a Bible college. They began by offering correspondence classes. Before the year was out, they moved into a large house with room for students. They founded the Bible Training College in Clapham, London.

In June of 1914, Austrian Archduke Ferdinand and his wife, Sophie, were shot dead while visiting Sarajevo, the capital of Bosnia. Austria, delivered an ultimatum to Serbia, and soon the two countries were at war. It was a time of intense nationalism, and one country after another took sides. The conflict erupted into the Great War (World War I) and involved 32 countries.

The disruptions caused by World War I left Oswald and Gertrude without students. They had to close the school. The YMCA offered Oswald a post as chaplain to British troops in Zeitoun, Egypt. He arrived in Egypt in October 1915, and his wife and their two-year-old daughter, Kathleen, joined him by Christmas.

Oswald Chambers

They had only two more years together. In 1917, Oswald Chambers died from complications following an operation for a ruptured appendix. His wife sent the news home by telegram: "Oswald, in His presence."

At the time of his death, Oswald had written but one book, *Baffled to Fight Better.* Mrs. Chambers returned to London. During their seven years together, she had taken shorthand notes of his messages. She combined her notes with his journals, sermons, lectures, letters, and poems. She began Oswald Chambers Publishing, and over the next 50 years, she compiled 30 published books that bear her husband's name.

My Utmost For His Highest is Oswald Chambers best-known book. It first appeared in small pamphlets that his wife circulated. The book was printed in Britain in 1923 and in the United States in 1935. Since then, it has remained one of the top ten most popular titles and the most popular devotion book of all time. It contains 366 Scripture-based devotions — one for each day of the year including leap day.

WILLIAM FOXWELL ALBRIGHT

1891–1971

Aᴍᴇʀɪᴄᴀɴ ᴀʀᴄʜᴀᴇᴏʟᴏɢɪꜱᴛ

Mᴀᴊᴏʀ ᴀᴄᴄᴏᴍᴘʟɪꜱʜᴍᴇɴᴛ: ɪᴅᴇɴᴛɪꜰɪᴇᴅ ʟᴏꜱᴛ ʙɪʙʟɪᴄᴀʟ
    ᴠɪʟʟᴀɢᴇꜱ

WILLIAM FOXWELL ALBRIGHT WAS born in Chile, where his parents were missionaries. He returned to the United States for his education when he was 12 years old. In 1916, he received a Ph.D. in archaeology at Johns Hopkins University. He also learned ancient Arabic, Hebrew, and Aramaic, as well as the modern languages spoken in the Middle East.

Albright developed an extensive range of skills in languages, classical scholarship, and archaeological techniques. From his base at the American School of Oriental Research in Jerusalem, he headed expeditions in Palestine, southern Arabia, and other areas in the Bible lands. Albright became adept at using pottery to identify ancient civilizations and to date when the civilization flourished.

He believed that a better understanding of ancient cultures would help in understanding the Bible. He noticed that most scientists assumed the Bible could not be trusted to guide them to lost Bible villages. The more he learned about the Bible and the history of an area, the more he realized that the history and the Bible converged.

He said, "The excessive skepticism toward the Bible by important historical schools of the eighteenth and nineteenth centuries, certain phases of which still appear periodically, has been progressively discredited. Discovery after discovery has established the accuracy of innumerable details, and has brought increased recognition to the value of the Bible as a source of history."

Because of his reputation, scientists often called upon him to settle debates about whether an artifact was misidentified. Albright became known as "the great authenticator."

In 1947, two shepherd boys discovered leather and papyrus scrolls in a cave in Qumrun, Jordan, near the Dead Sea. Although an interesting find, archaeologists did not attach much importance to the writing. They thought the material was about the same age as other manuscripts.

Albright, who was teaching at Johns Hopkins in Baltimore, Maryland, received two small photographs of the fragments. Albright examined the photographs with a magnifier. He recognized the text as from Isaiah. More importantly, he recognized the script as an ancient one and grew excited. He wrote back to Jerusalem that the date for the manuscripts was about 100 B.C. — 1,000 years older than any other Hebrew texts.

Scholars in Jerusalem had the actual Dead Sea Scrolls at their disposal, as well as the clay jars and other material to examine firsthand. The scholars had arrived at a tentative date much more recent than Albright's. They frantically searched for additional hidden manuscripts and took great care to preserve them. Over the next 12 years, additional clues such as coins, references in the manuscripts, and carbon-14 dating showed that Albright was entirely correct.

Albright published 800 manuscripts, including the books *The Archaeology of Palestine*, *Stone Age to Christianity*, and *The Bible and the Ancient Near East*. In his book *The Archaeology of Palestine*, Albright says, "Biblical historical data are accurate to an extent far surpassing the ideas of any modern critical students, who have consistently tended to err on the side of hypercriticism."

Albright retired from teaching at Johns Hopkins in 1959, after a teaching career of almost 30 years. He is considered one of the most successful archaeologists of the 1900s. His influence is still felt through the students he trained.

CORRIE TEN BOOM

1892–1983

DUTCH INSPIRATIONAL SPEAKER AND WRITER (IN LATER
LIFE)

MAJOR ACCOMPLISHMENT: SPOKE FOR RECONCILIATION
AND SPIRITUAL REHABILITATION AFTER WORLD
WAR II

CORNELIA TEN BOOM LIVED AN active Christian life in Holland.
Her father, Casper, was a watchmaker, and Corrie (as she was known)
became the first woman in Holland to qualify as a watchmaker. However, her vocation was as the supervisor of girls' clubs. The Chris-
tian-oriented clubs involved girls 12–18 years old in activities such
as gymnastics, music, hiking, and camping. Her efforts included
mentally handicapped young people. The clubs had members in
Holland and in Dutch Indonesia.

For 20 years Corrie filled her life with Christian service. She
was 52 years old when Germany suddenly and without provocation
invaded Holland. The country fell in less than a week. Her family
supported the underground resistance.

Because of her years of activity in the girls' clubs, Corrie had
extensive contacts with people she could trust. She was part of the
secret railroad helping Jewish people escape German persecution.
The ten Boom family lived in an old house. A hidden room behind a
swing-out bookcase was built upstairs in Corrie's bedroom. The fugi-
tives would escape to the room when the Nazi police arrived.

In February 1944, the entire ten Boom family was arrested for
their activities. The room was so well hidden that the Nazis could
not find the people hiding inside. Later, the people managed to reach
safety. The ten Booms, however, were not so fortunate.

Her father, Casper, was 84 years old. He died ten days after his
arrest. Corrie suffered from the flu and was held separate from the
rest for four months. The unheated cell had a bed of straw and one
blanket. Food was porridge in the morning and bread in the evening.
A nurse managed to smuggle in portions of the handwritten Scripture.

Corrie ten Boom

After Corrie recovered she was shipped to a labor camp to make radios for German aircraft. Corrie learned that her sister Betsie was in prison. She learned that her father had died, but the other members of the family had been released.

Prisoners at the work camp had a moment of hope when they heard explosions as the Germans blew up rail lines and bridges to stop advancing Allied troops. However, their happiness was short-lived. The men of the camp, 700 in all, were shot and the women were loaded into cattle cars and shipped to a concentration camp in Germany.

Each stage of her captivity had grown more desperate, and the Ravensbrook concentration camp could not have been more miserable. Prisoners who grew too weak to work were loaded on pushcarts and taken away. Later, gray smoke emitting from the tall chimneys above the gas chambers announced their fate. Corrie's sister did not survive the death camp.

One morning the guards summoned Corrie. When she reported, she was given a card that said "released" and a railway pass back to Holland. Later, she learned that a clerical error had released her. Other women her age had been consigned to the gas chamber.

Early in May 1945, Holland was liberated and by the end of the month Germany surrendered. Corrie had already decided what she wanted to do. She opened a large house to those who had suffered during the war. She knew that the aftermath of the war should be a time of healing and forgiveness. She worked toward that goal.

Many survivors of the prison camps could not function because of their bitterness. Her message of forgiveness brought about recovery so they could live again. She made the difficult decision to meet with the guards at the camp where her sister had died. She was invited to over 60 countries to speak, including Israel, where she was honored for her aid of Jewish people.

She wrote the book *The Hiding Place* that was made into a film of the same name and released in 1975. The title was taken from one of her father's favorite Bible verses during the time they worked with the resistance: "Thou art my hiding place and my shield: I hope in thy word" (Psalm 119:114). Two years after the release of the movie, Corrie settled in California. She died on her 91st birthday.

ARTHUR HOLLY COMPTON
1892–1962
AMERICAN PHYSICIST
MAJOR ACCOMPLISHMENT: RECEIVED THE 1927
NOBEL PRIZE IN PHYSICS FOR HIS STUDY OF X-RAYS

ARTHUR HOLLY COMPTON BEGAN college in 1910. The major achievements of the second scientific revolution during the ten years from 1885 to 1905 had made their way into college textbooks. It was an exciting time for scientists, although the nature of light still puzzled them. The wave theory of light explained every property of light except for the photoelectric effect that seemed to indicate light was made of particles.

Young Compton was a bright student with an inquisitive mind. Four years after the Wright brothers made their first flight, Compton began building model airplanes that flew. In high school, he designed a full-size glider that carried himself as pilot. He received a patent for one of his inventions to better control the airplane.

Compton had a deep faith, and the life of his family centered on Christian service. His father was a Presbyterian minister and Dean of Wooster College. While in college, Compton taught Sunday school. Although he had inspired several in his class to become missionaries, Compton did not know what course he should pursue.

His father told him, "It is in science that you will do your best work. Your work in this field may become a more valuable Christian service than if you enter the ministry."

After graduation from Wooster, Compton traveled to Princeton for advanced study. He was impressed by how many of the professors were active in the various Christian churches. Like them, he believed that the design of nature offered overwhelming evidence for the existence of an Almighty Designer. He said, "I believe that our universe is not a chaos but an ordered cosmos."

Compton experimented with x-rays shot into crystals. X-rays were a type of high-energy light. The regular arrangement of atoms in crystals scattered the x-rays. He measured the angle of their scattering. From the data, he hoped to learn about the arrangement of the atoms and electrons in the crystal. To his surprise, he found the wavelength of the x-ray going in did not match the wavelength of the x-ray coming out. Other scientists confirmed his discovery. They called it the Compton effect.

Compton could best explain the effect when he treated x-rays as particles. An x-ray hit the electron as if it were a material object with mass and momentum. Compton invented the term "photon" for a particle of light. Light had properties of both waves and particles. Compton saw no contradiction in this. In Sunday school classes, he taught three aspects of God: God as the ruler of the universe, God as a hero to be admired, and God as a guiding spirit. Could not photons have more than one aspect?

In 1927, Arthur Holly Compton won the Nobel Prize for his x-ray studies. By the time he received the Nobel Prize, Compton had taken up the challenge of cosmic rays. Over the next 20 years, he put together a dozen scientific teams to travel the world over and take readings. Each team carried identical instruments so their results could be compared. They climbed peaks of the great mountain ranges of the world: Himalayas, Andes, Alps, and the Rocky Mountains. They followed tunnels far into the sides of mountains. They rose into the upper atmosphere in balloons.

Compton and his wife traveled 40,000 miles collecting information. They visited Hawaii and Ecuador near the equator. They traveled to northern Canada for readings near the magnetic north pole.

The readings showed that more cosmic rays came in at the poles than at the equator. Compton proved that cosmic rays were extremely powerful subatomic particles, primarily protons that traveled through outer space at nearly the speed of light.

During World War II he was the chief scientist on the secret Manhattan Project. After the war, he became chancellor of Washington University in St. Louis, Missouri. In 1953, the year he retired, he wrote a paper in which he stated that a world that has science needs religion as never before. Science served the physical needs of people. Religion served their spiritual needs.

Arthur Compton enjoyed a life of science and Christian service. He said, "From earliest childhood I have learned to see in Jesus the supreme example of one who loves his neighbors and expresses that love in actions that count." He often spoke of his Christian faith.

In one example, as his life grew to a close, he compared his life to that of an airplane flight. Sometimes it was bumpy, but once he reached the landing field, family and friends who have gone on before would be waiting to greet him.

ERIC LIDDELL
1902–1945
BRITISH MISSIONARY AND SPORTS FIGURE

MAJOR ACCOMPLISHMENT: WON GOLD MEDAL IN

1924 OLYMPICS

ERIC LIDDELL WAS BORN IN Tientsin (Tianjin), China, where his Scottish parents were missionaries. When he was five years old, the family returned to the British Isles. His parents enrolled Liddell and his older brother in a boarding school in London for missionary children. Then his parents returned to China. During the 12 years at the boarding school, he saw his mother and father only about three times when they were on furlough.

In 1920, Liddell began studies in science at Edinburgh University. He had been an all-around athlete, playing rugby and running track. However, because of the press of his studies, he decided to concentrate on only one sport. He chose running. His best event was the 100-meter dash. At the championships in London in 1923, he set a record for the 100-meter dash. Everyone agreed he would have no trouble winning that event in the next Olympics.

He made plans to run the 100-meter individual and 100-meter relays at the 1924 Olympics in Paris. However, qualifying trials for those events would be held on Sunday. He had observed Sunday as the Lord's Day. He said, "I'm not running."

On the Sunday of the 100-meter trials, he spoke about his Christian beliefs in a Paris church.

He checked the schedule and saw that he could enter the 200-meter and 400-meter races. Liddell had an unusual running style. He ran with his head back and bobbing, his arms thrashing and his feet flying high from the ground. When asked how he could see the finish line, Liddell explained, "The Lord guides me." He unexpectedly finished third in the 200-meter for the bronze medal.

The 400-meter race, however, looked like a lost cause. He had drawn the outside lane. His position was the farthest from the starter's gun. The stagger put his competitors behind him, so during the race he would not be able to judge his position because he could not see them. Radio listeners to the race in England heard the announcer say, "They've cleared the last curve. Liddell is leading! He's increasing his lead! What a race!"

He finished five meters ahead of the field. He'd earned a gold medal, a world record, and the nickname "The Flying Scotsman."

The story of Eric Liddell's Olympic triumph was chronicled in the movie *Chariots of Fire*. The motion picture received several academy awards including Best Picture.

For Liddell, the Olympic win was not the end of the story, or even the main event of his life. The next year he graduated from Edinburgh University with degrees in science and religion. He returned to China as a teacher and missionary. Rather than staying in Tientsin, he hiked into remote Chinese villages to tell the story of Jesus.

It was a dangerous time in China. Japanese invaders patrolled the roads and challenged Liddell as a spy. Chinese warlords barely tolerated the British missionaries. Communist insurgents had infiltrated the rural areas. However, when friends accompanied him, he insisted that they be unarmed. "If you have that gun in your pocket you will depend on it rather than God."

In 1932, he married Florence Mackenzie, the daughter of Canadian missionaries. By 1941, Liddell decided it was too dangerous for his wife and three daughters. They left for Canada, although Liddell stayed behind. Two years later, the Japanese forces captured Tientsin and rounded up the foreigners. Liddell and 1,500 others were taken by train to the interment camp at Weihsien (Wei-fang). The entire camp occupied a stockade 150 by 200 yards.

Many of the other missionaries had not sent their children home. Some children had become separated from their families for four years. Camp life was hard on them, especially the teenagers. Even the slightest misbehavior could result in severe punishment by the Japanese.

However, Liddell convinced the Japanese to let him deal with the 70 young people, and the guards agreed. He supervised the daily roll call. To keep the children out of trouble, Liddell began science and math classes for them although he lacked a classroom or blackboard. He also became the youth minister at the camp church. The children called him "Uncle Eric." He taught them his favorite hymn "Be Still, My Soul."

Be still, my soul, the Lord is on thy side;
Bear patiently the cross of grief or pain;
Leave to thy God to order and provide;
In every change, He faithful will remain.
Be still, my soul: thy best, thy heavenly friend
Through thorny ways leads to joyful end.

He played games with the younger children and organized youth sports for the older ones. He repaired hockey sticks by tearing up his own bed sheets. He gave his running shoes to one of the boys.

After two years in the camp, everyone had become thin and sun blistered. Although he did not complain, it became clear that Liddell suffered from more than just the poor diet and primitive conditions. He had severe headaches. In 1945, he collapsed and was taken to the camp hospital. A few days later the news passed through the camp. Eric Liddell had died of a brain tumor. He was 43 years old. He was buried outside the interment camp.

Shortly before he died, a band of student musicians had marched by the hospital. A nurse passed a note to them: Eric Liddell would like you to play his favorite song. The students struck up the tune: "Be still, my soul, the Lord is on thy side. . . ."

GLADYS AYLWARD

1902–1970

ENGLISH MISSIONARY

MAJOR ACCOMPLISHMENT: OVERCAME PERSONAL
LIMITATIONS AND DANGERS TO SERVE AS
MISSIONARY TO CHINA

ALTHOUGH SHE REPUDIATED THE movie, Gladys Aylward is best
known by the dramatization of her story in the motion picture *The
Inn of the Sixth Happiness*. Ingrid Bergman played her in the movie.

Gladys Aylward was born near London. Her father was a mail
carrier and not particularly wealthy. Aylward became a maid in a
West End home.

When she was born again, she became convinced that Jesus
had a work for her to do. At the age of 26, she entered training to be
a missionary. However, after three months, the China Inland Mission
decided she was not missionary material. They rejected supporting
her or giving her any additional training.

She was disappointed but determined. She again took work as
a maid. During the next four years, she saved her money. She wrote
letters to individual missionaries and offered her services. However,
she received no encouragement, and her savings were woefully inadequate for travel to China.

The breakthrough came when she learned an overland trip by
railroad was less expensive than by ship. Even so, she still came up
short. Her friends, who were also domestics in low paying positions,
donated money to complete the purchase of her tickets. She left England with only two pounds and nine pence (a little over $10.00) in
her purse.

After a ferry ride across the English Channel, she began the trip
by rail across Russia and Siberia to Vladivostok. The route was not
direct because of fighting between Russia and China. In addition, she
had to walk a long section to catch her next train. She spent a winter
night in the Siberian wilderness with the calls of wolves around her.

Her goal was to team with Jeannie Lawson, an elderly Scottish
missionary. Lawson had written a letter requesting an assistant.

Aylward had responded that she was coming and then left without waiting for Lawson's approval. Lawson had lost contact with her sponsors and to some extent her sanity as well. During one of her more lucid moments, Lawson seized on the idea to reach Chinese with the gospel by opening an inn for travelers.

With Aylward's help, Lawson opened the "Inn of the 8th Happiness." (The inn became the "6th happiness" for the movie because the director thought six sounded better.) After Lawson died, Aylward continued running the place. Her sole help was a Christian cook named Yang.

Aylward began a determined effort to learn Chinese. She considered it a real miracle when she became fluent in the language in less than a year.

The inn in Yangchen, Shansi (Shanxi) province became a favorite place for mule drivers to stop and rest. She charged the going rate for the food and lodging, but offered added services such as watering the animals. The muleskinners also enjoyed the stories from the Bible that she told, which they more or less accurately repeated at other stops across China. In this way, the story of Jesus received wide circulation.

One day the local leader, the mandarin of Yanchen, sent a large escort to bring her to his palace. The mandarin had a special mission for her — foot inspector. He had ordered an end to the custom of binding female baby's feet to keep them small as the girl grew into adulthood. Aylward would be given free access into the women's quarters to inspect feet and see that the decree was being enforced. The mandarin's assignment gave her the opportunity to evangelize throughout the province.

The next year, 1933, the mandarin summoned her again. A prison riot had broken out. Several prisoners had died, and the guards were afraid to enter the stockade. The mandarin and the warden took literally her statement that Jesus was protecting her. They urged her to enter the compound and quell the riot. Aylward met with leaders of the inmates and learned about the overcrowding, the lack of anything to do, and inadequate food. She arranged for families to bring in food and asked for donations of looms so the men would have something to keep them occupied.

She began gathering orphans. She rescued an orphan girl who was being trained as a beggar. Aylward named the girl "Ninepence"

— the amount Alyward paid as a ransom. A year later, the girl came in with an orphan boy and promised to eat less if Aylward would take him in. The boy became known as "Less."

Alyward became a Chinese citizen and identified with the Chinese during the war with Japan. Her village was invaded, and on one occasion she was beaten and knocked unconscious by a rifle stock to the head. On another occasion, she was shot by the Japanese, but escaped. The Japanese put a reward on her head, dead or alive.

In 1940, the situation had become untenable in Yanchen. Aylward gathered the 100 children in her orphanage and began the trek to Sian (also spelled Xian). They had to climb a mountain range and cross the Yellow River (Huang He). The 27-day trip covered 100 miles of difficult and dangerous terrain. In addition to the physical demands of a mountain climb without food or adequate clothing, the band faced armed Japanese patrols and strafing by Japanese airplanes.

She arrived at Sian nearly dead. She was dehydrated, exhausted, malnourished, and then came down with typhus fever and pneumonia. After her health improved, she began a Christian church in Sian.

In the late 1940s, she returned to England. Alan Burgess featured her story as a war hero on a BBC radio broadcast. He wrote a book about Gladys Aylward called *The Small Woman*.

Aylward said of herself, "My heart is full of praise that one so insignificant, uneducated, and ordinary in every way could be used to His glory for the blessing of His people in poor persecuted China."

ALBERT E. BRUMLEY

1905–1977

AMERICAN HYMNWRITER

MAJOR ACCOMPLISHMENT: WRITER OF 600 GOSPEL
SONGS INCLUDING "I'LL FLY AWAY."

ALBERT E. BRUMLEY GREW UP on a cotton farm in Oklahoma. Both chopping cotton (eliminating the weeds with a hoe) and picking cotton (a totally manual operation) were mind-numbingly boring. To pass the time he would sing hymns. One of the songs was "If I Had The Wings of An Angel." As he surveyed the endless rows of cotton, his thoughts turned to literally flying away from his farm chores. The idea for his best-known song, "I'll Fly Away," was born.

He preferred singing (and practically anything else) to picking cotton, so by the time he was 17 he began to plan for a career in music. He imagined it would either be as a singer or vocal instructor. He studied music at the Hartford Musical Institute in Arkansas. After four years, he began teaching singing at a variety of schools in Arkansas, Oklahoma, and Missouri.

In 1929, he wrote "I'll Fly Away" but did not send it to a publisher. While in Powell, Missouri, at one of the schools, he met Goldie Schell. They were married in 1931. Her father ran a general store, and he offered Brumley a job at one dollar a day. Brumley accepted and made Powell his home. His wife encouraged him to find a publisher for his songs. "I'll Fly Away" was the first one published, and it became his most-requested song.

Writers of Christian hymns usually avoided contemporary references. However, Brumley published "Turn Your Radio On" in 1938. His use of the radio as an allegory for prayer breathed new life into Christian songwriting. It became immensely popular years later when sung by Ray Stevens.

He wrote about 600 songs, including "I'll Meet You In the Morning," "Jesus, Hold My Hand," and "If We Never Meet Again." He had strong religious convictions, so his songwriting revolved around Bible themes and spiritual principles. However, Brumley is considered one of the most influential songwriters of the 1900s. In 1970, he was inducted into the Country Songwriters' Hall of Fame.

WERNHER VON BRAUN
1912–1977
GERMAN AMERICAN ROCKET SCIENTIST
MAJOR ACCOMPLISHMENT: DEVELOPED SATURN V
ROCKETS THAT LAUNCHED APOLLO SPACECRAFT TO
THE MOON

WERNHER VON BRAUN GREW UP in Germany in a well-to-do family. He attended church regularly and gave his heart to the Lord at an early age. As a reward for Bible study, his parents gave him a telescope. The objects the telescope revealed in the night sky fascinated him. His interest in astronomy led to a curiosity about the possibility of space travel. The next year, the German rocket pioneer Hermann Oberth published *The Rocket into Interplanetary Space*. Oberth explained mathematically how rockets could gain enough speed to escape earth's gravitational pull.

Von Braun's schoolwork was merely adequate, and mathematics was his poorest subject. Oberth's book was filled with mathematical equations that von Braun could not understand. Von Braun tackled his studies with renewed vigor. Within a year, he led the class in mathematics.

After high school graduation, von Braun enrolled in the Berlin Institute of Technology. He joined the German Society for Space Travel, a group of rocket enthusiasts. Von Braun also worked as a volunteer with Oberth, who used money his book earned to experiment with liquid fuel rockets.

Von Braun received a doctor's degree from the University of Berlin in 1934. He wrote a research paper about the thrust of rocket engines. The German military concealed the nature of his research by giving it the title "About Combustion Tests."

Von Braun was assigned to the Pennemünde rocket testing grounds near the Baltic Sea. The military closed down the amateur rocket society and outlawed public rocket research and testing. He found his research into the peaceful exploration of space being turned into weapons of war. By 1944, the deadly V-2s were perfected, but by then it was clear that Hitler would be defeated.

The Gestapo, the feared Nazi police, arrested von Braun. They threw him into prison and accused him of being more interested in space travel than in building V-2s. The Gestapo released him when Allied forces invaded France and the Communists from Russia were closing in from the east.

Von Braun was well aware of the anti-religious nature of communism. Given a choice of being overrun by the Communists from Russia or surrendering to the Americans, von Braun and his team chose the Americans.

Wernher von Braun

The car in which he was fleeing crashed into a railroad embankment and burst into flames. Von Braun forced open the door and pulled the driver to safety. Braun's left arm was broken in two places and his shoulder shattered. The doctor set the arm in a cast, but doubted that the arm would heal properly.

Von Braun moved the rocket group to Oberammergau, a little village in the Bavarian Alps. His broken arm became infected. The little town was a ski resort, and village doctor was an expert at setting broken bones. Because of wartime shortages, the doctor had to reset the arm without painkillers. Von Braun gritted his teeth and let the doctor go ahead. This time it healed properly.

The Americans sent von Braun to the isolated White Sands Test Range near Roswell, New Mexico. During the 1930s, Robert H. Goddard had tested his rockets at the desert site. Goddard had died, but von Braun was very familiar with his work. He said, "Goddard was ahead of us all." However, he now felt his team was in the lead. "After all," he said, "we've had 15 more years of experience in making mistakes and learning from them."

By taking V-2s and adding smaller rockets on top of them, von Braun was able to launch scientific instrument packages to the very edge of space. He called for rockets to be used for peaceful purposes.

"As we study our equations and sail our space ships, we must always remember that our first concern is for man himself. Our science must increase man's blessings."

In 1947, von Braun was allowed to return to Germany briefly — to marry. After a time in the desert at White Sands, he moved his family to the green hills of Huntsville, Alabama. The countryside was more like what they had been used to in Germany. Soon they became a part of the community. They attended church regularly, and their German cooking became a favorite at church picnics.

He wrote *The Mars Project*. The book described in technical detail an expedition to the planet Mars. Most people considered the whole idea of space travel too fantastic. In all, 18 publishers turned down the book before the University of Illinois Press agreed to publish it.

Von Braun directed the army ballistic missile program in Huntsville. In 1955, his calculations showed that his most powerful rocket, the Redstone, could put a satellite into orbit around the earth. However, the United States government ordered him not to pursue this possibility.

October 4, 1957, USSR's Sputnik 1 became the first artificial satellite of the earth. United States citizens became outraged that America's Cold War adversary had been first and demanded action by the government.

The United States made its first attempt to put a satellite into orbit using the untried Vanguard rocket. On December 6, the rocket lifted two feet before falling back to the launch pad in a fireball. Another Vanguard could not be made ready for six months.

In desperation, government leaders called von Braun to Washington. They asked, "What can you do?"

He said, "We can use the equipment on hand and build a satellite-carrying rocket in 60 days." To most people, the claim seemed impossible. Most projects of that scope took years.

His team modified a Redstone rocket and renamed it a Jupiter-C. It was about as large as a bus. The Jupiter-C launched flawlessly on January 31, 1958, and placed America's first satellite, Explorer 1, into orbit. He did it in less than 60 days.

Von Braun, who had become a United States citizen, was made Director of the Space Flight Center in Huntsville. When the moon-landing project began, von Braun led the development of the Saturn

V. At 365 feet tall, with millions of parts, the Saturn V was the largest rocket ever built. In 1969, a Saturn V launched Apollo 11, the first craft to land human beings on the moon.

Von Braun was happy that his teacher, Hermann Oberth, had been able to come from his retirement home in Italy to watch the launch of a Saturn V. In addition to their interest in rockets, Hermann Oberth and Wernher von Braun had a strong spiritual faith. Oberth had published the book *Material and Life,* in which he argued against the philosophy of materialism on which communism was based. Oberth also believed that the soul could not be explained by science.

About his own religious views, von Braun said, "We must consider God as Creator of the universe and master of everything. Astronomy and space exploration are teaching us that the good Lord is a much greater Lord, and master of a greater kingdom."

DALE EVANS
1912–2001
American actress and writer
Major accomplishment: "Queen of the West"
actress and author of "Happy Trails"

DALE EVANS WAS BORN Lucille Wood Smith in Uvalde, Texas. Her name was changed to Francis Octavia Smith when she entered school. She grew up in Texas and Arkansas. She suffered a nervous breakdown at age 11, married at 14, became a mother at 15, and divorced at 17. She went through numerous name changes, and two more marriages, before becoming Dale Evans.

After gaining experience in Memphis, Tennessee, as a singer on radio, she toured with jazz musician Fats Waller. Then she became a vocalist in Chicago hotel ballrooms featuring big bands. By the mid-1930s she had become well known as a big-band singer. She signed with the Chase and Sanborn Hour that was broadcast nationally.

Her agent pitched her acting and singing abilities to Hollywood. He promoted her as being only 21 years old, and explained away her 14-year-old son Tom as her brother. She signed with Republic Pictures that filmed B-westerns. Women seldom had a lead in western movies, but Republic Pictures took a chance by writing an expanded starring role for her with Roy Rogers.

Roy Rogers (born in 1911 as Leonard Slye) started his career as the lead singer for the Sons of the Pioneers. They had recorded "Tumbling Tumbleweeds" and "Cool Water." He starred in the motion picture *Under Western Stars*. By 1943, he had earned the title "King of the Cowboys." The next year he teamed with Dale Evans in *The Cowboy and the Senorita*.

Roy Rogers had an adopted daughter, Cheryl, and two children by his wife, Arline: Linda Lou and Roy Rogers Jr. (called Dusty.) Arline died shortly after the birth of Dusty. Fourteen months after the death of his wife, Roy and Dale married on New Year's Eve 1947.

Dale gave birth to Robin, who had Down's syndrome. They adopted several children: Mary Little Doe (called Dodie), a Native

American; John David (called Sandy), a battered child from an orphanage in Kentucky; Marion, a foster child from Scotland; Debbie, a Korean War orphan.

In addition to combining their families, Roy and Dale combined their careers. They made 28 more movies together and began a radio program. While preparing for the radio program, Dale decided they needed a theme song. The title was easy because Roy signed his autographs with "Trails of Happiness." Scribbling on an envelope, she wrote the lyrics. The melody was the classical "Grand Canyon Suite" by Ferde Grofé. She had heard the music when big-band leader Paul Whiteman introduced it in 1931. She taught "Happy Trails" to Roy and the Sons of the Pioneers 40 minutes before show time.

Dale and Roy starred in 100 episodes of the weekly *Roy Rogers Show* that ran on television from 1951 to 1957. They imbued the shows with good-natured, non-threatening excitement. They were the most popular cowboy and cowgirl that television has ever known. At the end of each episode, they signed off with the song "Happy Trails."

Dale had been growing in Christian faith. She led Roy to Christ, too. Starting in the 1950s, they made an effort to speak about their religious beliefs. When they were guests on national television talk shows, they would tell about the love of Jesus. At news conferences, they would speak about their Christian beliefs even if reporters didn't bring up the subject.

At home, Dale told her children, "Your life is the only Bible some people will ever read." She wrote an alternate religious verse of "Happy Trails" that contains the lines "It started on the day that we met Jesus; He came into our hearts and then he freed us."

Dale and Roy's Christian faith became a source of strength during a series of trying events. She and Roy lost three of their children. Robin died of complications from Down's syndrome before she was 2. Debbie died in a church bus accident when she was 12. Sandy accidentally choked to death while in the military in Germany.

Dale wrote a book about Robin, *Angel Unaware* (1953). National newspapers did not include religious books when totaling sales for best-seller lists. Only later was it learned that the story of the girl with Down's syndrome had sales equal to a best seller. *Angel Unaware* was the first of 20 books by Dale.

Roy and Dale opened the Roy Rogers-Dale Evans Museum in Victorville, California. One of the items sold in the gift shop was a list of the Roy Rogers Riders Club Rules. It became the most popular souvenir. Number 9 on the list was "Love God and go to Sunday school regularly."

Roy and Dale were married for 51 years. He died in 1998, and she died in 2001 at her home in Apple Valley, California. She was 88 years old.

JAMES B. IRWIN
1930–1991
AMERICAN ASTRONAUT

MAJOR ACCOMPLISHMENT: SPENT THREE DAYS ON THE

MOON'S SURFACE AND FOUNDED THE HIGH

FLIGHT FOUNDATION

JAMES B. IRWIN WAS A MEMBER of the Apollo 15 mission to the moon. He and David R. Scott landed on the moon's surface on July 30, 1971. They landed in a narrow valley in rough terrain. The 15,000-foot tall peaks of Apinnine Mountains hemmed them in on three sides. A mile-wide canyon, the Hadley Rille, was on the remaining side.

Irwin became the first person to drive a vehicle on the moon. Irwin's and Scott's exploration in the battery-powered lunar rover carried them a total of 27 miles, a record for the Apollo program. At one point, they were beyond the horizon so that their base camp was not visible.

Irwin and Scott transmitted live pictures to earth. They kept up a running commentary so viewers on earth could live the experience with them. Irwin was especially awed by the lunar mountains. While on the radio with mission control in Houston, he quoted a favorite Bible passage: "I will lift up mine eyes unto the hills, from whence cometh my help" (Ps. 121:1).

At the end of the highly scientific mission, they presented a unique experiment. Scott held a falcon feather in one hand and a geologist's hammer in the other. He released them both at the same time, and they fell side by side. The moon had no atmosphere, and without air resistance the feather fell at the same speed as the hammer.

The *Apollo 15* flight was Irwin's only space mission. His book, *To Rule the Night*, details his experiences as an astronaut. In his speeches he would often say, "Seeing the earth [from space] has to change a man, has to make him appreciate the creation of God and the love of God."

He resigned from the space program shortly after he returned to earth. He founded the High Flight Foundation, a Christian evangelical organization. On two occasions Irwin led expeditions to Mount Ararat, Turkey, to search for Noah's Ark. Near the summit, he injured himself during a fall on a glacier. He said, "It's easier to walk on the moon."

He traveled extensively as a speaker. He said his experience on the moon moved him to devote the rest of his life to "spreading the good news of Jesus Christ."

Irwin lived in Colorado Springs, Colorado, the base of the High Flight Foundation. James Irwin died of a heart attack while at home in 1991.

EDWIN EUGENE "BUZZ" ALDRIN JR.

1930–

AMERICAN ASTRONAUT

MAJOR ACCOMPLISHMENT: CREWMEMBER OF

APOLLO 11, THE FIRST MOON-LANDING MISSION

DURING HIS CAREER, Edwin Aldrin, known as "Buzz," spent more than 4,500 hours in flight and 290 hours in space. He was the second human to walk on the moon.

Aldrin was born in New Jersey. He intended to be a pilot, but the air force, created in 1947, did not yet have a service academy. Aldrin entered the army and received a bachelor's degree with honors at West Point. He transferred to the air force and earned his pilot's wings in 1952. He flew 66 combat missions during the Korean War.

He was not selected as an astronaut in the first round because he had no test pilot experience. He wanted to remedy this by going to test pilot school. However, he had already entered the aeronautics program at Massachusetts Institute of Technology. The next four years were devoted to earning a Ph.D. in orbital mechanics. His thesis was on the techniques of space rendezvous. He dedicated it to those in the astronaut program: "Oh that I were one of them."

He was not accepted into the second round of astronauts, but did manage to become part of the program at the Houston Manned Space Center testing experiments for the Gemini program. Finally, Aldrin was accepted into the third group of astronauts. He was the first astronaut with a Ph.D.

He became part of a back-up crew with Jim Lovell. Due to an aircraft accident that killed two of the prime crew, the schedule was shuffled and Aldrin and Lovell flew aboard *Gemini 12*. Aldrin carried a prayer written by his nurse: "The light of God surrounds me; the love of God enfolds me; the power of God protects me; the presence of God watches over me; wherever I am, God is."

During a rendezvous test, the on-board radar failed. He manually recomputed the rendezvous and earned the title Dr. Rendezvous.

Aldrin was selected for the first moon-landing mission. On the morning of July 16, 1969, Edwin Aldrin, Neil Armstrong, and Mike Collins rode an elevator to the command module at the top of the 363-foot Saturn V rocket waiting on Pad 39A at the Kennedy Space Center in Florida. If all went as planned, Armstrong and Aldrin would be the first human beings to set foot on the moon. Collins would remain aboard *Columbia*, the command craft, as it circled the moon.

Each astronaut had packed a small PPK (Personal Preference Kit) with objects to take to the moon and bring back to earth. Each bag of white cloth was hardly bigger than a paperback book and had a drawstring to pull it closed. Weight restrictions on the moon flight forced everything to be small and lightweight.

Neil Armstrong, soon to be the first to walk on the moon, had been too busy to pack his kit, and his wife had done it for him. He thought she had put in some tiny American flags for friends and members of the NASA team. Michael Collins carried small shoulder patches as souvenirs of the trip.

Buzz Aldrin had taken special care to pack his PPK. He remained silent about its contents.

The journey lasted 76 hours and carried them 240,000 miles to the moon. On the final descent, the inboard computer became overloaded. It recycled to put the most pressing calculations first. Then, 20 seconds before touchdown, Armstrong saw the *Eagle* would be landing among boulders. He made a quick change and extended the flight to pass over the boulders.

The world was listening, and knew the landing was near when Aldrin said, "Picking up a little dust." The *Eagle's* footpads touched down on the moon at 3:18 Central Standard Time on Sunday afternoon, July 20, 1969.

Neil Armstrong turned off the engine. "Houston, Tranquility Base here," he said, his voice clear and calm. Then, with triumph, he added, "The *Eagle* has landed!"

The two astronauts immediately began to power down the ship to conserve energy. Aldrin finished his part of the power down. Then he removed four small objects from his PPK: a little silver cup, a small plastic container of wine, a small piece of bread, and a sheet of paper with a Scripture verse written on it. Aldrin laid the objects on the flat top of the computer.

Aldrin quickly prepared for his special communion. He had saved the bread and wine from a communion service with friends a week before at the church he attended outside Houston. The wine poured in slow motion because the moon has a gravity one-sixth that of the earth.

Aldrin spoke to Houston. "I'd like everyone listening in to pause a moment to contemplate the events of the past few hours and to give thanks in his or her own way." The people at Houston respected his request for radio

Edwin Eugene "Buzz" Aldrin Jr.

silence. Aldrin unfolded the tiny sheet of paper. As he took the communion, he read the verse of Scripture: "I am the vine, ye are the branches" (John 15:5).

Neil Armstrong was the first to set foot on the moon. Aldrin followed and spent two hours on the surface gathering lunar surface samples and setting up scientific equipment. Armstrong's photograph of Aldrin standing near the lunar module is the one often reproduced in historical articles about the moon landing.

After the successful moon exploration and return to earth, Aldrin and the Apollo crew received a hero's welcome. But the "what should I do next" question left him severely depressed. He wrote the book *Return to Earth* that candidly addressed his Apollo experiences and treatment for depression following the event.

The moon landing is considered one of the greatest events of human exploration. Aldrin insured that the first act of human beings on the moon was a remembrance of Christ.

JONI EARECKSON TADA

1950–

AMERICAN ARTIST, INSPIRATIONAL SPEAKER, AND
WRITER

MAJOR ACCOMPLISHMENT: OVERCAME QUADRIPLEGIA
TO BECOME A SUCCESSFUL CHRISTIAN ARTIST

JONI EARECKSON LEARNED at an early age the joy of exploring
nature. Her family took camping, hiking, and horseback riding trips
through the deserts and mountains of the western United States. Once,
they rode from Laramie to Cheyenne, Wyoming. Four-year-old Joni
was the youngest person on the 100-mile trail ride.

Another trip took her into the spectacular Medicine Bow Mountains. The trail brought them to an open meadow. The sights, sounds,
and smells of the wild country deepened her appreciation for God
and His creation.

Joni began carrying a sketchpad. She filled pages with sketches
of mountains, horses, and animals. In high school, her hours were
filled with study, friends, and sports. She played hockey and lacrosse.
She kept a horse and continued to ride.

Joni was an active girl who loved to swim. During the summer
after her high school graduation, she went swimming in a lake with
some friends. She paddled out to a floating dock. She could hardly
suppress the sheer joy of the warm July day. She dived into the water.
The water was shallower than she had expected. She struck her head
against the bottom.

As she floated face down in the water, she became panic-stricken.
She could not move her arms or legs. She thought a net was wrapped
around her. She held her breath, hoping a friend would free her. Finally,
someone noticed. They pulled her ashore and sent for an ambulance.

On that day Joni Eareckson's life changed forever. It was not a
net but a broken neck that kept her motionless. She spent three and
one-half months in the hospital. She could not move her arms or
legs, or bring food to her mouth. She could not comb her hair or
wipe away her own tears. Every day was the same as the previous
day. Be fed, watch TV, sleep.

She grappled with the fact that she would never walk again or regain the use of her hands. On a visit home, she arranged to sell her horse and dispose of the hockey and lacrosse sticks.

From long discussions with Christian friends, she realized that some people who could walk led lives without meaning. All they did was eat, breathe, and sleep. They were not aware of their empty days because jobs or school distracted them. The accident caused her to see her own life with new eyes. A purposeful life came from glorifying God. She realized that God had a purpose for her.

Joni Eareckson Tada

She had feeling in her shoulders. Those muscles could be trained to twist her arm and lift it. It took intense concentration and days of practice. A special leather glove with a strap to hold a fork and spoon allowed her to start feeding herself. She learned to operate an electric wheel chair. A great day came when she motored out of the rehabilitation center and down the sidewalk to the local fast food restaurant.

What next? Joni remembered those wonderful scenes from her days of exploring out west. She knew that the skill and talent of an artist was in the eye and brain. Hands merely transferred what the artist saw to paper. She could draw with a pencil in her mouth.

After a year and a half of trying, Joni's drawings began to capture the emotion that had been missing from her sketches before the accident. She gave the art to family and friends. She signed them with the initials PTL, "Praise The Lord." Joni showed her drawings at local fairs. It was fun. People came, looked around, and chatted with her before leaving.

One of her father's friends arranged to display her work. She secretly hoped that at this one-person show, she might actually sell some of her nature scenes.

When her father drove her to the event, the street was blocked. She didn't want to be late, so they turned down a side street. It was blocked, too. Then they saw the reason for the commotion. A huge banner proclaimed *Joni Eareckson Day!* A brass band played. Newspaper reporters, television crews, and a multitude of people all came to see her paintings.

With the encouragement of this successful show, Joni started a line of greeting cards and distributed prints of her work at bookstores. Soon she could barely keep up with the demand. The White House asked for one of her drawings. She was interviewed on television. Not only did Joni have the eye of an artist — she had the heart of a champion.

Joni was especially pleased by the questions people asked. They did not focus on the fact she was in a wheelchair. Instead, they asked questions any artist would expect. Where did you get your ideas? Have you studied art?

Although she had not gone to art school, Joni enrolled in college and took courses in public speaking. She became an effective speaker and a writer. She wrote more than 20 books. The book *Joni*, which told about her struggles following the accident, was printed in 40 languages. It became an inspiration to millions of people. She took her inspirational message to the public and was heard on 700 radio stations worldwide.

ALPHABETICAL INDEX

JOHN HUDSON TINER

1944–

AMERICAN MATHEMATICIAN AND WRITER

MAJOR ACCOMPLISHMENT: *FOR THOSE WHO DARE —*
101 GREAT CHRISTIAN LIVES IS HIS 50TH BOOK.

JOHN HUDSON TINER GREW UP on a farm. His most pleasurable times were when it was raining too hard for fieldwork. He would spend those days in the hayloft, reading books about faraway lands while rain sounded on the tin roof. He was educated in a small school with several grades combined into one room. He gave his heart to Jesus at an early age.

He married D. Jeanene Tiner, a teacher and photographer. They have visited some of those faraway places he had read about as a boy, including the fabled city of Marrakech in northern Africa.

During Tiner's 12 years as a teacher of science and mathematics, he received five National Science Foundation teaching fellowships that allowed him to study graduate chemistry at the College of the Holy Cross (Massachusetts), graduate astronomy at Sam Houston State University (Texas), and graduate mathematics at Duke University (North Carolina). He also worked as a mathematician and cartographer for the Defense Mapping Agency, Aerospace Center (St. Louis).

Today, Tiner is a full-time writer. His popular non-fiction books tell their stories through the lives of people who left the world in a better condition than they found it. He says, "After the research is finished, a wonderful moment occurs when the story takes over and the characters come alive. No longer am I a writer, but a time traveler who stands unobserved in the shadows and reports the events as they occur."

He has received numerous honors for his writing, including the Missouri Writer's Guild award for best juvenile book for *Exploring the World of Chemistry*, which was also published by Master Books.

The
Exploring
Series

$13.99 each
8-1/2 x 11

Exploring Planet Earth

Blending a creationism perspective of history with definitions of terms and identification of famous explorers, scientists, etc., this book gives an excellent initial knowledge of people and places, encouraging the reader to continue their studies in-depth. Supplemented with photographs, illustrations, chapter review activities, and an index. ISBN: 0-89051-178-0 • 168 pages

Exploring the History of Medicine

From surgery to vaccines, man has made great strides in the field of medicine. Quality of life has improved dramatically in the last few decades alone, but we should not forget that God provided humans with minds and resources to bring about these advances. A biblical perspective of healing and the use of medicine provides the best foundation for treating diseases and injury. The fascinating history of medicine comes alive in this book, providing students with a healthy dose of facts, mini-biographies, and vintage illustrations. Includes chapter tests and index. ISBN: 0-89051-248-5 • 168 pages

Exploring the World of Chemistry

Chemistry is an amazing branch of science that affects us every day. Without chemistry, there would be no rubber tires, no tin cans, no televisions, no microwave ovens, no wax paper. Find out why pure gold is not used for jewelry or coins. Join Humphrey Davy as he made many chemical discoveries, and learn how they shortened his life. See how people in the 1870s could jump over the top of the Washington Monument. Includes many illustrations, biographical information, chapter tests, and an index. ISBN: 0-89051-295-7 • 144 pages

Available at Christian bookstores nationwide